1st Edition

CHILD CUSTODY

Building Agreements That Work

by Mimi E. Lyster

NOLO PRESS ⚖ BERKELEY

Your Responsibility When Using a Self-Help Law Book

We've done our best to give you useful and accurate information in this book. But laws and procedures change frequently and are subject to differing interpretations. If you want legal advice backed by a guarantee, see a lawyer. If you use this book, it's your responsibility to make sure that the facts and general advice contained in it are applicable to your situation.

Keeping Up-to-Date

To keep its books up-to-date, Nolo Press issues new printings and new editions periodically. New printings reflect minor legal changes and technical corrections. New editions contain major legal changes, major text additions or major reorganizations. To find out if a later printing or edition of any Nolo book is available, call Nolo Press at (510) 549-1976 or check the catalog in the *Nolo News*, our quarterly publication.

To stay current, follow the "Update" service in the *Nolo News*. You can get a free two-year subscription by sending us the registration card in the back of the book. In another effort to help you use Nolo's latest materials, we offer a 25% discount off the purchase of any new Nolo book if you turn in any earlier printing or edition. (See the "Recycle Offer" in the back of this book.) This book was last printed in October 1995.

	FIRST EDITION
Second Printing	OCTOBER 1995
Editor	STEPHEN ELIAS
Illustrations	MARI STEIN
Book Design	TERRI HEARSH
Cover Design	TONI IHARA
Index	SAYRE VAN YOUNG
Proofreading	BOB WELLS
Printing	DELTA LITHOGRAPH

Lyster, Mimi E.
    Child custody : building agreements that work / by Mimi E. Lyster.
 -- 1st national ed.
     p.   cm.
    Includes index.
    ISBN 0-87337-283-2
    1. Custody of children--United States--Popular works.   2. Divorce
settlements--United States--Popular works.   I. Title.
KF547.Z9L97 1995
346.7301'7--dc20
[347.30617]

               95-107
               CIP

Dedication

To Dan, who's support and ability to pick up as I left off made this book possible; and to our daughters Katelyn, Alysha and Nichelle who were almost always willing to "wait just a minute".

Acknowledgments

Special thanks go to Kevin Elkus, John Helie and Steve Elias for helping to crystallize a vague idea into "virtual" reality. Steve Elias and Robin Leonard are the remarkable editors who made this book readable. Peg la France provided invaluable research assistance for the state-by-state legal comparisons. Nolo Press is an institution that I have admired as a consumer, and appreciate even more as an author. I am deeply indebted to Jan Shaw for making an indelible impression of the kind of mediator that I hoped to be, and to the parents whose mediations shaped my understanding of separate parenting and the power of mediated agreements. I am also grateful to the members, staff and researchers of the 2020 Vision Commission who forced me to transform my thinking about families, access to justice and the role of appropriate dispute resolution in the 21st century, and to Goeff Ball for his pioneering work with situation-solution (pairs).

Finally, I wish to acknowledge the important pioneering work done in the field of parenting agreements by Dr. Isolina Ricci, author of the seminal work, *Mom's House, Dad's House.*

Table of Contents

7 Understanding Your Children's Needs

8 Multiracial, Multicultural and International Families

9 Nontraditional Families

10 State and Federal Laws Affecting Child Custody

11 Help Beyond the Book

A Appendix: Tear-Out Forms

Worksheet 1: Describe Your Child

Worksheet 2: Describe Your Relationship With Your Child

Workshhet 3: Adding the Details

Worksheet 4: Checklist of Issues for Your Parenting Agreement

Parental Agreement

Index

Introduction

This is a book for parents who want to reach the best possible agreement about how they will share and divide their parenting responsibilities during or after a separation or divorce. This book will help you to evaluate your current situation and choose from among a wide range of possible solutions so that you, the other parent and your children can put many, if not all, of your parenting disputes behind you and look to the future with confidence.

This type of agreement can have many names. Most commonly it is called a Custody Agreement, but increasingly, it is known as a "Parenting Agreement," a term coined by Dr. Isolina Ricci, author of *Mom's House, Dad's House* (Macmillian, 1980).

Regardless of its label, a parenting agreement typically addresses issues such as:

- taking care of the children
- making necessary decisions on the children's behalf
- making sure the children spend time with both parents, and
- meeting the children's medical, psychological, educational, spiritual, physical and social needs.

This book takes you step by step through the process of creating a parenting agreement. It also explains how your agreement can serve as a blueprint for your future parenting relationship with your children and with their other parent. When thoughtfully prepared, a parenting agreement becomes the centerpiece of a separation or divorce involving children.

A. Make Your Own Custody Decisions If Possible

When parents first turn their attention to custody and parenting issues, they are typically angry, hurt and overwhelmed with both the divorce or separation process and their own feelings. Often a parent's first instinct is to try to gain the upper hand by demanding full custody of the children. And all too often the other parent responds in kind. These instinctive reactions create a substantial risk of a long, expensive and emotionally draining journey into the world of child custody litigation, the result of which is likely to please no one.

When parents take parenting issues to court rather than resolve them on their own, they are short-changing themselves. They must rely on a judge or court-appointed evaluator to understand the family's situation and each parent's

position within a few minutes or hours, and then to make wise decisions with the children's best interests in mind. It is very difficult for a judge to "get it right" under this condition.

Each state has guidelines for its judges to follow when making custody decisions. Nonetheless, judges have considerable discretion in interpreting these guidelines and imposing their own views of what constitutes a good environment for children. The chance that a judge's decision will be ideal for your specific situation is relatively slim.

Most researchers—especially those who study the effects of divorce on children—believe passionately that using the court to resolve custody issues is a mistake in all but a few cases. It is far better, in the opinion of these researchers, for parents to negotiate their own parenting agreement, with the help of outside experts such as mediators, counselors and lawyers on an as-needed basis. Court intervention is appropriate, however, if the children's safety or well-being is at risk and their parents cannot agree on a way to reduce that risk.

B. Parenting Issues and Financial Issues

In addition to parenting issues, separation and divorce often require the parents to deal with financial issues such as dividing property, paying marital debts and providing for support. Although this book focuses only on the parenting issues, by starting with an agreement that serves your children's best interests you may find that many of the financial issues are easier to tackle and resolve.

For example, if you choose to have one parent take on the majority of the daily parenting responsibilities, you may decide that that parent will live in the family home. But if your children will be spending approximately equal amounts of time with each of you, you reasonably may choose to sell the family home (especially if it is your primary asset) and use the money to rent or buy a home for each parent that can accommodate the children.

Clearly, decisions about financial issues affect parenting issues just as decisions about parenting issues can affect financial issues. This book assumes that, to the greatest possible extent, the "people" issues should come first and your agreement about how to best meet your children's needs should set the stage for deciding the money issues. Especially when it comes to support, for example, the larger

the role a parent plays in the lives of his or her children, the more likely that parent is to cheerfully contribute to their support.

C. Why This Book Is Unique

This book has a number of innovative features not generally found in other books addressing separate parenting and related custody issues. To begin, you can use this book whether you are thinking about separation, preparing to negotiate your first agreement or modifying an existing agreement. The six other unique features of this book are described below.

1. This Book Offers Real World Solutions to Parenting Issues

Parenting encompasses a complex mix of relationships and responsibilities. From the cosmic to the comical, from the monumental to the mundane, the essence of a parent's role is the same—whether or not the parents remain partners.

This book reflects the trials and tribulations of real parents who have encountered and resolved the same issues

that you and your children's other parent now face. It presents the research and observations of professionals who help parents resolve separate parenting issues, and describes the solutions that these parents have fashioned for themselves.

2. The Book Is for Married and Unmarried Parents

Many couples in the United States parent without getting married. These parents do not legally separate or divorce, but their needs for parenting plans are just the same as their separated or divorced counterparts. Although most of the examples are written as though a legal marriage had taken place, (and the terms "separation" and "divorce" appear throughout the book), parents who were never married can assume that the terms and examples include their relationship.

3. The Book Is for Nontraditional Families and Families With Different Cultural Backgrounds

This book is not just for Caucasian, middle class and heterosexual-parented families. Incorporated throughout the text, as well as in chapters devoted to multicultural, multiracial and nontraditional families, is an understanding that all kinds of families need parenting agreements.

4. This Book Is for Families With One Child or Many Children

For convenience, this book is written using the word "children" rather than "child" or "child(ren)." If you have only one child, you can assume that every reference to children includes your child.

5. This Book Can Be Used With or Without Professional Help

This book was written to help you negotiate your own parenting agreement, with or without the help of professionals such as mediators, counselors, attorneys, arbitrators and courts. It includes worksheets you can use for your own negotiations, to record your agreement or to help any outside professional who might become involved. The book helps you assess whether or not your agreement will work, lists resources for getting outside help if necessary, and explains how you can finalize your agreement if you are involved in a court proceeding.

You may be surprised to find that this book doesn't sound like what your attorney, or divorced friends say is important about separation, divorce and separate parenting. That is because this book is focused on you, your children and their other parent—not on the law.

Many people who have been through divorce, and the lawyers who represent them, focus on terms like "custody" and "visitation" and ask the one question "who gets the kids?" While these are certainly important, this book helps parents to first understand their children's needs, and then to structure their agreement accordingly. After you and the other parent have been able to agree about most aspects of your separate parenting relationship, this book will help you to assign the labels which seem to make the most sense.

6.   The Book Is a Work in Progress

This book is part of a growing database of real-world solutions to separate parenting problems. If you come up with an issue or a solution we haven't included, let us know on the Reader Contribution Card you will find in the back of the book. If we use your issue or options in future editions, we will acknowledge your contribution (if you wish).

D. A Word to Skeptics

Many parents who go through separation or divorce feel that books like this and processes like mediation won't work for them. This feeling may be based on one or more of the following beliefs:

- The emotional conflict between the parties precludes any approach except all-out legal warfare.
- One or both parents are unwilling to budge on core issues.
- Each parent's bottom line includes the same result (usually sole or primary custody of the children awarded to that parent).

Fortunately, none of these situations is an automatic barrier to negotiating an agreement on your own or to reaching an agreement through mediation or an avenue other than court.

1.   If You Think the Conflict Is too Intense to Negotiate on Your Own

Intense conflict is a natural and normal part of separation, divorce and separate parenting. To presume otherwise

would do you, the other parent and your children a disservice. But conflict—even intense conflict—is not reason enough to assume you cannot negotiate a parenting agreement.

Chapters 4 and 6 contain information on how you and the other parent can handle your own negotiations even if your conflict is bitter. Chapter 4 explains how to conduct an effective meeting and improve your communication style, and offers specific strategies for managing conflict. Chapter 6 explains the process of mediation and how it can be used to bring parents together for the benefit of their children.

If your pessimism is especially high as you read these words, skim Chapters 4 and 6 before continuing. Hopefully, you will gain some reassurance from what you find there, and be willing to return here and work through the rest of the book.

2.   If the Other Parent Is Inflexible

Being adamant about a certain position is not necessarily bad. If the less flexible parent can describe his or her concerns, goals and perceptions of the situation in some detail, you will often have a good list of issues that must be addressed and resolved to reach a lasting agreement.

Perhaps the most effective way to put your discussions on a positive footing is to shift the focus to your children. The worksheets in Chapter 3 help you to identify and describe your concerns, describe your children's needs and acknowledge the unique situations that your family is experiencing. 1Chapter 7 helps you gain insights into what children need and experience at different ages, and how you might structure your agreement to best meet those needs.

By focusing on your children while negotiating parenting arrangements, you'll probably find that you can adjust your positions enough to produce a good parenting agreement.

3.   If You Want the Same (Mutually Exclusive) Things

Sometimes, both parents want the same thing—often "sole" custody of the children. In this situation, you and the other parent have several options, each of which might be enough to get your negotiations on track. First and foremost, you must focus on meeting your children's needs. As mentioned above, Chapter 3 helps you to identify those needs and Chapter 7 gives you a perspective on the needs children have at different ages. Often, when parents are very clear about which of their children's needs they want to meet, they adjust their own demands to meet those needs.

Parenting separately is challenging, but it is a job worth doing well. By making the commitment to put your children's best interests first, and by taking the time to educate yourself about your options, you, your children and the other parent may find that you can develop a parenting agreement that each of you feels is essentially fair.

E. Icons Used in This Book

Look for these icons to alert you to certain kinds of information.

 When you see the "fast track" icon, you'll be alerted to a chance to skip some material you may not need to read.

 This icon introduces a family.

 The caution icon warns you of potential problems.

 The briefcase lets you know when you need the advice of an attorney.

 This icon refers you to other books or resources. ■

Taking Stock of Your Situation

Before getting into the nuts and bolts of building an effective parenting plan, you need to understand the context within which your parenting decisions will be made.

A. You Are Not Alone

For the last quarter of a century, the expectation that two people would meet, marry, raise a family and grow old together has changed. In 1993, Maccoby and Mnookin, researchers at the Stanford Center for the Study of Families, Children and Youth, studied 1,000 families filing for divorce in California. They found that couples usually divorce after seven years of marriage, and that two thirds of these families have at least one child under the age of six. They also reported that the parents of approximately one million children a year get divorced in the United States.

Other researchers have commented on the changing structure of the family in the 1990s. During the last 25 years, the divorce rate has quadrupled, births outside of marriage have increased by 22%, and many families relocate every few years, which deprives these families of the many benefits derived from a geographically-close extended family. A family in which biological parents stay together and raise their children is now only true for about one-third of all couples. The reality is that most parents never marry, marry and later divorce, or create their family through artificial insemination or adoption.

B. Keep Your Parenting Plan Focused on Your Children

You and your children's other parent are about to undertake a difficult but very important project—making adult decisions that will be the best possible ones for your children to live with. Of course, it may be hard to separate the desire to have nothing more to do with your ex from the task at hand. After all, separation and divorce were not created to meet children's needs but rather to resolve adult problems.

Even if your separation or divorce will be better for your children in the long run, for the short term, most children feel that few things are worse. Divorce or separation can shake a child's confidence that he or she will continue to be loved, cared for and safe. This is true even when children understand the adult reasons behind the decision.

You and the other parent can greatly ease your children's insecurity by using this book to formulate a parenting plan which is focused squarely on meeting your children's individual needs. The more attention you pay to those needs, the more likely you are to build an agreement that works for you as well.

You and the other parent must honestly assess your relationship as parents, as well as your ability to work together. To keep your agreement focused on your children, you must be willing to trust each other and to set aside your anger, frustration and pain. If you've just separated, you may think it will be impossible to trust and cooperate with the other parent. In fact, however, trustful and cooperative separate parenting relationships usually do evolve over time. (See Section C, below.) One of the most effective strategies for moving toward this kind of relationship is to build on points of agreement until you craft a comprehensive parenting plan.

DIVORCE AND SEPARATION AREN'T ONLY ABOUT ENDING AN INTIMATE RELATIONSHIP

Every divorce or separation is actually a series of mini-divorces or mini-separations. The partners are rejecting or severing their emotional, financial, legal, social, and intimate relationships. Unless you and your ex (or soon to be ex) prepare for each of these, you will find that you feel helpless to chart your own course. You may not be very happy with the results if you don't take an active role in shaping your own and your children's future.

C. Know That It Gets Easier Over Time

When parents initially separate or divorce, the process is often traumatic. Many people behave irrationally or are unstable. As time passes, however, many parents can entertain a more rational and dispassionate view of their options.

Let's look more closely at the typical emotional stages parents pass through upon separation, and how these stages might affect each parent's ability to reach an effective, child-focused parenting plan.

1. The First Few Weeks

Just before or just after the initial separation, you are likely to feel confused by a seemingly endless array of decisions, each of which appears the most important. Like most parents, you are probably riding a roller coaster of emotions that includes intense feelings of rage, depression, abandonment, relief, grief, guilt and excitement. In short, deciding to end a relationship, or having one ended for you, can leave you feeling as though you might be going crazy!

Now is not the time to worry about charting a permanent course for your children's future. Your own emotional survival—as well as that of your children—is very much at stake and must be your first priority.

GET HELP
A number of books have been written to help parents going through separation or divorce cope at the beginning. See Chapter 11 for references.

2. The First Few Months

Several months after the initial separation, your life will probably be a little calmer, but you may still find that your relationship with the other parent can enrage either or both of you. One reason is that while you distance yourself from the other parent, you continue to share your children. They can be a constant reminder of what has gone on (or has gone wrong) and what remains to be done. If you are experimenting with a new partner or approach to how you live your life, you may feel annoyed at the damper on your newfound freedom that you think the other parent's presence introduces.

At the other end of the spectrum, you or the other parent may still feel angry, sad, powerless or abandoned as you did when you first separated. If so, either of you may suspect that every action or inaction by the other is another ploy to retaliate or undercut your newfound stability.

If you try to negotiate a parenting plan during this phase, you may find it extremely difficult to reach agreement on any but the easiest issues. Many parents, nevertheless, negotiate workable temporary parenting arrangements early on, especially to resolve a particular issue, such as where the children will attend school.

3. One Year Later

A year or more after the initial separation, you may be far more clear-headed about your situation than you were when you first separated. You and the other parent will have firsthand experience with your initial (or temporary) parenting arrangements. You can gauge the effects that these arrangements have had on your life and on your children. You will probably be ready to address most, if not all of the issues presented in Chapter 5.

4. The Second Year and Beyond

Two years or more following a separation, most families have settled into their first parenting arrangements, and many realize that their arrangments need at least a few changes in order to accomodate the changes in their own or their children's lives. In fact, many mediators report that significant numbers of families renegotiate their first parenting agreement around two years after their separation.

No matter what stage of the separation you are in, remember that the one constant element of separate parenting is change. Neither you, the other parent, nor your children can expect the first agreement to be the last. You can never anticipate all of the decisions you will have to make on behalf of your children. Certain provisions will work for the long term while others will need to be revised regularly.

The changes that can trigger the need to modify a parenting agreement are many. One of the most common is the presence of a parent's new partner. Children often have strong opinions about new stepparents, boyfriends or girlfriends. Additionally, when one parent has a new partner—especially if that is the parent with whom the children primarily live—the other parent may need reassurance that he or she will not be replaced by the new partner.

Other changes that tend to trigger the need for a modification of an existing arrangement include:

- a parent's desire to move to change jobs or go back to school
- a parent's desire to move to be closer to relatives
- a child's special needs, or
- a child's desire to live with the other parent.

D. Learn How to Negotiate

Negotiation is the process of reaching an agreement which is acceptable to the people involved. The more successful the negotiation, the more acceptable the agreement. For the following three major reasons, negotiation is an integral part of separate parenting:

- Most parents tend to be involved with their children, at some level, well into their early adulthood. Parents who stay involved in their children's lives must find a way to work together.
- Children usually want to maintain a relationship with both parents and suffer when their parents constantly fight. The better the parents are at negotiating satisfactory solutions to their differences, the better their relationships will be with their children.
- When parents are unable to agree on basic decisions regarding their children's health, education and wel-

fare, a court will step in and impose decisions. These decisions, though aimed at protecting and preserving the best interests of the children, are often very different from what the parents want or feel is appropriate.

Negotiating your parenting agreement is covered in detail in Chapter 4.

USING MEDIATION TO HELP YOU NEGOTIATE

There are several basic approaches to negotiating a parenting agreement. Some parents resolve the issues on their own. Others ask a counselor to help, work with attorneys or use mediation. Mediation is a process that uses a trained neutral person (someone who has nothing to gain or lose by what you decide) to help you identify the issues to resolve and reach solutions. It offers many advantages because you control the decision-making process.

Mediation is available in all states, either through the court or from private practitioners, and has become popular because it is less adversarial than courtroom litigation. It is discussed in Chapter 6.

E. If the Other Parent Is Absent

This book assumes that both parents are at least minimally involved in their children's lives. This, however, is not always true. Some parents leave their families and are never heard from again. Others are around so infrequently that they have abandoned their families in most respects. If this describes your situation, you will probably need the help of an attorney to get a divorce (if you're legally married) and obtain child support.

With respect to daily parenting, consider talking with one of the children's grandparents, a favorite aunt or uncle or a very close friend about sharing the parenting. If it works, you'll have adult help and your children will have the benefit of another adult's influence while growing up.

F. If There Is Violence or Abuse in the Family

Situations involving violence or abuse usually call for outside help. Most of the information in this book assumes that your family situation is conducive to negotiating and reaching a parenting agreement. In some families, however, serious issues such as child abuse or ongoing violence between the parents make negotiating nearly impossible.

In these circumstances, you will want to consult with a mental health professional, an attorney or your court to learn about available options. See Chapter 11 for suggestions on finding outside resources. If your family situation stabilizes to the point that you are able to negotiate a parenting plan, this book can then be of help. Issue 15 in Chapter 5 will help you and the other parent to address domestic violence. ■

An Introduction to Parenting Agreements

broadest sense, a parenting agreement is the sum total of the arrangements parents make about parenting separately. Common convention and state laws describe these arrangements as "custody." The term "parenting agreement" better reflects the needs and involvement of all concerned, because it implies that the agreement is both comprehensive and tailored to meet each family's needs.

A. What Parenting Agreements Cover

Parenting agreements may be vague or detailed, casual or legalistic. Your agreement will reflect your (and the other parent's) preferences and your state's requirements.

As mentioned in the *Introduction*, a parenting agreement addresses:

- taking care of the children
- making necessary decisions on the children's behalf
- making sure the children spend time with both parents, and
- meeting the children's medical, psychological, educational, spiritual, physical and social needs.

Increasingly, parenting plans address many more issues, such as transporting the children between parents' houses, the roles of parents' new partners and how parents should communicate when issues arise. Comprehensive agreements offer clarity, anticipate the needs of the parents and children over time, and pave the way for better communication and understanding.

B. Advantages of Parent Negotiated Agreements

Parents are almost always in the best position to know what arrangements are preferable for their children. You know your children's interests, hopes, strengths and weaknesses. You know how your children deal with change and what makes change easier for them to accept. If you can work with the other parent to plan for your children's future, you will provide them the best possible springboard to adjust to your separation or divorce and reassure them that they are loved and cared for.

1. Minimize Court Involvement

You may be surprised to find that we suggest you consult the law and courts last when considering how you resolve parenting issues. This is because, the law, for all its express protections for children, doesn't know your individual children. This is where your experience as a parent comes to the fore. When you and the other parent focus first on understanding and meeting your children's needs and second on finding ways to cooperate to meet those needs, you pave the way for a successful separate parenting relationship.

Cooperating eliminates the need for an outside person with limited information, such as a judge or court-appointed evaluator, to make decisions for you. This doesn't mean, however, that parent-negotiated agreements are completely independent of the legal system. Rather, they are created in the "shadow of the law." This means that a court retains the authority to review your agreement and make sure it is in your children's best interests. If the court finds that it is not, the court will reject your plan and impose its own.

All states have their own criteria for determining the best interests of the children. Determining what is or is not in your children's best interests is an inexact process. Some of the factors to be considered, however, include:

- age
- temperament
- relationships with each parent
- special needs or activities, and

• religious and social values.

In "Parent-Child Relationships in Family Mediation," by Michelle Samis and Donald Saposnek, *Mediation Quarterly* (1987), the authors list several simple but key characteristics of agreements they feel protect a child's best interests. Parents and parenting agreements must take into account that separation or divorce is a stress on children. Therefore, parenting agreements must try to anticipate and reduce conflict, allow for continuing relationships with both parents and other adults with whom the children have significant bonds, and allow everyone to find "normalcy" in their new relationships through consistent routines.

Each state's laws are summarized in Chapter 10. Skim that chapter before you draft your plan. Then read it carefully after you complete your agreement so you can make any necessary adjustments.

2. Reduce Conflict

Many parents initially doubt they can negotiate their own parenting agreement. In addition, parents often question whether any plan can transform the anger, pain, confusion and disarray of the break-up into a viable way of parenting. Take heart! The experiences of the vast majority of families who separate or divorce show that conflict, legal or otherwise, is far less than the media—or lawyers—would have us believe. In fact, study after study shows that only about 15% of custody agreements are the product of a full court trial. In most instances, parents negotiate their own agreement, often with the help of an outside professional, such as an attorney, mediator or counselor.

MOST FAMILIES SEPARATE WITHOUT SIGNIFICANT CONFLICT

Dividing the Child, by Elenor Maccoby and Robert Mnookin (Harvard Press, 1992), studies custody and visitation. The researchers measured conflict levels within divorced families by interviewing both parents at three separate times over a three-year period. The researchers found that 51% of families experienced "negligible" conflict, 24% experienced "mild" conflict, 10% experienced "substantial" conflict, and only 15% of families were locked in "intense" conflict.

3. Increase Fairness

Parents, children and professionals all agree that the most successful agreements are those that the parties can describe as fair, meaning that even if they didn't "win" everything, they feel that they have gained something. If your parenting plan is clear and detailed, you will find that day-to-day living is simpler and everyone's responsibilities are well understood. While most children hope for reconciliation, they can probably adapt to almost any plan if they are confident that you believe it to be fair.

C. Goals of a Successful Parenting Agreement

Although every parenting agreement is different, the most successful parenting plans emerge out of a commitment by both parents to:

- reduce the conflict between the parents
- encourage good parent-child relationships between the children and both parents, and
- make the changes inherent in a separation or divorce easier for the children to accept.

1. Reduce Conflict Between Parents

Reducing conflict is undoubtedly your most important goal in separate parenting. Despite this, parents sometimes continue to battle long after their separation or divorce. Often, it is because they:

- cannot accept the reality of a separation or divorce
- want to remain involved with the other parent, at any cost
- have unresolved anger
- have incompatible parenting values
- fear for the well-being of their children when they are with the other parent
- have a history of violence between them, or
- blame the other for the failed relationship.

Holding onto these feelings is perfectly normal, and quite common. If you let negative feelings linger months and even years after a divorce, however, your ability to cooperate in child-rearing will be impaired. Your children will bear the brunt of the anger, blame and acrimony that you display, and will carry the scars for a very long time.

HOW CHILDREN REACT TO CONFLICT IN DIVORCE

In *How It Feels When Parents Divorce*, by Dr. Jill Krementz (Alfred A. Knopf, 1984), the author presents the statements of children she interviewed after their parents had divorced.

Zach, aged 13, voiced a common feeling that children share about being fought over when he says: "...If they had fought over us, I know that I would have felt like I was a check in a restaurant—you know, the way it is at the end of a meal when two people are finished eating and they both grab for the check and one says 'I'll pay for it,' and the other one says 'No, this one is mine,' and they go back and forth, but secretly neither one wants it, they just go on pretending until someone finally grabs it, and then that one's stuck."

Tracy, aged 16, fears that she may never escape the conflict that already exists in her family. She says "... The worst thing by far about my parents' divorce is that it's still going on. I mean, my parents don't talk. If they have to talk, it's like screaming. I thought that once the divorce was over, my Mom and Dad could just get on with their lives, but it hasn't worked out that way. I think the fighting will never stop."

2.   Encourage Good Parent-Child Relationships

The fear of losing contact or a relationship with one parent usually looms large in the minds of children whose parents are undergoing a separation or divorce. Even well-intentioned parents can inadvertently communicate the idea that their children will hurt them if they show open affection and regard for the other parent.

In *Divorce and Your Child*, by Sonja Goldstein and Albert Solnit (Yale University Press, 1984), the authors present two very compelling arguments against undermining the relationship with the other parent. First, if you succeed in curtailing or preventing visits with the other parent, your children might lose trust in you, fearful of what other harm you might do. Children have relatively little control over how their lives will be structured under any circumstances, let alone after their parents separate or divorce. Your children will watch you very carefully to see if they can trust you to structure their world so that it includes the people they love.

Second, when children are cut off from a parent, they often feel deprived of an important piece of themselves. Many children who are cut off from contact with one parent following a separation or divorce act as adopted children do, searching for their roots by seeking out their biological parents. If you force your children to abandon contact with their other parent, your children may blame you for the lost relationship.

Children will go to great lengths to avoid appearing to "choose" one parent over another. They will often tell you just what they think you want to hear—that the other parent is not as good as, not as well liked as, and maybe even more dispensable than are you. While it is certainly preferable "not to say anything if you can't say something nice," if you are not careful, your children will get the message that the other parent's existence is to be denied in your home if they are to remain in your good graces.

This aside, some parents discourage or prevent children's visits with the other parent out of concern over the environment in that parent's home. Knowing when your concerns are justified is not always easy. If you fear for your children's physical or emotional safety, then you may be right to seek supervised, restricted or no visits with the other parent. If the dangers are less obvious and threatening, you will need to examine your own motives very carefully, looking at the situation through your children's eyes whenever possible.

3.   Make Changes Easier for Your Children to Accept

The key to helping your children accept the changes that accompany separation and divorce is to work very hard to develop a parenting agreement that everyone feels is fair and workable. Children can adapt to their changed circumstances and to the differences in their parents' living arrangements, house rules and expectations if they see that you are doing your best to be sensitive to their needs. Children can accept that:

- the rules in one household are not necessarily the same as in the other
- each parent is his or her own person and has his or her own style
- each parent has his or her own strengths and weaknesses, and
- their needs can be met even if their parents live in different homes because there will be an expanding world of people who love and support them.

D. Parenting Agreements and Custody

When parents separate or divorce, the term "custody" often serves as shorthand for "who gets the children." Legally, the term has a much broader meaning because it applies to the total relationship parents have with their children. All parents are obligated to provide for their children's physical and emotional needs, and to protect and preserve what is fundamental to their best interests—medical care, education, food, shelter and safety. Custody implies all of these responsibilities.

When parents separate, the custody they jointly exercised over their children must change to accommodate the new living arrangements and the new relationship between the parents. The modification may be minor if the parents live near each other and can communicate well, or profound if ongoing conflict prevents cooperation in parenting. For most parents, it's somewhere in between.

In a divorce or legal separation, courts commonly order either sole custody or shared custody. Under a sole custody arrangement, one parent is the primary care-giver and the other parent's visits are defined by a set schedule. Under a shared custody arrangement, both parents enjoy significant amounts of time with their children and make decisions together.

Some states distinguish between the legal authority to make decisions and providing physical care of the children. In these states, courts can make any of the following orders:

- **Sole legal and physical custody.** In this arrangement, one parent assumes the decision-making responsibility, and children spend most of their time with that parent.

- **Shared legal and sole physical custody.** Parents share decision-making authority, but the children spend most of their time with only one parent.
- **Shared legal custody and shared physical custody.** Parents share decision-making authority, and the children divide their time fairly equally between their parents.

Chapter 10 contains information on the different forms of custody each state authorizes.

If parents cooperate in drafting and implementing a detailed parenting agreement, the court (if authorized) is likely to issue a shared custody order. On the other hand, if the parents show an inability to reach agreement on important child rearing issues, the court may issue a sole custody award to one parent, allowing the other "reasonable" visitation. Clearly, a sole custody award heavily favors the "custodial" parent in caring for and making decisions on behalf of the children.

In some states like New Hampshire and New Mexico, the court must begin with the premise that it will order shared custody unless it would not be in children's best interests. In 21 states, a court may order shared custody even when one of the parents disagrees. (See Chapter 10.) So in all of these states, even if you don't successfully negotiate a parenting plan, you may end up with a shared custody order if you are in court.

In Chapter 5, you will select a specific custody arrangement to include in your parenting plan—assuming you and the other parent are ending a legal marriage. Additional information is in Chapter 7, *Understanding Your Children's Needs*, and (if applicable) Chapter 9, *Nontraditional Families.*

MOST OPPOSITE-SEX COUPLES SELECT SOLE CUSTODY TO MOTHER

For a variety of reasons, most opposite-sex parenting couples agree that the mother will have custody after a separation or divorce and that the father will exercise reasonable visitation. For some, this happens because fathers presume that mothers will be awarded custody. In others, it happens because of the mother's fear that she will be judged poorly if she is not the primary caretaker. In still other situations, the parents agree that the mother has more time, a greater inclination or a better understanding of the children's daily needs.

E. Parenting Agreements and Money

While this book does not deal directly with child support or alimony, or the division of marital or otherwise jointly acquired property, how you resolve these issues certainly can affect your parenting agreement. This aside, some parents equate their obligation to pay child support with the "right" to visit the child, while others equate owing child support with having lost the "right" to visit the child. In fact, neither position is accurate or reflects a consideration for your children's best interests.

Adequate financial support is certainly a critical element of any child's care. Providing support is also the legal responsibility of every parent, regardless of custody arrangements. For this reason, all states separate child support issues from custody and visitation issues in a separation or divorce. Additionally, no state allows a parent to withhold visitation because the other parent owes support, or withhold support because of disputes over visitation. Quite simply, children need financial, physical and emotional support, but children are not to be traded or withheld for money. Happily, the more noncustodial parents are involved in their children's lives, the more seriously they take their child support obligations.

Maccoby and Mnookin (*Dividing the Child*, Harvard Press, 1992) discovered a telling relationship among custody and visitation arrangements, levels of conflict and payment of court-ordered child support. In their findings, most families opt for custody with the mother, while the father pays child support. On average, fathers paid between two-thirds and three-fourths of the awarded support amounts, but their compliance fell off over time. Fathers tended to continue paying child support when they had regular and frequent daytime and overnight visits with their children. The less involved with their children's lives they became, the less apt they were to keep paying support.

The implications of this research for building successful parenting agreements are obvious. The more involved a parent is in his or her children's lives, the more likely he or she is to continue paying child support. The less involved a parent is in his or her children's lives, the more likely he or she is to stop.

MOTHERS FARE WORSE AFTER DIVORCE THAN DO FATHERS

Much has been made of the changed circumstances, financially, when families separate or divorce. Initially, both parents experience substantially reduced economic resources. Over time, this may change significantly depending on new jobs, better pay, remarriage, public assistance, the sale of property or other factors. One disturbing fact, however, emerges consistently. Although the economic well-being of divorced mothers and their children increases over time, the income of mothers who do not remarry remains substantially below the father's income. By contrast, the economic well-being of divorced fathers (over time) remains substantially above pre-separation levels. Despite this significant discrepancy, custodial mothers remain the primary support for their children in the years following the divorce. Even if paid in full, child and alimony represent only a fraction of the mother's post-divorce household income.

In Dr. Jill Krementz' interviews with children who live in divorced families (*How It Feels When Parents Divorce*, Alfred A. Knopf, 1984), Ari, aged 14 says "... the worst part of the divorce is the money problem. It's been hard on my Mom because lots of times she can't pay her bills and it makes her angry when I stay with my father and he buys me things. She gets mad and says things like 'If he can buy you things like this, then he should be able to pay me.' And I feel caught in the middle.... I can't really enjoy whatever my Dad does get for me, and ... I don't know who to believe."

Preparing to Build Your Parenting Agreement

As any good builder will tell you, you need the right tools and supplies at hand before you start to build, or the building is likely to fall. Your first tasks when preparing to build your parenting agreement are to review all relevant documents and take stock of your relationship with your children. Below are four worksheets to help you with this task.

WHEN TO CONSULT AN ATTORNEY

The ideal situation for taking stock would be one in which you can take the time to evaluate all options before making any decisions. You may not have that luxury right now, however. Consult an attorney as soon as possible if you are in any of the following situations:

- court hearings or deadlines require you to make decisions quickly
- you are involved in court proceedings you don't understand
- you are not sure of what you want or what your rights are
- you feel overwhelmed and unable to adequately represent yourself
- you have been sued for paternity
- a high degree of conflict between you and the other parent absolutely precludes negotiations
- the other parent has hired an attorney
- you are the subject of a "home study" or other custody evaluation, or
- the court is considering terminating your parental rights.

A. Organize and Review All Pertinent Documents

To successfully negotiate with the other parent, or to work well with any professional, you will want to collect and review all relevant documents. These include:

- court documents you have filed or received, such as a "summons," "petition," "complaint," "response," "answer," "declaration" or "affidavit"
- correspondence from an attorney, counselor, mediator or court official regarding a separation, divorce, paternity, child support, custody or visitation
- court orders regarding a legal separation, divorce, paternity declaration or award of custody
- previously mediated, arbitrated or negotiated agreements between you and the other parent

- documents dissolving your religious marriage, or describing your marital status and your options according to your religious denomination, and
- reports, letters or evaluations from school officials, counselors, therapists or others who have an insight into your children.

Carefully read the documents you gather. If you need help in finding or understanding any of them, an attorney, court clerk, paralegal, marriage counselor, mediator, member of the clergy or other professional might be useful. Chapter 11 offers tips on finding people and resources to help you.

You won't necessarily need all of these documents to develop a parenting plan. Nevertheless, having them can help expedite matters, especially if you are going through a legal separation or divorce. For example, if you or the other parent have already initiated a court proceeding, you may have a deadline for submitting your parenting agreement. If you begin negotiations and they seem to be going well, you will probably want to ask the court for an extension of time (called a "continuance") to let your negotiations continue. In short, you need to know where you stand right now so you can take all necessary steps to finalize your agreement, assure your rights and satisfy all legal requirements.

B. Take Stock of Your Relationship With Your Children

Now it's time to take stock of your relationship with your children on the four worksheets set out below. Some of this will be fun, especially when you describe your child. Some of it may be painful. Some of it will be mundane, especially when you gather basic facts and figures. All of this information is important, however, because it will highlight the issues and concerns that your parenting agreement must address. The issues and options you go through in Chapter 5 to build your parenting agreement refer back to answers on these worksheets which might help during your discussions with the other parent.

There are no right or wrong answers for the questions on these worksheets. What is most important is that you try to answer each question thoughtfully and completely. The more information you have at hand when you build your parenting agreement, the better your agreement will meet your needs and your children's needs.

Parenting agreements are meant to focus on children, so you will begin by describing your children. You will need to visualize how the world looks through their eyes. A school counselor or teacher, trusted adult friend, religious leader or other adult who knows your children might be able to add some objective insights.

HOW CHILDREN EXPERIENCE DIVORCE

Drs. Judith Wallerstein and Joan Kelly were the first researchers to investigate and document children's views and reactions to divorce. As a result of their work, therapists, attorneys, parents and courts have a new understanding of the effects of divorce on children. Wallerstein and Kelly found that children experience shock, depression, denial, anger, low self esteem, shame and guilt (though guilt is primarily experienced by younger children), regardless of their outward behavior.

Behaviorally, different children respond differently to divorce or separation. Some become overly good, some lash out at anyone and everyone nearby, some withdraw into a shell and some regress to a younger behavioral age. These realities can make the task of understanding your children quite difficult. You may have to play detective as well as parent.

To help you clarify your feelings and your goals for your future relationship with your children, complete the four worksheets. You can use them in your own negotiations, or to educate any mediator, counselor, lawyer or other person who might help you develop a parenting agreement.

Each parent should complete a separate copy of Worksheets 1, 2 and 3. Working independently lets you each focus on your own feelings and impressions. It also takes some of the pressure off by allowing you to think for yourselves without having to agree about how to answer each question.

Worksheet 4 is meant to be filled out together. You and the other parent use your answers from the first three worksheets to generate a checklist of the core points to include in your parenting agreement. You can start the process by reading each other's completed Worksheets 1, 2 and 3. The answers that you record on Worksheet 4 should reflect both parent's views. If you disagree, put down both responses.

For parenting agreements to work, they must be relevant to you, the other parent and to your children. If sharing

your answers to Worksheets 1, 2 and 3 is difficult or provokes arguments, consult Chapter 4, *How to Negotiate a Parenting Agreement,* or consider bringing in a mediator or counselor. Chapter 6 has information on finding a mediator and making the most of mediation. Chapter 11 has material on finding a counselor.

Below are sample completed worksheets. Blank copies are in the appendix. Before filling out any of the worksheets, make at least the number of photocopies suggested in the instructions. You can make more to allow for mistakes.

The questions on the worksheets are mostly open-ended and are meant to make you think. Fill out the worksheets in order, as each one builds upon the previous.

⚠ RESIST THE URGE TO MOVE QUICKLY

Most separating and divorcing parents reach a point when they want to just get it over with and move on with their lives. Those feelings are natural and tempting, but unrealistic. By demonstrating some patience now, you and your children will be far happier as the years go by.

1. Worksheet 1: Describe Your Child

Worksheet 1: *Describe Your Child,* asks you:
- what kind of a person your child is
- what puts your child at his or her best, and
- what makes change easier or harder for your child to accept.

Each parent needs one blank copy of this worksheet for each child. For example, if you have three children, you will need six copies.

If you have more than one child and want to put the same answer for one child as you gave for another, write "same as (child's name)" to indicate which worksheet contains your answer.

👪 FAMILY PROFILE

This family consists of a mother, a father and their only daughter, Susan, who is now 11 years old. Susan's parents live in the same community, and Susan can easily ride the bus to either parent's home after school. Since her parent's separation, Susan has been living with her mother one week and her father the next week. Susan's mother completed this form.

WORKSHEET 1: DESCRIBE YOUR CHILD

Child's name: Susan

1. What kind of person is this child?

    Happy, intelligent, but concerned about what is going to happen after our divorce is final.

2. What makes this child special?

    She has a great sense of humor, likes sports, likes to help others, loves animals.

3. How does this child like the current parenting arrangements?

    She is not very happy about having to change homes all of the time, but seems to understand
    that it's necessary now. She complains about not knowing which house to come home to after
    school and which room to decorate. She is embarrassed about having to give friends two
    numbers to call. Although she doesn't like having to spend holidays or her birthday with just
    one of us at a time, she doesn't seem to mind that she gets to celebrate twice!

4. How has this child's behavior changed since the separation or divorce?

    She has been a lot quieter than usual. She seems to be trying to find ways to get us back
    together. Her behavior has been pretty good, and I have really appreciated not having to fight
    with her all the time over the little things like what to wear or who she should play with. She
    has been helpful around the house and keeps her room clean.

5. Has this child expressed any preferences regarding the future?

    Other than wishing that we would get back together, she hasn't had much to say about the
    future.

6. How does this child react to change?

    She seems pretty resilient. As long as you tell her what is going to happen and why, she
    handles it O.K.

7. What makes change easier for this child to accept?

    She needs to be told ahead of time and allowed to ask questions.

8. How does this child let you know that something is wrong?

    She usually says something, but sometimes I have to try and figure it out because her behavior
    gets worse or she starts fighting with her friends.

9. Who else is important in this child's life?

    Her grandparents on her father's side, her cousins Nick and Tim, my brother and Susan are
    especially close, and she has lots of friends around where we live.

2.   Worksheet 2: Describe Your Relationship With Your Child

Worksheet 2: *Describe Your Relationship With Your Child,* asks you about your relationship with your child, including:

- things that you like to do together
- plans you have for this child's future
- details about your parenting style with this child
- how you would propose to share your parenting responsibilities, and
- whether you are happy with the current parenting relationship.

Each parent needs one blank copy of this worksheet for each child. For example, if you have three children, you will need six copies.

If you have more than one child and want to put the same answer for one child as you gave for another, write "same as (child's name)" to indicate which worksheet contains your answer.

FAMILY PROFILE

This family consists of a mother, a father and two boys, Jimmy aged 6 and Nathan aged 14 months. The worksheet was completed by the father and describes only his relationship with Jimmy. Jimmy's parents have been divorced for 6 months; Jimmy's mother has custody and the father has asked that they renegotiate their current arrangements.

WORKSHEET 2: DESCRIBE YOUR RELATIONSHIP WITH YOUR CHILD

Child's name: Jimmy

1. What do you and this child like to do together?

    We go to the park, the zoo and to his T-Ball games. I try to take him to see my folks at least once a month so that he can play with all of the cousins.

2. What are your plans and wishes for this child's future?

    I want him to grow up knowing that both of us love him. He should go to college, but he can be whatever he wants.

3. What do you think are the most important things for this child to achieve?

    He should be able to move on with his life and not let our divorce affect him so much. He should know that he can come to either of us with his problems. He should be able to grow up in exactly the same way as if we had stayed together.

4. How do you and this child handle and resolve conflict?

    For the most part we just talk about it. Sometimes I have to discipline him, but that doesn't happen too often.

5. How do you handle discipline with this child?

    Usually he gets sent to his room or loses a privilege, like playing with his friends or riding his bike.

6. How did you share parenting responsibilities and time with this child during the time you were married or living together?

    I did a lot for Jimmy. I always gave him his bath, helped him with his homework and played games with him. Sometimes I fixed the meals and I did the housework. I was always involved in something to do with raising Jimmy.

7. How do you and the other parent share parenting responsibilities and time with this child now?

    We share the responsibilities just fine. I try to keep up with all of Jimmy's activities. I help out with the T-Ball team and go to the open houses at his school. I try to get in at least one parent-teacher conference a year. Since Jimmy has so many friends here, I always know how things are going with his buddies.

8. Are you happy with the current arrangements? (Please explain)

    Not entirely. I want more time with Jimmy since I am so active in his life. I still feel like I'm being treated like the "other parent" and that's not fair. Although we don't fight as much about Jimmy, I still feel a lot of tension between us on this subject.

9. Is this child happy with the current arrangements? (Please explain)

Jimmy says that he misses me a lot and that he wants to spend more time with me. I think
that would be better because I spend more quality time with him than his mother does.

10. If changes are in order, what would you suggest?

I think Jimmy should live with me most of the time. The school district for my area is better,
which means he'll have a better basis for being successful in college. Also, my job is more
flexible and I have made Jimmy my priority.

3. Worksheet 3: Adding the Details

Worksheet 3: *Adding the Details*, has you identify miscellaneous information needed when drafting a parenting agreement, such as:

- important documents
- work schedules and living arrangements
- your children's activities, needs and interests
- yourself and your children's religious denomination
- counseling histories, and
- histories of domestic violence or substance abuse.

Each parent should start with at least one blank copy.

FAMILY PROFILE

The sample family represented in this form consists of a mother (Marilyn), a father (Sean) and three children: Jennifer (age 12), Brandon (age 10) and Matthew (age 4). This form has been completed by Marilyn. Marilyn and Sean were married for 14 years and are about to finalize their divorce. They have been separated for almost a year. Since Sean moved out, the children have been living with Marilyn in the family home. The entire process has been hard for everyone, and the parents have a difficult time talking about anything without arguing.

WORKSHEET 3: ADDING THE DETAILS

1. List of existing court documents, orders or agreements: (Note that the terms listed here might be different in your state. See Chapter 11 for the terms used in your state.)

    Divorce Petition, Response, Separation Agreement

2. Parent's name, occupation and work schedule.

    Marilyn, Accountant, Tuesday - Saturday 8:00 - 3:30

3. Schedule of children's activities (such as school, religious training and after-school activities).

    Jennifer: school, after school sports, 4-H; Brandon: school, after school sports;

    Matthew: day care

    all three children go to Sunday School and participate in the youth group

4. Children's special needs or interests.

    Brandon needs his ADD medication each day; all three children like to spend as much time as

    possible riding their bikes and playing with their friends when their homework is finished and

    they have no other commitments.

5. Religion.

    Parent—Methodist   Children—Methodist

6. Where do you live now?

    123 Main Street, Smithtown

7. Do you have any plans to relocate from the area? (Please explain)

    I might have to move out of the area for work. I won't know that for a year though because our

    firm hasn't yet decided whether to open a branch office.

8. Do you have any plans for remarriage?

    Not at this time.

9. Are there any adult relatives or friends with whom the children should or should not have close contact?

    The children should continue to see their cousins and grandparents on both sides. They should

    not be around Aunt Rachel or Uncle George if they have been drinking.

10. Counseling for children.

All three children received counseling from school counselor and Dr. Jones regarding the divorce and the level of conflict in our home over the last year. I think we should offer them additional counseling, but not force them to go.

11. Counseling for parents.

We received counseling from Dr. Jones regarding the divorce from July-December of last year. I'd be willing to go again if Sean would agree to it.

12. Do you want to address domestic violence issues in your Parenting Agreement? If yes, why?

Yes. We only seemed to have serious problems at the end, but I'm worried about what might happen now that we're both single parents.

13. Do you want to address the use or abuse of drugs or alcohol in your Parenting Agreement? If yes, how do you think these issues should be handled in your parenting agreement?

Yes. Sean should start attending Alcoholics Anonymous meetings.

14. Do you have any special concerns about your parenting arrangements?

Yes, I think that all three children need a parent around as much as possible. I don't believe in leaving them alone to take care of themselves like Sean does when he has the children.

15. Do you have any special concerns about your relationship with the other parent?

All three children are doing fairly well, but I think that Sean must be blaming the divorce on me because they seem so angry with me. I wish that Sean would stop bad-mouthing me in front of the children and that we could limit our conversations to the children.

4. Worksheet 4: Checklist of Issues for Your Parenting Agreement

In Worksheet 4: *Checklist of Issues for Your Parenting Agreement*, you and the other parent work together to identify the issues you want to cover in your parenting agreement. Before you start, you should each read the other's answers recorded on Worksheets 1, 2 and 3. Also skim the table of contents for Chapter 5, which lists 40 issues you can include in your parenting agreement. As you build your parenting agreement in that chapter, you will be reminded to review your answers on these four worksheets.

Make at least two copies of Worksheet 4. Record your answers on one copy unless you disagree. In that case, put one answer on the main copy and the other parent's answer on the second copy, or squeeze both answers onto the main copy. Try to avoid arguments. Your goal in this worksheet is to identify issues, not to start negotiating your agreement.

FAMILY PROFILE

This family consists of a mother (Gloria), a father (Sam), and two boys: David (age 9) and Zachary (age 5). Gloria and Sam were married for ten years and have been separated for six months. They are both Catholic and are seeking an annulment of their marriage through the Church. Two years ago, Gloria reached the conclusion that she was a lesbian but did not tell her family until just prior to the separation. She moved out of the family home and lives alone. Sam and Gloria tried counseling off and on for a year prior to their separation. When they separated, they negotiated a temporary parenting agreement and obtained a court order formalizing their agreement. Currently, David and Zachary live with Sam during the week and with Gloria on the weekends. Gloria would like to negotiate a permanent agreement and to expand her time with the children.

WORKSHEET 4: CHECKLIST OF ISSUES FOR YOUR PARENTING AGREEMENT

1. Existing court documents, orders or agreements which must be changed to accommodate your parenting agreement.

   Temporary Order awarding child custody.

2. Existing agreements to consider while negotiating this parenting agreement.

   Temporary parenting agreement reached at the end of marriage counseling.

3. Steps you will have to take to resolve legal or religious issues such as divorce, legal separation, annulment, etc.

   We will have to get a permanent court order and an annulment of the marriage through the Church.

4. Any concerns or recommendations made by a counselor, school, therapist or other interested adult regarding your children's emotional, spiritual or physical well-being.

   The marriage counselor thinks that we need to continue some form of counseling to help the children deal with the divorce and the fact that Gloria has realized that she is a lesbian.

5. Each child's current relationship with each parent.

   David has a good relationship with both of us. As long as we are not fighting, he seems able to get along with each of us. He likes to have Sam help out with his sports and other activities, and wants Gloria to stay active in his school events.

   Zachary seems to be taking the divorce harder than David. He has a good relationship with each of us, but his relationship with Gloria has suffered the most. Zachary is defiant with Gloria most of the time. Sam has an easier time getting Zachary to behave.

6. Each child's feelings, reactions or concerns about separation or divorce.

   Both boys are angry about the divorce but understand why we don't want to live together anymore. They are uncomfortable being around Gloria's new partner, but seem willing to work the situation out as a family. David is closest to Sam. Zachary alternates between being angry with both of us and wishing we could forget about the past and get back together.

7. Changes you think would be good in each child's current relationship with each parent.

David's relationship with both parents will probably improve on its own over time. Zachary needs to get over his anger so that he can regain his positive relationship with Gloria.

8. Changes that may be necessary in each child's current relationship with each parent.

Gloria and Zachary will have to find some way that they can comfortably spend time together, even if Gloria's new partner is around.

9. Current problem areas for children.

Both boys are having difficulty getting along with their friends right now. David's grades are not poor, but they could be much better. Zachary needs to be able to accept discipline from Gloria.

10. Current areas of conflict between the parents.

There is still a lot of conflict over Gloria's new life, although both of us agree that the other is a good parent and that we can find some way to both be heavily involved in raising the boys.

11. Changes either parent would like to see in current parenting relationship.

Gloria doesn't want to have to answer questions from Sam about her partner and her new life. Sam would like Gloria to have her partner around less often until the boys are more comfortable with the situation.

12. Times when either parent is available to care for children: _____

Both parents are available on Saturdays and Sundays and most weekday evenings.

13. Times when only _____Gloria_____ is available to care for children: ___Tuesday evenings___

14. Times when only _____Sam_____ is available to care for children: ___Wednesday evenings___

15. Other adults children will be spending time with.

David and Zachary are very close to both sets of grandparents. Gloria's parents usually take the boys on a one-week vacation each summer.

16. Adults or minors the children should not spend time with (or be alone with).

    No one.

17. Any problems with violence, abuse or neglect that would have to be accommodated.

    None.

18. Other comments or issues to be included.

    We should offer the children counseling, but they should not be forced to go if they don't want to.

How To Negotiate a Parenting Agreement

This chapter suggests ways to make your negotiations lead to a parenting agreement that works. When a parenting agreement works, the children's basic needs are met and both parents feel that it is an essentially fair way to do what is in the children's best interests. The keys to making your negotiations successful are preparation and a willingness to work at overcoming impasse.

A. Good Negotiations and Lasting Agreements

Good negotiations are built upon several key elements. First, you must put aside your anger or resentment in order to think clearly about what you are discussing. Second, you must remain focused on your goal of making decisions in your children's best interests. In good negotiations, both people feel that:

- they have been heard
- their positions are understood, and
- they understand the other's position (even if they don't agree with it).

For an agreement to last, it must rest on a foundation of understanding and mutual gain. Almost everyone will uphold agreements when they can see the advantage of doing so. For example, most parents will accommodate small changes in the parenting agreement if they feel that the agreement is generally fair and that both the children's and the adults' needs are being met.

Even when you disagree on an issue, you must listen in order to understand the other's position. Further, your solutions must help everyone to gain something by having the agreement succeed. Your successes will most likely be measured in terms of your children's happiness and well-being, and in the relationships they maintain with both parents.

In *Getting To Yes*, by Fisher and Ury (Penguin Books, 1981), the authors explain the advantages of creating agreements where everyone feels that at least some of their needs are being met. Often these are called "win-win" agreements—meaning that, each party has "won" something which they value.

Your agreement is most likely to last if:
- all issues have been addressed
- the solutions are achievable
- everyone feels valued
- everyone will gain something if the agreement succeeds

- everyone's roles and responsibilities are clearly defined
- it includes methods to evaluate whether everyone's needs are being met
- it includes ways to resolve future conflicts, and
- it includes ways to make changes.

GAME THEORY OFFERS INSIGHTS FOR IMPROVING YOUR NEGOTIATION STRATEGIES

People who study game theory construct a very simple game to measure which strategies produce the best results for each player. Although life is far more complex than any research game, research games offer valuable insight into winning strategies that can be applied to real life situations—and your negotiations with the other parent.

By playing a game called "Tit for Tat," invented by Canadian professor Anatol Rapoport, researchers studied the best ways to "win" one-on-one contests. In the short term, playing for one's own advantage produced the best score. Over time, the high score eroded, usually because the other players also played "selfishly." In the long run, "niceness" scored better than "selfishness." Most significantly for parents, players who matched a "nice" move for a "nice" move and a "selfish" move for a "selfish" move tended to score better than when acting only "nicely" or "selfishly" alone. When players allowed their opponents to get away with one "selfish" move before retaliating with a matching "selfish" move (thus approximating the concept of forgiveness), they scored highest of all. The single most important factor influencing a player's score, other than responding in like kind with a small amount of "forgiveness" built in, was having a predictable game strategy.

For more information on game theory, see *The Prisoner's Dilemma*, by William Poundstone (Doubleday & Company).

For many, negotiations and agreements need only be judged by whether they produce the best possible results at the lowest possible cost. Little thought is given to how the other party fares in the process. As long as you don't need to rely upon the other person during any future relationship, this philosophy may work. If, however, you and the other person will have an ongoing relationship (as is the case with your children's other parent), ignoring the other person's needs and interests could lead to ongoing conflict. If you accept the suggestions offered by game theory experts, you will have a higher probability of success in negotiating a good parenting agreement if you:

- remember that parenting is a long-term relationship
- approach the negotiation process in good faith
- try to maintain a predictable and "open" negotiation style, and
- allow each other a few missteps before responding in a negative fashion.

B. Preparing Your Negotiations to Succeed

The most successful negotiators draw upon an extensive array of problem-solving tools. Among them are the abilities to listen, generate ideas, find solutions and have empathy for others. By planning your negotiations, and in particular identifying effective negotiation strategies, you will improve your chances of reaching an agreement.

Below are ten specific strategies to help your negotiations succeed.

1. Identify the Facts, Issues and Desirable Solutions

To negotiate successfully, you must first identify the major issues to be addressed in your negotiations, and the ideal solutions to these issues. (You may have listed these issues in Worksheet 4, in Chapter 3.) Specifically, you must:

- list the specific issues you want covered in your agreement, and the impact each issue will have on you or your children
- acknowledge any conflict associated with a particular issue and identify what can be done to minimize the conflict
- explain what a good solution would achieve for everyone, and
- generate solutions which are acceptable to you.

For example, if you and the other parent cannot agree on who will make day-to-day decisions concerning your children, preparing for the negotiations might consist of:

- recognizing that making decisions together means being able to set aside conflict
- acknowledging that past efforts at making decisions together often ended up in arguments

- learning communication and negotiation techniques for making discussions more productive
- defining "success" in terms of lack of conflict, focus on the children and timely resolutions, and
- resolving that you both will read and follow the suggestions in this chapter, and restrict your conversations only to issues concerning the children.

Next, think about how to present your ideas to the other parent. Your goal is to have thought through the issues from the other parent's perspective, and to anticipate his or her concerns. The Native American admonishment to "walk a mile in another's moccasins" before presuming that you understand that person's perspective is a good one. Although you may have known the other parent very well at one time, you may not know how the world looks to him or her now.

Often one parent assumes that the other is making decisions or taking actions only to get revenge. Although revenge is a powerful motivator, parents act on these feelings a lot less often than most would expect. More often than not, parents make decisions based upon how they interpret the overall situation. When people feel threatened, they usually respond defensively and then attack the other's position. When people are distrustful, they are often suspicious of the other's motives and react to each comment or action as if it represents a direct threat. By taking the time to understand how the other parent views your proposed or actual separate parenting arrangements, you can often anticipate issues or concerns that the other parent might raise—and prepare a response.

John Haynes, an attorney-mediator and well known author on the subject of mediation, uses two strategies with his clients. First, he suggests that each parent describe how he or she would convince the other parent to accept a particular proposal. Second, he asks each parent to think of what he or she can offer to the other in exchange for going along with the proposal. This exercise requires each parent to try very hard to understand the other's point of view about what makes a particular proposal acceptable.

To see the issues and potential solutions from the other parent's perspective, you must:

- identify what is important to the other parent
- anticipate the other parent's objections
- develop responses to those objections, and
- suggest alternative solutions that might appeal to the other parent.

If we consider the example of resolving who will have day-to-day decision-making authority for the children, your thought process might be as follows:

From _____'s (other parent) perspective, I know that the divorce has been hard on both of us and that, as a result, our conversations have been much more difficult than they used to be.

We used to be able to make decisions fairly easily as long as we focused only on the children.

When I talk to _____ (other parent), I will let him/her know that I realize he/she would prefer not to deal with me now, but I will emphasize that our children's interests will be better served if we continue to make decisions together and limit our conversations to the children.

If either of us wants to raise other issues, that person can let the other know in writing.

2. Choose Your Setting for Your Negotiations

Choosing when and where you will meet to talk with the other parent is very important. You must find a time and location that is convenient, comfortable and allows you to talk without interruptions. This may mean a pleasant restaurant or coffee shop with tables that offer privacy, but don't choose a restaurant that you used to frequent as a couple.

Other options for your meeting location include:

- a meeting or conference room at the public library
- a meeting or conference room at a community center, or

- a picnic table in a park (assuming your children are not present).

3. Set an Agenda

Your discussions will be more productive if you set out a list of issues that you will cover (called an agenda), and then stick to that agenda. You can use the worksheets in Chapter 2 or the parenting agreement worksheet in Chapter 5 to help you set your agenda, or you can develop your own agenda based on your needs at the time you meet.

Regardless of how you develop your agenda, start each meeting by agreeing on which issues you will discuss at that time. Part of each agenda should be devoted to reviewing your progress so far, and part should be devoted to deciding what should happen next. A sample agenda is below.

SAMPLE AGENDA

1. Review of progress to date.
2. Review each parent's evaluation worksheets.
3. Develop a checklist of parenting issues (Worksheet 4).
4. Discussion of:
   a. medical, dental or vision care   d. surname
   b. psychiatric care   e. religion
   c. education
5. Summarize decisions made.
6. Outline issues and set date and time for next meeting.

---

4. Give Yourself Enough Time

Negotiations over most parenting issues require that you set aside enough time so you can carefully consider each decision. Don't schedule your meeting for an hour before one of you must leave to catch a plane—give yourself time to be heard and to listen. If any issue on your agenda is likely to involve much discussion, limit the number of issues on your agenda for that sitting.

5. Don't Try to Solve Everything at Once

Speed is less important than completeness when negotiating parenting issues. You and the other parent will be happier with your agreement if you pace yourselves. You should negotiate a few issues at a time and allow sufficient time to fully consider possible resolutions. If you have not completely resolved an issue when your meeting has ended, do the following:

- make notes about what you have resolved
- decide what each of you will do before the next meeting to work toward a solution (such as developing a proposal for the other parent's review), and
- anticipate how much more time you need to conclude your discussion.

6.   Choose Your Words Carefully

Language is a very powerful tool. It can make communication easier, or it can make communication difficult, adversarial and confusing. By choosing your words carefully, you will be better understood and will be less likely to get into an argument. The following are specific ideas to improve your communication skills.

a.   Be an Active Listener

Listening involves more than hearing the words spoken—you must also understand them. Simple though it may sound, most people need to practice this skill. This is especially difficult when you negotiate with someone you have known—and argued with—for a long time. Try not to fall into the trap of assuming that you know what the other parent will say or what he or she "really" means.

To be sure that you understand the other parent's comments or concerns, ask. Simply say: "It sounds as though you are saying '___,' is that right?" Once you truly hear and understand the other, you can be sure that you are reacting to something real and can make your decisions accordingly. Who knows? You both might be pleasantly surprised to find that some things have changed!

b.   Say "Yes, … If" Instead of "Yes, … But"

Consider the following conversation between two parents:

PARENT A: *"I want the children to live with me during the week and you can have them on the weekends."*

PARENT B: *"But I want to be able to see them during the week sometimes too."*

PARENT A: *"There you go again—you always argue. Why can't you just let me have one decision go my way?"*

PARENT B: *"I wasn't arguing! You are as impossible to talk to as always! You can forget it now—the kids will live with me and you can see them when it's convenient."*

When parents are angry or distrustful, it is easy to jump to the conclusion that "yes, … but really" means "no." In fact, the reverse is usually true. When people start sentences with "yes, … but," they are often trying to describe the conditions upon which they might agree—rather than saying "no." You can avoid confusion and the other parent's negative reaction by saying "yes, … if" when you want to condition your approval.

As an alternative, these parents might have approached their discussion like this:

PARENT A: *"I want the children to live with me during the week and you can have them on the weekends."*

PARENT B: *"That might work, if I can also see them sometimes during the week."*

PARENT A: *"Well maybe, if I know about it in advance."*

PARENT B: *"I could call at the beginning of the week when I know I will have an afternoon free and the kids could ride the bus home to my house instead."*

In this second conversation, the parents were careful to phrase their responses positively. Their negotiations are almost certainly going to result in an agreement that is clear and acceptable to both.

c.   Use "I" Statements and Give Information

When a parent wants to convey anger, frustration or some other negative emotion, he or she is often tempted to start sentences with "you," as in "You are so irresponsible!" By turning these into "I" statements, you will find that you are much more effective because the other parent can better understand how you feel and why. Consider how much more effective you can be if you were to say, for example: "I get angry when you are late to pick the children up because I have to deal with their disappointment!" rather than "You don't even care enough about the children to show up on time!"

d.   Identify Bothersome Behavior and Suggest Solutions

When registering complaints, you will have greater success at finding a solution if you clearly state the problem and suggest solutions.

EXAMPLE: *I get angry when you are late picking up and returning the kids for two reasons. First, it seems to me that you don't think my time is valuable. Second, it doesn't matter to you whether the children get to bed at a reasonable hour on a school night. If you are going to be late, I need you to call at least an hour before, so the children don't sit waiting for you. If you can't get them back again at the agreed-upon time, I need you to agree that they will always be home at least half an hour before their bed time.*

7. Look to the Future While Learning From the Past

Focusing on the past is valuable, but only if you use it to plan for the future. In fact, getting stuck in the past is a common reason for failing to agree about the future.

When starting in on familiar arguments, many parents say "Oh no! Not this again!" and stop listening for issues or concerns that can be resolved. Instead of rehashing old issues, shift your focus to making the future work better by asking one or two strategic questions.

EXAMPLE: *I remember that in the past your concerns were "A," "B" and "C." Is this still true? If it is, what should we change so that "A," "B" and "C" are no longer issues?*

A realistic and successful parenting agreement will emphasize the things that work well for your family, and will try to compensate for the things that don't. For this to happen, you and the other parent must work just as hard to identify things that you do well together, as to point out things that are "wrong." When the situation seems especially dismal, remind yourselves of the things you can take credit for, such as:

- how well your children are doing
- how much of the decision-making process you are handling on your own, or
- how much you really agree on about raising your children.

8. Don't Be Thrown Off Course by "Backsliding"

"Backsliding," or changing your mind about things that you've already agreed on, is very common and is not usually a sign of bad faith in negotiations. Rather, backsliding is often a signal that someone is struggling with a very difficult issue. If one of you is retreating from what seemed to be an acceptable resolution of an issue, take the opportunity to:

- reopen the issue
- discuss what doesn't seem right about the resolution
- try to identify the real concerns, and
- ask what alternative solutions might better meet each person's needs and concerns.

9. Conduct an Effective Meeting

The negotiations that you and the other parent conduct on your own must be structured to be productive. The following list of strategies can help your meetings to go smoothly and your negotiations to be more likely to result in lasting agreements:

- Allow each other to speak without interruption.
- Don't criticize each other, even while talking about problems or situations you don't want repeated.
- Describe each problem in terms of your reaction (such as "When you are late I get angry because the children are disappointed and it seems you don't value my time").
- Use "I" statements (as opposed to "you" accusations).
- Focus on the issues.

10. Expect Success

While some people are naturally optimistic, others tend to see the gloomy side of things. Looking only for problems and threats can be enough to sour almost every negotiation. With practice and conscious effort, however, many people learn to see that challenges and past conflicts offer opportunities to succeed in the future.

People who succeed more often than they fail tend to expect success and to use past mistakes and conflict as opportunities to learn (unpleasant though the experiences may have been). When you expect to succeed, you will work hard to find solutions to your problems. If you expect to fail, you will usually give up looking for solutions, thereby guaranteeing failure.

When you and the other parent are actually making decisions and developing your parenting agreement, you can set your agreement up to succeed if you:

- develop an action plan and assign responsibilities
- find ways to describe what "success" means for your children
- establish how you will know when a problem is really solved, and
- schedule reviews of your parenting plan and make changes when needed.

C. Overcoming Impasse

Impasse, or a disagreement which seems completely unresolvable, is challenging but also common during negotiations. In fact, you should probably expect at least one or two serious disagreements during your negotiations. If you hit a dead end, first review the preparation techniques described in Section B, above. If reviewing the preparation suggestions doesn't get you over the hump, consider adopting one of the problem-solving strategies discussed below.

1. Set the Issue Aside for Awhile

One of the easiest ways to deal with an impasse is to set the issue aside for awhile. When setting your agenda, consider resolving the easy issues first—the ones on which you generally agree. This lets you rack up some successes and helps build momentum for resolving the more difficult issues. As you confront increasingly difficult topics, remind yourselves of your successful negotiations to date. Use the decision-making strategies that worked on the easy issues to tackle the hard ones.

2. Reestablish Trust

Trust is an essential element to effective communication and decision making, and yet trust is usually eroded or lost during separation or divorce. This can create enormous problems for parents trying to negotiate and implement a parenting agreement. Fortunately, there are ways for parents to recapture enough trust in each other to be convinced that the other will fulfill the agreement.

a. Understand the Problem

Some parents confuse trustworthiness with acceptable behavior. If the other parent's lifestyle or career changes do not meet your expectations, this does not necessarily mean that the person is not worthy of your trust. If you define trustworthiness with words such as "reliable" and "honest," and by characteristics such as a love for your children, common decency and values you have in common, you may find you are able to trust the other parent again.

b. Measure Trustworthiness

Once you understand the problem, you may be able to resolve your concerns about trustworthiness by describing how you will demonstrate trustworthiness in the parenting relationship.

EXAMPLE: *I am having trouble trusting my children's father because he keeps changing the visiting schedule. To resolve this problem, at a minimum, he would have to call within 72 hours of any change and limit his changes to once a month.*

My trust in our son's mother is gone because she describes her time with him one way and he says something else. These inconsistencies worry me because I don't know who to believe. She would relieve my anxieties by letting me speak to my son periodically during the course of a visit.

Forcing yourself to define exactly what the other parent can do to regain your trust will go a long way toward helping you overcome impasse.

c. Agree on Simple Tasks Each Parent Must Carry Out

One way for a parent to believe that the other can be trusted to honor a parenting agreement is to identify simple tasks for each parent to complete in a timely and appropriate manner. One example might be filling out Worksheets 1, 2 and 3 in Chapter 3 in preparation for completing Worksheet 4 together. Other examples include:

- maintaining an on-time visitation schedule for a month
- scheduling and keeping appointments with teachers to learn of your children's progress in school, or
- entering and completing a substance abuse rehabilitation program.

For this strategy to work, the tasks must be clear, achievable and meaningful. State your goals in positive terms by describing the actions that a parent will take, not those the parent will refrain from. For example, you can say that a parent will be on time, rather than a parent will not be late.

3. Find your "BATNA" or "WATNA"

Often, problems that arise in the course of negotiations become easier to solve when the parties consider the alternatives. Fisher and Ury, *Getting To Yes*, (Penguin Books, 1981), of the Harvard Negotiation Project, suggest you consider your "BATNA"—or Best Alternative To a Negotiated Agreement. John Haynes suggests identifying your "WATNA"—or Worst Alternative To a Negotiated Agreement.

An example of a BATNA, or best alternative, might be an evaluation and recommendation by a custody evaluator after observing both parents' homes and relationships with their children. This kind of assessment can be very valuable, assuming it does not polarize you further. One way to avoid increasing the conflict after receiving a professional evaluation is to use it in mediation as a means of breaking the deadlock.

One common WATNA to a negotiated parenting agreement is a full-blown court trial. Considering what a court trial involves often proves to be an effective motivator for parents to negotiate an agreement: seeking a decision by a judge will cost a lot of money, take a lot of time and heighten the conflict. There is also the risk that the judge will make a decision that neither parent likes.

4. Play to Your Strengths

List what your current parenting arrangements have going in their favor. Your list might include items such as:

- shared love for your children
- agreement about house rules and expected standards of behavior for your children
- agreement about the community in which you want your children to grow up
- agreement about what school your child will attend, and
- agreement about what religious training your children will receive.

Each area of agreement strengthens your chance of finding further areas of agreement, and reduces the chance of future conflict.

5. Break the Cycle of Constant Arguing

For some parents, arguing is an ever-present feature in their parenting relationship. In an article written for family mediators and therapists, Howard Gadlin and Patricia Ouellette ask parents to consider two brilliant, yet simple, questions: "Who enjoys arguing the most?" and "What would be missing if all of the arguing stopped?" ("Mediation Milanese: An Application of Systemic Family Therapy Approach to Family Mediation," *Mediation Quarterly* (1987))

Below are several strategies you might try stop the fighting.

a. Understand the Consequences of Continual Fighting

As you continue to fight, you should realize that:

- the conflict spills over and affects your children
- you are delaying deciding important matters (such as where your child will attend school), or

- you are spending as much time resolving your parenting issue as you would on a second career.

b. Bring in a Neutral Person

Many parents find it easy to focus on making good parenting decisions rather than blaming each other for their short-comings if a neutral person, such as a counselor or mediator, moderates the discussion.

c. Get Help With Anger

Some parents cannot break the cycle of constant arguing until they obtain counseling to deal with their own anger or other feelings about the end of the relationship.

d. Recall Times When Negotiations Were Easier

For some parents, the pain, anger and confusion of a separation or divorce is so intense that they forget the times when they were able to agree. Remembering what made past discussions more successful, other than being in love, is often enough to move parents toward an agreement.

e. Create a Divorce or Separation Ceremony

Most cultures have complicated rituals associated with marriage to help the partners to feel committed to each other. But few societies have separation or divorce rituals. To help themselves untie the ties that have bound them, some parents plan and conduct a divorce or separation ceremony.

For some, merely planning the ceremony provides enough closure to the relationship. Others need to read statements to each other, have witnesses present or sign a formal decree.

f. Remove Value Labels Such as "Good" and "Bad"

Many parents experience a wide range of sometimes conflicting emotions and unusual behavior during separation, divorce and after. They are tempted to label those emotions or behaviors as being either "good" or "bad." If you can remove the labels, however, and accept them as part of what you experience, you may have fewer problems accommodating them into your parenting relationship.

6. Expand Your Options

One effective strategy for overcoming impasse is to think broadly—most problems have a myriad of possible solutions. If, for example, your homes are not too far apart and your conflict is because one parent feels he or she is not seeing the children enough, consider adding a regular midweek dinner or having the other parent provide after-school care. If your discussions have broken down because one parent wants to move out of the area, consider having both parents move—assuming they can both find jobs.

7. Balance the Power

For any number of reasons, one parent may be at a distinct disadvantage when trying to negotiate with the other. If domestic violence or emotional abuse have been present, then the threat of force or intimidation might be very real. If one parent is articulate and the other is not, the latter parent may have trouble presenting his or her views and interests, or protecting the interests of the children. Also, some parents consider that they have few options because they fulfill a stereotyped role of "Mother" or "Father."

If these or similar situations are present, consider one of the options below.

a. Enlist the Help of a Mediator or Counselor

Counselors and mediators have different strengths when it comes to balancing power between two individuals. Counselors can offer parents a safe setting within which they can

vent their feelings and deal with emotional as well as practical parenting issues. Mediators can support one or both parents in their efforts to identify—and communicate more effectively about—practical parenting issues. Because mediators also manage the communication process, they can insure that each parent is given ample time and opportunity to explain a position.

b. Enlist the Help of Attorneys

An attorney can represent a parent's interests in negotiations. This is especially helpful when one parent feels incapable of representing himself or herself. If one parent is represented by counsel, then both should be represented. Be aware, however, that once attorneys get involved, parents may lose control over the kinds of decisions that are made, the kinds of resolutions they can consider and the costs of reaching an agreement.

While increasing numbers of attorneys support their clients through less adversarial proceedings such as mediation, many still feel more comfortable in a courtroom and may steer their clients that way. Chapter 11 has suggestions on how to find attorneys who are willing to approach separation or divorce cases in the least adversarial way possible.

c. Seek Individual Counseling or Therapy

Some parents have never learned how to stand up for themselves in a discussion or while negotiating an agreement. It may be because this parent cannot deal with the emotional content of the discussion or the stress associated with the separation or divorce. If emotional issues make your negotiations particularly difficult, you may need individual counseling prior to, or as part of, negotiating your parenting agreement.

d. Negotiate Separately

In some situations, especially when domestic violence or emotional abuse has been present, it is best that the parents choose a neutral facilitator and negotiate separately. With this option, each parent meets separately with a mediator or other facilitator to present his or her views, interests and objectives. The mediator or other facilitator helps both parents generate a list of issues and resolutions. ■

Building Your Parenting Agreement

Raising children to adulthood involves a myriad of parenting issues. Some of these are simple, clear-cut and noncontroversial (at least between the parents). Many others can be hotly contested and lead to expensive, emotionally draining battles. The more parenting issues you can discuss and resolve now, the fewer disagreements you will have later.

This chapter takes you issue-by-issue through the process of building your own parenting agreement. These issues include who your children's medical providers will be, where they will go to school, where they will live and how they will spend time with both parents. Following each issue are several options for you to consider. As you work through the issues and options, you will find references to questions on the worksheets in Chapter 3 which may help you to address your particular concerns.

In general, parenting agreements have come a long way from the days of "sole custody awarded to mother with reasonable visitation for father." Although some agreements and court orders still use this extremely general approach, more and more agreements are detailed. The reasons for this shift are many, but three stand out:

- "Sole custody with reasonable visitation" lets the sole custodian virtually strip the other parent of a parental role.
- Vague agreements are frequently contested and often lead to arguments over what constitutes "reasonable" visitation.
- Parents denied custody and given only minimum levels of visitation have little incentive to maintain contact with their children or to pay child support.

A. What Works in Building a Parenting Agreement

Two artifacts of a large, steady volume of divorce cases are seeing what works and being reminded frequently of what doesn't. The three key elements that contribute to a successful but separate parenting relationship are outlined below.

1. Cooperate! Cooperate! Cooperate!

It is difficult, but essential, that you and the other parent set aside your differences as you plan for your children's future. Ideally, you will find a way to trust each other. For most parents, this is hardest during the first weeks follow-

ing a separation or divorce. Fortunately, feelings of anger and pain usually diminish over time.

Most parents find that settling into a new life after separation or divorce makes it easier to untangle their "couple" issues from their parenting issues. Regardless of how you feel right now, keep in mind that many parents, feeling just the way you do, have found solutions that benefit everyone—at least in the long run.

2. Get Outside Help

Negotiating parenting agreements can be difficult and complicated. Chapters 6 through 9 cover some of the very complex issues in greater detail. If this is not enough, Chapter 11 provides a list of books, professionals and other information sources.

The parenting agreement in this book does not conform to any specific court's filing requirements. If you are getting a divorce or legal separation, you must check with your local court, the law library, a forms service, a paralegal or an attorney to find out if your agreement must be prepared in any special way.

In addition, because your parenting decisions may have legal consequences, consider having a family law or matrimonial attorney review your agreement. The attorney can help you make sure that the agreement conforms to your state's laws regarding child custody and visitation, says what you want it to say and accomplishes your objectives.

In addition, your agreement, by itself, will not be enforceable the way a business contract is enforceable. However, the attorney can help you turn the agreement into an enforceable court order.

3. Keep Your Agreement Current

You don't need a crystal ball to predict that your children's needs and interests will change over the years. So will yours. For these reasons, few parents negotiate a single agreement that stands, unaltered, until their children reach adulthood. In fact, many parents make at least one major change in their parenting arrangements within the first three years after their separation or divorce. Changes might also be appropriate if a parent intends to move, if work schedules change significantly or if a child wants to live with a different parent.

Section B, below, contains 40 issue/option sets which make up the parenting agreement. Some of these may not be relevant now. As time goes on, however, you, the other parent, or your children may discover that previously ignored issues have a new importance. For example, if you have pre-school children, you may not care to spend time now deciding about owning and operating a motor vehicle. Similarly, if neither parent is in a new relationship, planning for how to handle new partners may be impossible. Both of these issues, however, may become very important later.

You and the other parent should periodically review your agreement to see if changes are necessary. Issue 38, Making Changes, lets you build a review schedule into your agreement.

Also, keep this book handy for when you want to make changes. Your goal is to create a workable parenting agreement now, and to anticipate the need for changes as time goes on. Agreements that contemplate future changes are better able to respond to your family's changing needs, circumstances or concerns. The earlier you address a request for a change, the greater chance you have of keeping conflict to a minimum. If this edition of the book becomes outdated, you can trade this copy in for the newest edition at a 25% discount. The new material will include legal changes and new issue/option sets contributed by readers and professionals.

B. Complete the Parenting Agreement

You may want to skim the blank parenting agreement in the Appendix or the chapter table of contents to see what issues are covered. If issues important to you are not included, use our format to describe the issue and your solution. At a minimum, your agreement should include Issue 11 (Making Decisions), Issue 14 (Where Our Children Will Live) and Issue 37 (Labeling the Custody Arrangement).

As you fill out your parenting agreement, you can select one or more of the options listed or you can include your own solutions. If you have more than one child, you may make different decisions for each. In this case, use the blank lines to record your different decisions or attach additional sheets.

We'd like our database of issue/option sets to keep growing! You can mail in your comments on our pre-addressed reader contribution card, fax your comments to (510) 548-5902, or e-mail your suggestions to (feedback@NoloPress.com).

Look over the parenting agreement carefully before you begin. The order that the issues are presented in may seem a little strange, or at least different from what an attorney tells you is important, but there is a reason for it. The vast majority of parents who successfully negotiate parenting agreements handle the less heated issues first—usually issues about decision making. Accordingly, in our agreement, decision-making issues come first and living arrangement issues follow.

You can negotiate your agreement in the order the issues are presented, or you can skip around, tackling the issues that are easiest for you first. Regardless of which approach you take, use the worksheet to record your agreement as it takes shape, not to dictate how you will structure your negotiations.

Here is a suggestion for filling out your worksheet as you go through each issue/option set. Use an uppercase "X" in the space to the left of each item to note which issues you will address. Use a lower case "x" to identify all options you want to include in that portion of your agreement. When you have finished the entire agreement, go back and number the issues and letter the options you will include. For example, your provision regarding your children's surname might read as follows:

_X_   Our children's surname is ___Garcia_____.

Any decision to change that surname will be made as follows [choose all that apply]:

_____   Our children will keep this surname until they become legal adults.

_____   Our children may choose their surname.

_X_   Our children may choose their surname after age ___16___.

_X_   We will discuss and agree on any change of surname.

_____   _____ [parent] has the authority to change our children's surname.

_X_   We further agree that [specify]:

Our children must inform us before submitting any documents to obtain a legal
name change.

_____

You will work through this section most efficiently if you:

- have Worksheets 1 through 4 from Chapter 3 close at hand (for each issue, refer to the "Worksheet Cross-Reference" chart)
- make at least six copies of the blank parenting agreement
- give the other parent two agreements and keep two for yourself
- complete one copy as you negotiate with the other parent
- write or type your final agreement on one copy, and
- get outside help when you need it.

Issue 1:   Medical, Dental and Vision Care

Most parents want their children to receive competent medical care, when they need it and at a reasonable cost. Making it happen, however, might not always be easy. Use your parenting agreement to specify the details, including:

- your children's medical providers
- who has authority to make decisions regarding your children's medical care
- how you will exchange medications your children take
- how much medical information you will share (such as every cold and scrape or only major illnesses and accidents), and
- who will take the children for their regular checkups.

ISSUE 1 CROSS-REFERENCES

Worksheet	Questions
Worksheet 3	4
Worksheet 4	4

a.   Choose Health Care Providers

When parents live in the same city or within a reasonable distance, they often agree on the primary medical, dental or mental health care provider for their children. If you and the other parent live a considerable distance from each other, however, it makes sense for you each to find providers so that your children can receive consistent care. If you each select medical providers, exchange names, addresses, phone numbers and releases so the providers can exchange records and information. Your doctor should have a release for you to sign.

b.   Routine and Special Care

Specify who has the authority to seek routine care for your children, such as immunizations, annual physical exams and blood tests. Many parents agree to let either parent handle routine care for the children without first discussing it with the other. Some circumstances, however, such as immunizations, require coordination to avoid duplication.

You also need to specify how your children's special medical, dental or vision care needs, such as hospitalization, surgery, medication or experimental treatment, will be met.

Most parents who share legal custody (or joint custody in states that do not differentiate between legal and physical custody) require discussion and agreement before allowing this level of treatment. (See Chapter 2, Section D, for definitions of joint, legal and physical custody.)

c. Emergency Care

Clearly state how much authority each parent has to seek treatment in a medical emergency. If the children spend a fair amount of time with both of you, you will probably want to allow either parent to obtain emergency treatment without first consulting the other. If you choose to restrict a parent's authority to seek emergency treatment, the parent who must make, or be consulted about, emergency decisions, must include a medical release during visits with the other parent, or be available at a moment's notice.

d. Ongoing Medical, Dental or Vision Care

Some children have medical or physical conditions (such as diabetes, a physical disability, poor vision or periodontal disease) which requires attention for months, years or even for the rest of their lives. In such situations, you must decide whether medications, physical supports or enhancements (such as crutches or prosthetics) will be kept in each home or will travel with the children.

Issue 2: Psychiatric and Other Mental Health Care

Psychiatric or other mental health care can be a source of serious disagreement. If you and the other parent discuss this issue, keep in mind that you need to decide the following:

- whether you will permit or require psychiatric or other counseling for your children
- whether you will permit or require psychiatric or other counseling for either parent
- who may provide the care, and
- how you will determine when the need for counseling has ended.

Counseling for parents is included here because a parent's state of mind and mental health can have a significant impact on children. Whether the parents attend counseling together, or articulate goals to strive for in separate counseling sessions, time spent in counseling will usually result in better parenting plans.

Specific provisions in your parenting plan might:

- identify the issues to be addressed (such as anger, frustration, jealousy or violence)
- allow the counselor and patient to agree when the these issues are resolved, and
- provide for a letter from the counselor to the other parent stating that the counselor and the patient agree that the counseling has accomplished its objectives.

ISSUE 2 CROSS-REFERENCES

Worksheet	Questions
Worksheet 1	4
Worksheet 2	9
Worksheet 3	4, 10, 11
Worksheet 4	4, 6, 9

Issue 3: Education

School obviously dominates every child's life. Whether your children attend a public school, private school or home school, parental involvement in children's education is critical. Making decisions about your children's education is more complicated than simply deciding on the type of school they will attend. In addition, you must consider:

- how you will make decisions about changing your children's school
- how you will address your children's special needs or talents
- who will participate in, and remain informed about, your children's school activities and performance
- whom the school should contact in the event of an emergency
- how you will define and encourage your children's good school performance
- the kind of post-high school education you will consider, and
- how you will pay for post-high school education.

ISSUE 3 CROSS-REFERENCES

Worksheet	Questions
Worksheet 1	2, 9
Worksheet 2	2, 3, 10
Worksheet 3	3, 4
Worksheet 4	10, 18

a.   Public, Private or Home Schooling

Although most children attend the local public school, many do not. If you are not content with the local public school, investigate before assuming you have no other options.

Some public school districts are large enough to allow for specialized schools (such as schools that emphasize art, science or math). Other school districts allow parents and students to choose from more than one school.

Private schools come in all sizes and configurations. You can choose from parochial, secular, same-sex or co-ed schools. The school may let students live at home, or require them to live in residence on the campus.

Home schooling is an option when a parent is willing and able to commit to full time teaching. Home schooling requires an enormous commitment by one or both parents, and the curriculum must adhere to state educational standards.

You must consider your children's educational needs, academic needs and preferences before settling on a solution. If your option costs money, you must make sure that you put aside adequate funds. Specify your arrangement in your parenting agreement and your child support agreement, and be sure to include the same decision in both places.

If either parent or the children want to change schools, you can plan now for how that decision will be made. You can establish criteria (such as the child attaining certain skills or staying within a budget), or specify who will be authorized to make the change.

b.   Supporting Special Needs or Talents

Some children need help with keeping up with certain skills or subjects. Others have special talents which can be cultivated through extra classes or activities. Parents need to be sensitive to these possibilities, as well as to the children's changing needs.

If your children have special needs or talents, consider:

- requesting support from their current school
- supplementing the school resources with private tutors, counselors or after-school activities, or
- switching schools.

c.   Participating in School Activities

You and the other parent must agree on who will:

- participate in any parent-teacher associations
- help in the children's classroom
- attend parent-chaperoned functions, or
- attend other similar activities.

d.   Attending Parent-Teacher Conferences

You and the other parent must also decide who will attend parent-teacher conferences. Some parents attend together, some designate one to attend and inform the other parent of the matters discussed, and some opt for separate conferences.

e.   Listing Parents' Names on School Emergency Contact Forms

You and the other parent must determine who will be listed on the school's emergency contact forms and in what order these persons will be listed. The school will also need to know who has authority to make medical decisions in the event of an emergency. (See Issue 1.)

f.   Encouraging Good Performance in School

Parents often disagree about how to encourage good school performance or what the consequences will be for poor performance. For example, some parents give their children money or other rewards for earning good grades. Some parents withhold allowances or other privileges if their children get poor grades. If you and the other parent decide to reward or punish good or poor school performance, you will want to define the terms and specify the rewards or punishments you will use.

g.   Sex Education

If you or the other parent want to prevent your children from participating in sex education classes, specify it here. In addition, you must find out whether you will be asked to give permission for your children to take the class or your children will take the class unless you deny permission.

h.   Post-Secondary Education

Although most children and parents think about post-high school education for their children, such as college or technical training, many families fail to plan until their children reach high school. In fact, there are many planning options available, some of which require more preparation and thought than others.

Consider setting up a special account which you will use to pay for your children's education. If you do this, you will want to indicate how money will be deposited into that account. You can also investigate different loans, grants or scholarships. If the type of training your children receive is important to you, you can specify what programs you are willing, or refuse, to pay for, such as:

- pay-to-learn apprenticeships
- trade schools, or
- two-year or four year institutions.

Issue 4:   Surname

Many parents never question what last name their children will use after divorce or separation; however, the issue does come up. In general, courts require that a child's surname be chosen with the child's best interests at heart.

In some families, everyone has the same last name. In other families, they are all different. Some of the options you can consider after separation or divorce include:

- give the children one parent's surname
- create a new name from both parent's surnames (such as a hyphenated name), or
- have the children use one parent's last name from a new relationship or marriage.

After separation or divorce—especially if one or both parents changed names when the couple married or began living together—either or both parents might choose to return to a previous name. Additionally, a parent who begins a new relationship after divorce or separation might change his or her last name to match the new mate's surname.

Your children will need to know what their last name is and who has the authority to change that name. Some parents let their children choose their name; others allow the children that choice only after they reach a certain age.

Some parents change their children's last name without the other parent's consent. Later, they register the children in school, with the doctor or elsewhere under the new name. Asking children to assume a new last name without the other parent's consent can be confusing for the children and often provokes an argument with the other parent. It also means that your children's school, medical and other records might be difficult to piece together.

In most states, when you change a minor's last name, you must obtain court approval.

ISSUE 4 CROSS-REFERENCE

Worksheet	Question
Worksheet 3	8

Issue 5:   Religious Training

After separation or divorce, parents may need to plan for their children's religious training. For some parents, this is easy; for others, it presents difficult choices. In many families, parents have different religions. Whether you will expose your children to one religion, agree to disagree, teach two religions, give your children no formal religious training or let your children choose for themselves, religion can be an important aspect of a child's development. Additional information on multicultural families is in Chapter 8.

ISSUE 5 CROSS-REFERENCES

Worksheet	Questions
Worksheet 1	9
Worksheet 2	1, 2, 3
Worksheet 3	3, 5
Worksheet 4	3, 4, 18

a. Teach One Religion

This is quite probably the approach you will take if the parents have the same religion. But even if your religions differ, you may choose, for the sake of simplicity or because one parent has stronger religious ties, to raise your children with only one religion. This is especially common when children have two Christian parents who belong to different denominations, or have one parent who strongly identifies with being Jewish while the other parent has nominal ties with a Christian denomination.

b. Teach Both Religions

Some parents agree that while neither plans to convert to the other's faith, they want their children to grow up understanding both parents' religious beliefs. If this is your choice, consider whether either parent will be allowed to confirm, convert or otherwise formally indoctrinate the children in a particular faith.

c. Agree on Basic Tenets and Allow Children to Choose Denomination

Some parents have no strong preferences about which denomination their children must be raised in, as long as the principal values follow a general religious belief, such as Christian, Moslem, Jewish, Hindu or Buddhist. In this situation, consider who will expose the children to the faith and take them to services. Also consider what you will do if your children express an interest in a particular denomination.

d. Let Children Choose Religious Participation

Some parents do not subscribe to any particular faith, are not active in any congregation or have no interest in providing religious training for their children. In this situation, decide how you will respond if your children some day express an interest in religion. You might decide to take them to religious services of their choice, expose them to several different religions or refuse to let them participate. Also, if you and the other parent *do* participate religiously but you want to let your children choose for themselves, consider what you will do if your children select no religious training.

Issue 6: International Travel and Passports

Some families want or need to travel out of the U.S. with their children. Almost all foreign travel requires a passport—even for children. International travel becomes a concern if you fear that a trip abroad might become an attempt to change custody or to take the children away from you altogether. If your children have dual citizenship, you may have a hard time enforcing your court orders outside of the U.S., as there might be a question about which country has legal authority to make decisions.

ISSUE 6 CROSS-REFERENCES

Worksheet	Questions
Worksheet 2	2
Worksheet 3	6, 7, 14
Worksheet 4	10, 18

We Assume Good Intentions

This books assumes that neither parent intends to take the children out of the country to steal them from the other parent. If this is an immediate concern, see a lawyer for help in securing a court order that will minimize this possibility.

a. Issue Passport but Set Limited Travel Time or Destination

With this option, parents might permit travel out of the U.S., but incorporate restrictions specifying permitted countries or amounts of time their children can be abroad, or both.

b. Issue Passport but Require Supervised Travel

Your parenting agreement might require that an adult accompany your children and the other parent for international travel. If this is your inclination, you might seriously rethink whether issuing a passport is advisable at all given that it might not be possible for a travel "supervisor" to prevent child snatching under all circumstances.

c. Require Both Parent's Permission to Obtain a Passport

In the event that one parent seriously fears flight or abduction of a child, then that parent should seriously consider requiring that both parents give permission before passports are obtained for their children. International agreements provide some relief if this happens, but are not as effective as withholding the passport in the first place.

d. Instruct the State Department to Withhold a Child's Passport Unless Requested by the Custodial Parent

If one parent has sole custody, he or she can inform the State Department not to issue a passport for the children unless it is the custodial parent who applies for it.

Issue 7: Driving and Owning a Car, Motorcycle or Off-Road Vehicle

Parents often disagree about when their children will be allowed to drive or own a car, motorcycle or off-road vehicle. While most parents let their teens take driver's training with their peers, the rules regarding when, how far and under what circumstances they may drive without an adult vary. Parents also often disagree on the following:

- whether or not their teens may own a car, motorcycle or off-road vehicle
- under what circumstances the teens may own a vehicle (for example, only if it is brand new, if it is formerly the "family car," or if a teen pays for it), or
- who will pay the insurance, tickets, repairs and other costs—the parents or the teens.

Because driving and owning a vehicle can be very important for your children in their teen years, this decision is especially worth thinking through in advance.

ISSUE 7 CROSS-REFERENCES

Worksheet	Questions
Worksheet 1	4
Worksheet 2	5
Worksheet 4	4, 9, 18

Issue 8: Military Service

Minor children need a parent's permission to enter the military. Some options you can consider would allow your minor children to enlist as follows:

- without restriction
- in the event of war
- after a certain age
- with the approval of one or both parents, or
- never.

Issue 9: Allowing Underage Marriage

You have at least five options when considering whether you will let your minor children get married, including:

- allow it at the child's discretion
- allow it in the event of a pregnancy
- allow it after a certain age
- allow it with consent of one or both parents, or
- not allow an underage marriage.

Because teenage pregnancy and underage marriage are such emotionally charged issues, you might make a tentative decision now and reevaluate that decision if the issue actually arises.

ISSUE 9 CROSS-REFERENCES

Worksheet	Questions
Worksheet 1	9
Worksheet 2	2, 3

Issue 10: Insurance

Insurance coverage can help with both the predictable and unpredictable expenses of child rearing. Parents can provide insurance for medical, dental, vision and psychiatric care, and for prescription drugs. Parents can insure their own lives for the benefit of their children, and can get life insurance policies for their children which they can later convert to cash to pay for college.

Insurance coverage might be available through a parent's employment, secured as a stand-alone individual policy, or converted from employee coverage to an individual policy if a parent changes jobs. Some parents agree that both will obtain whatever insurance coverage they can as long as it is available at low or no cost through their employer. If you both have insurance, you will have to agree on submitting claims, seeking treatment on the child's behalf and paying deductibles and other uncovered expenses.

⚠ Insurance and Child Support

Most states require one or both parents to provide health insurance for their children as an obligation of child support. If you are also making a child support agreement, make sure your decisions in this section are consistent with what is in your child support agreement.

A list of resources that answer insurance questions is in Chapter 11.

ISSUE 10 CROSS-REFERENCE

Worksheet	Question
Worksheet 3	4

Issue 11: Making Decisions

When parents are married or living together, they work out their own system for making decisions. Only rarely does a court or other outsider, such as a therapist or physician, get involved in either the process or the actual decision.

When parents separate or divorce, however, they have to figure out how the big and little decisions affecting their children will be made, and who will make them. The question of who makes decisions is especially relevant if either or both parents have new partners. The parents also have to accept that only the larger decisions can be made in advance. Most decisions will be made as the issues arise.

Good decisions take your values and needs, and your children's values and needs, into consideration. Good decisions also stand the test of time because everyone involved gains something important. Whenever possible, the advantages of a decision should outweigh the disadvantages for everyone concerned.

You can take some of the guesswork out of the decision-making process by building a sound decision-making framework. To build this kind of framework ask and answer the following questions for each decision which must be made:

- What must this decision accomplish?
- Who will gain by the decision?
- Who might lose by this decision?
- Whose needs must be met by this decision?
- How will I know that this decision has accomplished my objectives?

Take, for example, the need to choose between two schools for your children. Your answers to the above questions might go something like this:

- What must this decision accomplish? ("The school must provide a good college preparatory education.")
- Who will gain by the decision? ("Our children will gain a good education.")
- Who might lose by this decision? ("We will lose money if we choose an expensive private school. If we select a public school where only one of us lives, the parent who doesn't reside in that district may lose weekday contact with the children.")
- Whose needs must be met by this decision? ("Our children's needs must come first; but we must be able to afford any private school and have money left over to continue most other important activities.")
- How will I know that this decision has accomplished my objectives? ("We will see the children's grades and test scores improve, and the school counselor will be confident that the children will have a good chance of getting into a good college.")

There are basically four models for making decisions, each with its own advantages and disadvantages:

- the parents reach an agreement
- one parent decides and later informs the other
- one parent decides but need not tell the other, or
- another responsible adult (such as a grandparent, aunt or close family friend) has the authority to make decisions.

ISSUE 11 CROSS-REFERENCES

Worksheet	Questions
Worksheet 1	5
Worksheet 2	6, 7, 8, 9, 10
Worksheet 3	12, 14, 15
Worksheet 4	1, 2, 3, 4, 10, 17

a. The Parents Reach an Agreement

Provisions which require the parents to agree work well when both parents are active in their children's lives, can set aside their conflict, and have the same child-rearing values regarding raising their children. This does not mean you must see things identically, but that you are generally able to reach agreements on your own.

The best way for your parenting agreement to succeed is for you and the other parent to work together to find solutions that are in your children's best interests. Additionally, you both must remain informed about health care, school and outside activities so you can make decisions with an understanding of how they are likely to play out over time.

You can structure this option in any way that feels comfortable—just be specific. If, for example, you want to let a parent make everyday decisions when the children are with that parent, but will require discussion and agreement for significant decisions, you must describe what you mean by "everyday" and "significant" decisions.

Parents usually agree that in an emergency, the parent caring for the children at the time will handle the situation and inform the other parent as soon as possible thereafter. Conversely, parents usually require consultation and agreement on major decisions, such as a change in residence, surgery, remedial tutoring, support for special talent or participation in a hazardous activity.

Parents can choose to meet in person, talk by telephone, or start out their discussions by letter. Writing letters is good if you and the other parent are currently arguing. If you must communicate in writing because of constant arguing, however, reevaluate whether you and the other parent can actually make this decision-making model work.

b.   Parent With Primary Care of Children Decides and Informs the Other Parent

This option allows parents who argue frequently over child rearing to make sure that decisions get made, while both parents remain aware of what is going on in their children's lives. It keeps both parents in the loop and eliminates opportunities for perpetuating the conflict. The parent who makes the decisions may have to provide the other parent with a medical release when the children are in the other parent's care. Otherwise, you can handle emergencies as described in Section a, above.

c.   Parent With Primary Care Makes All Decisions

This option may be necessary with parents who have a history of harassment, abuse or violence between them, or when a parent has had little involvement in raising the children. It allows decisions to be made for the children without fear of fighting or interference.

When the parent who does not have the authority to make decisions on the children's behalf spends time with them, that parent may need a medical release from the other parent to cover emergencies. This decision-making model is consistent with agreements that include supervised, or otherwise very limited, visitation.

d.   Parents Choose Another Responsible Adult to Make Decisions

In some families, the parents are either unwilling or unable to make decisions on their children's behalf. Sometimes, this is the case with very young parents who need to grow up themselves. Other parents are incapable of making responsible decisions because of illness, abuse, substance

abuse or neglect. In this situation, a court often determines who will take over the parenting role.

Issue 12: Resolving Disputes When Making Decisions Together

Even the most experienced negotiators may find themselves unable to resolve a particular issue. This is called impasse. You and the other parent must plan for how you will resolve an impasse, that is, how necessary decisions will be made even when you cannot reach agreement on these issues on your own.

Part of the problem when trying to resolve a difficult issue is understanding the nature of the conflict. In addition to differing views, values and cultures, we are all driven—at least in some part—by jealousy, anger, bitterness or revenge. Often we may insist that our views are in the best interests of our children when, in fact, they are not. Many disagreements between parents are motivated by a desire to improve their adult lives rather than to meet the needs of their children. One effective strategy you can use to resolve conflict is to examine your motives for taking a particular position.

You have several options for resolving disagreements. As you consider these options, make sure that the option you choose allows for decisions to be made in a timely fashion. Your options include:

- giving the primary caretaker authority to decide
- giving each parent final authority on different issues
- mediating disagreements
- seeking advice from a counselor, therapist or attorney, or
- arbitrating disagreements (in the few states that permit it).

ISSUE 12 CROSS-REFERENCES

Worksheet	Questions
Worksheet 2	6, 7, 10
Worksheet 3	7, 12, 15
Worksheet 4	3, 10, 17

A COURT'S ROLE IN MAKING DECISIONS

When parents cannot resolve their parenting issues, they can consider taking the issue to a court. Courts will not decide what clothes your children may wear to school, friends they may spend time with or sports they can play. A court, however, will decide who has authority to make decisions affecting your children, where your children will live and how they will spend time with both parents.

Most parents and professionals use the court as a last resort for resolving disputes. Going to court can be quite expensive and take a lot of time. More importantly, the judge making the decision will not know either you or your children, and will have little time in which to hear the matter and make a decision. As a result, you risk getting a decision that is less sensitive to your particular needs than might be the case if you and the other parent reached an agreement on your own. Furthermore, if you already have a court order, a court will not modify it unless you show that there has been a substantial change in circumstances.

Many states provide their judges with some guidance in making custody and visitation decisions. Some judges are urged to avoid contested proceedings whenever possible. These judges usually rely on the recommendations of a custody evaluator when making their decisions. Also, most judges give significant weight to a teen's preference about custody and visitation.

a. The Primary Caretaker Has Authority

If your children will spend significantly more time with one parent than the other, consider giving that parent final authority to make decisions when you otherwise can't agree. Alternatively, you could give one parent final authority on certain issues when you disagree and give the other parent similar authority for different issues.

To put some limits on the parent with decision-making authority, you could require that before making a final decision the parent consult with someone whose opinions both parents value, such as a counselor, religious leader or family member. Even when parents cannot agree about something, they can often agree on whose advice they will trust and follow.

b. Mediate Disagreements

Many parents select mediation as a method to resolving disagreements. When the mediator has no authority to make an independent recommendation to the court, the process allows parents to control their own decisions. As a result, the parents are able to focus on their children and on persuading each other of what choices should be made.

Mediation is covered in Chapter 6.

c. Use a Counselor, Therapist or Attorney

One option is to ask for an evaluation of your situation from a trained professional, such as a psychiatrist, marriage and family counselor or other mental health professional. You can accept any recommendation that the evaluator makes, use the recommendation to try and reach an agreement on your own or bring the recommendation into mediation.

Another option is to each consult with an attorney—or meet with one attorney together—to get information about the law. (Be aware that many lawyers refuse to meet with both parties in a divorce dispute.) Many parents insist on knowing "what the law says" before making a decision. For example, if your state requires that a noncustodial parent be given a certain minimum amount of visitation, consulting an attorney might help you by guiding your decision about where the children will live (Issue 14), holidays (Issue 22) and vacations (Issue 23).

d. Parent A/Parent B Plan

This tool for resolving impasse involves assigning parental roles involved in a particular issue to two hypothetical parents—Parent A and Parent B. Once these roles are assigned, you can then start deciding, based on the situation, which real parent is best suited to be Parent A and which Parent B. For instance, if you decide that the child should spend Christmas with Parent A and three weeks in the summer with Parent B, you would then decide which role is most appropriate for you and the other parent—that is, who would be the best Parent A and who the best Parent B.

The Parent A/Parent B approach is in fact most often employed when deciding where the children will live a majority of the time (Issue 14). Especially if you have trouble making that decision when you get to it, you may wish to return here and review this decision-making option.

EXAMPLE OF HOW TO USE PARENT A/PARENT B PLAN

Sometimes, parents cannot agree on where their children will live, not because they differ, but because they want the same thing. For example, you and the other parent might decide that "Parent A" will be the primary caretaker for the school year and "Parent B" the primary caretaker for the summer. You agree on how the children will visit each parent when they are with the other, and how they will spend holidays, weekends, special occasions and vacations. The only question remaining is who gets the nine-month chunk of time with the children, and who gets only three.

In deciding who will be Parent A and who will be Parent B, you might consider the following:
- who provided most of the daily child care when you were a couple
- who lives near the better public schools
- whose home is more conducive to studying
- who lives closer to community recreation programs and sports facilities in which your children participate, and
- who lives closer to the children's friends or in a neighborhood with similar-aged children.

e.   Arbitrate Disagreements

A few states allow parents to submit parenting decisions to an arbitrator when they cannot reach agreement on their own. Unlike mediators, arbitrators are decision makers. In arbitration, each parent presents his or her views to the arbitrator, who resolves the issues in dispute.

WHEN CONSULTING OUTSIDERS

If you turn to an outsider for help in resolving disputes, be sure you maintain control over the process. No matter what type of outsider you use—mediator, counselor, therapist, attorney or arbitrator—you must decide the following in advance:
- how the outsider will be chosen—will you require any minimum qualifications
- how the outsider will be paid
- exactly which issues the outsider will be helping you resolve, and
- the scope of the process—will you limit the number of mediation or counseling sessions? Will certain legal rules apply in arbitration? Will attorneys be present in arbitration?

See Chapter 6 for more information on mediation and arbitration, and Chapter 11 for information on working with therapists and counselors.

Issue 13: Exchanging Information

Both parents will need and want at least some information about their children's health care, school, outside activities, interests, abilities and special needs.

Talking with the other parent can be difficult. When parents are angry or hurt over the separation or divorce, or still hope for a reconciliation, they may use information exchanges about the children as an excuse to rehash the adult issues. While discussing the adult issues is fine under many circumstances, you might easily get sidetracked and forget to discuss your children and their needs. Also, some parents use information exchanges about the children as a chance to criticize or pry into the other's new life, partner or activities. When this happens, the children's interests suffer or are forgotten altogether.

Parents often need to find new ways to communicate effectively. Below are a few options to consider putting into your parenting agreement. Consider choosing more than one so you can use one when things are going well and another when communication is difficult.

For additional help, consider the following:

- review Chapter 4 on negotiations
- evaluate your agreement to see if it addresses everyone's needs
- get help from a mediator or counselor, or
- consult with any other third party whose opinions you respect.

The more ideas you can generate to solve problems the better.

ISSUE 13 CROSS-REFERENCES

Worksheet	Questions
Worksheet 1	8
Worksheet 2	6, 7, 10
Worksheet 3	12, 14, 15
Worksheet 4	4, 9, 10, 17

a. Don't Put Your Children in the Middle

One of the worst mistakes you can make—and lots of parents make it—is to put your children in the middle by having them carry messages. You and the other parent must find a way to keep each other informed without passing messages through your children.

Children are apt to forget, distort or misunderstand your message. Children also soon resent the role and cringe when they deliver a message that the other parent doesn't want to hear. Some children may temporarily like the power of being the "information highway," but that soon fades. If you need to change plans, collect child support, find out about the other parent's activities or understand what discipline is being used in the other parent's home, talk to the other parent directly.

b. Establish a Businesslike Relationship

Many therapists, mediators, counselors and attorneys know that to let hostilities cool, the relationship between the parents has to change from intimate partners to business partners. Parents who have been through this can tell you how difficult that change can be. Nevertheless, the strategies for bringing this new relationship about are fairly simple.

You and the other parent must learn to make your conversations brief, focused only on the children and courteous. You must make an effort to inform each other about the little things, such as what your children have been doing for fun or have accomplished recently, as well as the significant information about illnesses, behavior, special events and report cards.

If things don't go well when you talk in person, consider scheduling telephone calls. If that doesn't work, exchange notes through the mail, via e-mail, at a convenient drop off, or, as a last resort (and only if your children can't read yet), in your children's suitcase.

c. Establish Separate Relationships With Activities and Care Providers

For some parents, exchanging information about health care, school, counseling or outside activities doesn't work. These parents must establish separate contacts with the children's health care providers, school officials and event and activity coordinators.

Many schools, doctors, counselors, club leaders or coaches are not set up to communicate with parents separately. You may need to be persistent. Keep in mind, however, that scout leaders, coaches, doctors and others dread getting between parents battling over control of their children. You will have an easier time dealing with these people if you make your contacts brief, friendly and to the point. Don't rely on these people to give you information about the other parent or to relay messages. If children resent being made into message carriers, outsiders resent it even more.

Issue 14: Where Our Children Will Live

Perhaps the most hotly contested provision in a parenting plan establishes living arrangements. If you and the other parent agree to a sole custody (or sole legal and physical custody) arrangement, then this issue will be obvious. With any other custody arrangement, however, be prepared for some intense, but critical, negotiations.

Your goal is to have your children spend as much time as possible with each parent, without ignoring their needs for stability and routine.

In evaluating the options below, consider:
- the ages, needs, wishes and temperaments of your children
- the distance between your homes
- available transportation
- what you can afford, and
- how well you and the other parent work together.

With a little creativity, you should be able to come up with several possible solutions, each presenting advantages and disadvantages.

In Issue 11, option d, we discuss the Parent A/Parent B method for resolving impasse around custody issues. If you find that you reach impasse on where the children will live, go back and review that discussion. Essentially, the Parent A/Parent B method asks you to first assign parental roles to hypothetical parents and then examine the circumstances to determine which of you would best fit each role.

ISSUE 14 CROSS-REFERENCES

Worksheet	Questions
Worksheet 1	3, 5
Worksheet 2	1, 3, 4, 7, 8, 9, 10
Worksheet 3	2, 3, 4, 6, 7, 14
Worksheet 4	1, 2, 4, 5, 6, 7, 8, 12 ,13, 14, 15, 17, 18

AVOID CREATING A "VISITING" PARENT

Sometimes, changing the way you view the parenting agreement and living arrangement is as simple as changing the words you use. In *Mom's House, Dad's House*, by Dr. Isolina Ricci (Macmillan Publishing, 1980), the author recommends that parents and children describe the time spent with each parent as "living" with that parent. Further, she points out that when parents and children describe their arrangements to others, they should acknowledge that they have two families, one with each parent. If at all possible, avoid the notion that children live with one parent and just visit the other. By making one parent the everyday parent and one parent the visiting parent, you run the risk that you and your children will either resent or exploit the lopsided roles and relationships that follow.

"Everyday" parents are sometimes viewed (and often view themselves), as the only ones responsible for the day-to-day realities of child rearing. As a result, it is easy to assume that the everyday parent is the only real parent. Some everyday parents prefer to control all substantive aspects of their child's life. Others feel overwhelmed and that they are being taken advantage of by missing out on relaxation times, especially if the children live with their other parent on weekends and holidays.

"Visiting" parents are sometimes accused of becoming the fun or party parent. The reasons some visiting parents adopt this role are as varied as the people who live with these arrangements. Some visiting parents are so starved for time with their children that they try to cram every conceivable activity into short periods of time. Some parents miss the giving that is part of daily care taking, and compensate with gifts that are more frequent, more expensive, and sometimes problematic.

Although no one can fault parents who seldom see their children for wanting to make every minute count, their relationships with their children will be far more balanced and fulfilling if they can intersperse fun activities with the routines of everyday life. Familiar, daily routines often provide an opening for conversations about thoughts and feelings. If all visits are filled with activities, the parent and children will have few opportunities to "talk," and are apt to drift apart. As a result, visiting parents often become "special," but less significant influences in their children's lives.

a. One Primary Residence

For many children and parents, designating one home as the primary place that children live makes the most sense. This arrangement can take on many variations, including the following:

- Live in home "A" except for alternating weekends, alternating holidays and a portion of the summer. This allows some geographic distance, and accommodates parents who don't get along too well or children who don't want or need more frequent contact.
- Live in home "A" except for midweek overnights, alternating weekends, alternating holidays and a portion of the summer. This allows for some geographic distance between the homes, but may require both parents to live in the same school district.
- Live in home "A" and visit other parent for short or daytime visits only. This accommodates extreme geographic distance or situations where violence, abuse or neglect require limited and/or supervised visitation.

b. Dual Residences

Some families prefer to have their children live for extended periods of time with each parent. Again, there are many possible variations. These living arrangements require extensive coordination between the parents and a willingness to regularly run into each other and any new partners. Some common dual-household arrangements include the following:

- Children alternate living in home "A" and "B" at approximately equal intervals such as every week, two weeks, month or six months. This requires homes in close proximity, especially if children are school-aged.
- Children live in home "A" during the week and in home "B" on the weekends. This option allows somewhat more geographic distance.
- During the school term, the children live in home "A" during the week and in home "B" on the weekends. In the summer, the children live in home "B" during the week and in home "A" on weekends. This option will work only if there is a moderate geographic distance between the parent's homes, and probably won't work if the children attend school year-round.

c. Children Live With Someone Other Than a Parent

For some families, it makes sense for the children to live with an adult other than a parent. This third adult may also have custody of the children or may be appointed their guardian.

If this option appeals to you, make sure your parenting agreement specifies the arrangements. The more specific you are, the more everyone will understand their responsibilities to the children and to each other. For example, if one or both parents are struggling to finance separate apartments, get jobs and recover from a drug addiction, having the children live with a grandparent could be a good idea—as long as you specify how each parent will maintain a relationship with the children.

d. Bird Nesting

Bird nesting means that the children remain in one home and the parents alternate moving in and out. The parents might have separate homes, sleep at a friend's house or stay with a relative.

Bird nesting is chosen infrequently, but can be especially good for infants or very young children. It requires an unusual degree of coordination and cooperation between the parents. And you must be clear about who will make decisions regarding the layout, furnishing and routines of the household.

Issue 15: Domestic Violence, Child Abuse and Child Neglect

Domestic violence, child abuse and child neglect are serious issues that affect all members of a family. Reports of violence, abuse and neglect are on the rise nationwide. Domestic violence, child abuse and child neglect happen in all kinds of families, from all parts of the country and at all income levels. Domestic violence can be directed at women, men and children. It may or may not be associated with drug or alcohol abuse. Some estimates show that approximately one in five marriages will experience at least five violent episodes each year. Other statistics estimate that in approximately 50% of the families in which a mate is abused, so are the children.

Get professional help if there is abuse in your home. Do not assume that violence directed at an adult does not affect the children. Children are very aware of their surroundings. Furthermore, violence, abuse and neglect come in many forms. Hitting, molestation, name calling, intimidation, abandonment, kidnapping, neglect of basic needs for food, shelter, care and protection all harm children—whether or not they are the intended targets.

KIDNAPPING IS A FORM OF CHILD ABUSE

Jill Krementz' book profiling children's experience with separation and divorce is instructive (*How it Feels When Parents Divorce*, Alfred A. Knopf, 1984). Jimmy, a ten year old, was the object of repeated kidnapping by both of his parents. As his parents fought over who should be his primary caretaker, he was taken from one home to the other—always in secret. Court battles and orders followed each abduction—and placed his father deeply in debt.

Jimmy relates how this nightmare began when he was seven: "... the court decided that I should live permanently with my Dad, but keep seeing my mother on weekends. Well, that made my mother so mad that she decided to steal me. One weekend while I was visiting her, she and Don packed up their car with a lot of stuff and we all piled in.... I remember asking her, 'What about Daddy?' And she just said 'Don't worry about it.'" After having been "stolen" at least three times, Jimmy was finally settled in his father's home. He lost a year of school—and all contact with his mother.

Families with a history of violence, abuse or neglect often use mediation, counseling or attorneys to make their parenting decisions. Mediation can be a problem, however. A battering victim may be intimidated when making decisions with the batterer in the room. If your state requires mediation in custody and visitation disputes (see Chapter 10), ask for separate meetings with the mediator so you can speak without fear or feeling intimidated.

In some states, judges appoint a social worker to evaluate both parents' homes and make a custody or visitation recommendation to the judge. In that situation, be honest about what has gone on and your concerns for the future. If you would feel more comfortable with a support person with you during an evaluation, ask the judge or social worker if it's possible. It's unlikely you'll be told no.

If your children are a target for either parent's uncontrolled anger, sexual advances or violence, consider bringing in someone trained in assessing domestic abuse to help you decide whether or not your children will be safe in that parent's care. (We explain how to find domestic abuse experts in Chapter 11.) If violence or abuse against any family member was or is a fairly common event, the expert can recommend a treatment plan so that children are not placed into the same situations with that parent's new home or family setting.

If you were the target of violence or abuse in this family relationship, get help of a counselor or therapist to make sure that the decisions you are making on behalf of your children are not based on fear or intimidation. You should also find out about what protective court orders might help out during the time when these decisions are being made, and afterwards.

ISSUE 15 CROSS-REFERENCES

Worksheet	Questions
Worksheet 1	4
Worksheet 2	5 10
Worksheet 3	4, 9, 12, 15
Worksheet 4	1, 3, 4, 5, 7, 8, 9, 10, 11, 16, 17

a. Make Protective Orders Work

If you are concerned about violence or abuse, you can get a protective order from a court that tells an abuser to stay away. While a piece of paper is not a guarantee that the abuse will stop, most abusers adhere to the terms of an order.

Whether you are trying to negotiate or implement decisions regarding your children, protective orders can help in the following ways:

- provide time and space to let a situation cool down
- keep specific people away from each other
- require supervised visits with the abuser, and
- limit telephone calls between the abuser and victims.

A court may issue a temporary protective order, to be modified or extended as needed, or to be made permanent. An attorney, court clerk, battered women's shelter or police department can help you obtain this kind of order.

b. Require Counseling or Emotional Support

One of the best steps you can take in stopping violence, abuse or neglect is to deal with the issue openly and honestly. Many parents agree to undergo counseling to learn how to change their behavior. (See Chapter 11 for more information.) A parent who doesn't volunteer may be ordered to go by a court.

The abusive or neglectful parent may not be the only one who needs counseling. No doubt, so will the victims. If the abuse or neglect has ended, the parents may need joint counseling to learn how to work together.

c.   Find a Safe Way to Care for the Children

You must find a way that your children can be cared for without losing safe contact with both parents. Often this translates into supervised visits between the abuser and the children. You should also identify an adult whom your children can call if they ever fear for their safety while in a parent's care. Be sure your children know that they will never be punished for calling this adult, even if their fears were unfounded.

d.   Get an Independent Evaluation

A trained professional can provide parents with an objective opinion about how to deal with violence, abuse or neglect. Depending on the issues involved, parents can learn new strategies for dealing with stress, disciplining their children and understanding their children's behavior. Unless you are low income and qualify for financial help, you will probably have to pay for this kind of evaluation.

e.   Require Supervised Visitation

Supervised visitation means that when your children spend time with an abusive parent or a parent who presents a serious threat of kidnapping, another adult is with them. Your court may recommend specific people who have been trained to perform this function. If not, you and the other parent must find your own supervisor. This might be a relative or friend, or a social worker or battered women's shelter employee whom you may need to pay. Some courts will require the supervisor to file a report with the court describing the visit and the children's reactions to being with the parent.

f.   Take a Break

If the violence you're experiencing is the result of the stress of separation or divorce, take a break. After the parents have established new homes, get some counseling and then slowly resume visits between the children and the abusive parent.

Issue 16: Alcohol or Drug Abuse

Many parents have an alcohol or drug problem. For some, it is an ongoing problem. Others use alcohol or drugs to escape the pain of the separation or divorce. You and the other parent will be more successful in dealing with these issues if you allow the addicted parent to help define and control his or her own recovery.

ISSUE 16 CROSS-REFERENCES

Worksheet	Questions
Worksheet 1	4
Worksheet 2	5, 8, 10
Worksheet 3	9, 13, 14
Worksheet 4	4, 10, 16, 18

a.   Attend a 12-Step or Similar Recovery Program

Throughout the country, a myriad of 12-step recovery programs, such as Alcoholics Anonymous, meet daily. (Chapter 11 provides information on how to locate these types of programs.) Some programs will provide a written record of a person's attendance to whoever needs to verify it. In some instances, this will be the court while in others it might be the other parent.

b.   Require Counseling or Emotional Support

Consider requiring a parent to get counseling. Some courts require the completion of a particular course of counseling or group therapy. If you agree to counseling without court intervention, check with a mental health agency, doctor, hospital, police department, community organization or church to find a qualified counselor.

Your agreement will be more likely to succeed if it:
- describes what specific behavior must stop
- describes what issues must be covered (such as ending the substance abuse and dealing with feelings of anger, jealousy and abandonment), and
- gives the addicted parent and the counselor a method of defining when the problem is under control.

c.   Limit Access to the Children

Getting a handle on a substance abuse problems can take a long time, and you may want to establish certain conditions before allowing the parent with the problem to care for the children. Here are some suggestions:

- The parent with the alcohol or drug problem will not operate a vehicle containing the children within 12 hours of consuming any alcohol or nonprescription drugs.

- The parent with the alcohol or drug problem will not consume alcohol or nonprescription drugs within 12 hours prior to, or during, any visit with the children.

- The parent with the alcohol or drug problem will submit to alcohol or drug testing if the other parent so requests. If that parent passes, the other parent will pay for the test. If that parent fails, he or she will pay for the test and forfeit scheduled visits until he or she can pass a test. (Alcohol or drug testing might be available through your police department, hospital or public health facility. You will have to investigate what services are available in your area as there is no universal way these services are made available to the public.)

- You can limit visits, or require them to be supervised (see Issue 15, option e), until the parent with the alcohol or drug problem successfully completes a rehabilitation program.

- Identify an adult whom your children can call if they ever fear for their safety while in a parent's care. Be sure to let your children know that they will never be

punished for calling this adult, even if their fears were unfounded.

- The parent with the alcohol or drug problem will not allow any person to consume alcohol to excess or nonprescription drugs in the children's presence.

Issue 17: Maintaining Contact When the Children Are With the Other Parent

Neither children nor adults can be two places at once. Therefore, your agreement should include a schedule for how each parent will remain in contact with the children when they are with the other parent. You will also want to make sure that calls happen at a convenient time.

ISSUE 17 CROSS-REFERENCES

Worksheet	Questions
Worksheet 1	3, 4, 5, 8
Worksheet 2	1, 2, 7, 8, 9, 10
Worksheet 3	3, 4, 7, 8, 14
Worksheet 4	4, 5, 6, 7, 8, 9, 18

a. Set Up a Contact Schedule

Many parents agree to a minimum number of calls between the children and the other parent. For example, you might agree that the parent with whom the children aren't living would initiate at least one call per week to the children. Many parents allow their children to initiate additional calls whenever they like.

In some families, the problem isn't too little communication, but too much. Calling a child too frequently may cause problems. If you call as often as once or twice a day, you may be communicating that you fear for your children's safety while in the other parent's care, or that you are desperately lonely. By pacing your calls, you can stay in touch without introducing unnecessary worry or anxiety. If, in fact, you are extremely lonely or anxious, discuss the situation with a trusted advisor or mental health professional.

b. Set a Regular Contact Time

Some parents forget that calling their children when they are eating dinner, doing homework, doing chores or getting ready for school can be disruptive. To avoid this, many parents schedule regular times each week when they can be reasonably sure that their children will be free to talk. Telephone time is set up to be as convenient as possible for both parents and their children. It may take some planning to find this time, but it usually pays off in enjoyable conversations and a minimum amount of disruption in daily routines.

c. Give Children Their Own Telephone Line

It is common for many parents to have less than friendly feelings for the other parent after separation or divorce. Therefore, receiving calls from the other parent, even for the brief moment of calling your children to the telephone, can be distasteful. To avoid this, consider getting your children a separate telephone line, or a line with a different ring, so that when it rings, only the children answer.

If you choose this option, be prepared to establish ground rules on acceptable telephone use. Your telephone company may have ideas for regulating telephone use and blocking certain types of calls (such as 900 numbers).

d. Schedule a Mid-Week Dinner

When the parents' homes are in the same general area, scheduling a regular mid-week dinner might be a great way to shorten the time between visits and create a special occasion for everyone. If you set up regular mid-week dinners, you must specify who will transport your children, as well as the pick up and drop off times. (See Issue 26.)

e. Plan for Contact During Trips

Parents need to plan for how they can stay in touch with their children when they are away on a trip with the other parent. The simplest solution is to leave an itinerary and include telephone numbers for where and when the children can be reached.

Issue 18: Reinvolving a Previously Absent Parent

Parents drop out of their children's lives for a variety of reasons. Some parents are better able to cope with the separation or divorce if they have little or no contact with their family. Others leave or are kept away because of substance abuse, violence, child abuse or incarceration. Regardless of the reason, reinvolving a parent is often a difficult task.

While children are remarkably adaptable, flexible and loving, they typically experience a mixture of hurt, anger,

happiness, confusion, hope, jealousy, anxiety and anticipation by a parent's absence and return. So does the parent who remained. Both parents will need a lot of time to get used to the other parent's return. Consider incorporating many of the options below into your parenting agreement.

a. Deal With Your Feelings

Everyone—the children, the parent who remained and the returning parent—can benefit from counseling. The children and the parent who remained may need to talk about their fears and hopes. The returning parent may need help in understanding both his or her own feelings, and the feelings of the children and the other parent.

b. Develop a Businesslike Relationship With the Other Parent

When a parent returns, tension with the other parent is both natural and common. Parents need time to develop trust, resolve the issues that existed before the parent left, and come to terms with the changes that are inevitable when only one parent remains to care for children.

Often, returning parents want to pick up where they left off. A parent who remained often resents the underlying assumption that the returning parent can just "waltz back in, become an instant parent and be a hero!"

To help ease this transition, you and the other parent can behave like business partners. Maintain your separate adult lives, but work together to raise your children. As with all good business relationships, the partnership works best when the parents can exchange information, respect each other's privacy and relationship with the children and keep a cool head when conflicts arise.

c. Go Slowly and Respect the Children's Feelings

Children often act out to avoid being hurt again. Young children may feel that they can't get enough of the returning parent, and not let that parent out of their sight. Older children, on the other hand, may test the parent's commitment through weeks, or even months, of short tense visits before resuming a normal relationship. The returning parent may develop a deep and satisfying new relationship with the children if he or she respects the children's feelings. You might ask your children how much contact they can handle.

If you are the parent who has been absent, be prepared to talk honestly about what happened and to answer your children's questions—even if it takes awhile for the questions to surface.

d. Keep an Open Mind

If you are the parent who remained, you probably have mixed feelings about the other parent's return, although anger may be high on the list. Depending on the length of the absence, your life and your children's lives may have changed considerably.

You need to maintain an open mind about the possible ways in which the other parent might reenter the children's lives. At the same time, be realistic and keep your support systems in place. The other parent may find the transition back too hard and may leave again or assume a very limited parenting role. If, however, the other parent wants to take an active role in your children's lives, consider ways to accommodate this request, as long as it is not harmful to the children.

e. Negotiate Short-Term Agreements

When a parent reenters his or her children's lives, it is a good idea to negotiate simple, short term agreements. These agreements allow both parents and children to test the waters and to learn what works best.

Trust, a critical element of any parenting relationship, is built over time. By adhering to these short-term agreements, returning parents demonstrate trustworthiness—and make more reliable negotiators for long term agreements.

f. Consider Reevaluating Your Sole-Custody Arrangement

Parents who remain behind have de facto sole custody of their children, whether or not a court makes such an order. If the returning parent appears to be reestablishing a long-term parenting role, you might consider modifying the custody arrangement.

Knowing whether a parent is back for good can be difficult. One way to test it is to negotiate and adhere to several temporary agreements, as described in option d, above. After everyone is satisfied that the returning parent is reliable, it may make sense to give that parent a larger parenting role.

The parent who remained behind may balk. But researchers repeatedly find that parents actively involved in

their children's lives maintain regular visitation schedules, pay a higher percentage of court-ordered support and have more satisfactory relationships with their children than do parents less involved in their children's lives.

Issue 19: Child Care

Child care is an important issue for many parents as they go their separate ways. In some families, a grandparent, other relative or friend has been a frequent care provider, and will continue to be available after the separation or divorce. In other families, finding child care providers that are acceptable to both parents is more difficult.

Below are some options that parents commonly consider. For ideas and information on finding child care providers and what qualifications you might want in a child care provider, see *Nolo's Law Form Kit: Hiring Child Care & Household Help*, by Attorney Stephen Elias (Nolo Press).

ISSUE 19 CROSS-REFERENCES

Worksheet	Questions
Worksheet 1	3
Worksheet 2	6, 7, 9
Worksheet 3	2, 3, 7, 8, 9, 12, 13, 14
Worksheet 4	1, 4, 9, 12, 15 ,16, 17

a. Agree on Care-Provider's Minimum Qualifications

Parents may not have a clear idea of who will provide child care, but may be able to agree on certain minimum qualifications. Parents often consider the care provider's age, physical location and licensure. Depending upon the distance between your homes, you can use the same provider (offering more continuity in your children's care) or each find a provider with the minimum qualifications you agree upon.

b. Agree on Ineligible Care Providers

You may be more anxious about preventing certain people from caring for your children than defining who can provide care. If this is the case, name these individuals in your parenting agreement or describe the characteristics you find unacceptable, such as being under the age of 17, using drugs or alcohol or operating a child care facility more than 10 miles from your home.

c.   Address the Role of a Parent's New Partner

Sometimes, the care provider that a parent wants to exclude is the other parent's new partner. This can fuel a fairly intense battle, so approach the situation with caution.

First, ask yourself your motive for not wanting the new partner to care for your children. If your concerns are motivated by jealousy, rivalry, or a fear of being "replaced" as a parent, consider more direct and productive ways to express and resolve your fears than to exclude that person as a care provider. Feeling jealous of the other parent's new partner is common, even if you don't want to have the other parent back as a partner. Similarly, a fear of being displaced is natural, and can be handled by:

- agreeing that your children will never be told that you are anything other than their parent
- finding special names for the new partner other than "Mom" or "Dad," and
- talking directly to your children about your fears.

Additional decisions about new partners are in Issue 36. If you find yourself unable to manage your feelings about the other parent's new partner, a counselor might be able to help.

d.   Agree to Call the Other First for Child Care

When parents homes are close by, they can consider providing child care for each other. For some parents, this means that one parent provides all after-school care until the other returns from work. For others, it means that one parent "covers" for the other for business or vacation trips.

This option offers several advantages:

- It allows parents to extend the time they spend with their children.
- It provides for greater continuity in care, which is especially important for young children.
- It keeps child care costs down.
- It shows children that their parents can still cooperate—at least about them.

There are at least two disadvantages. First, some parents use the chance to be called whenever child care is needed as "proof" that the other parent leaves the children too often. Second, you may find it difficult to maintain a separate life if the other parent is constantly around and able to keep track of your activities.

e.   Find an Adult Neighbor Who Can Check On Your Child

Some children are old enough to stay home by themselves for short periods. Others can take care of themselves with a neighbor's help. If your children need only minimal supervision, consider asking an adult in the neighborhood to call or stop by to see how things are going, or to be available by telephone in the event of an emergency.

⚠ DON'T PUT YOUR CHILDREN AT RISK

Do not leave your children home without adult supervision unless they are fully capable of caring for themselves and know who to call in the event of an emergency. Although you may have difficulty finding child care, unless your children can each care for themselves, or your oldest child is truly capable of caring for younger siblings, you could be taking a dangerous risk by leaving them unattended. Chapter 11 contains referrals to books which can help you to assess your children's readiness to stay home alone.

Issue 20: Moving

Some parents want to move away after a separation or divorce. A career change, job change, enrollment in school, new partners' job change, desire to be near a parent who can provide child care, inability to afford to live in the community or desire to just start over are common reasons for wanting to move.

Any parent who wants to move should examine his or her motives and options carefully. If moving is not critical, you may be making it unnecessarily difficult for your children to spend time with both parents. In some states, a court can prevent a parent with custody from moving out of the area unless the parent can show that the move is in the children's best interests. (Chapter 10 includes information on these states.)

ISSUE 20 CROSS-REFERENCES

Worksheet	Questions
Worksheet 1	3, 4, 5, 6, 7, 8, 9
Worksheet 2	1, 2, 6, 7, 8, 9, 10
Worksheet 3	1, 3, 4, 6, 7, 8, 9, 10, 12, 14, 15
Worksheet 4	1, 2, 4, 5, 6, 7, 8, 9, 11, 12, 13, 14, 15, 17, 18

a. Both Parents Relocate

In some parts of the country, the economy is so depressed that both parents may have to leave following a separation or divorce. Or, if both parents are originally from the same area, both may want to move back to that area after the divorce or separation to take advantage of the support that may be forthcoming from family members or old friends who have remained there.

You and the other parent can consider several options, including relocating together to a city or other area large enough to support you both and let you pursue your own lives. Many parents consider this alternative when they agree that their children need to have frequent contact with both parents, and feel that they might each benefit by making a move.

b. One Parent Relocates

With this option, the parents agree that there is no compelling reason for both parents to either remain in the same area or move to the same new area. You must choose a living arrangement that accommodates the distance between your homes. Issues 14 and 17 suggest options.

c. Parents Remain and Find New Ways To Meet Their Goals

You may decide that although you or the other parent might prefer to relocate, the children's interests would be better served if both parents remain in the area. You'll need to adopt some creative solutions to address the concerns of the parent who considered moving. Here are a few suggestions:

- The parent who wanted to move could return to school to gain new job skills to find employment in the area.
- The parents could alter the living arrangements to allow the parent who wanted to move to "commute" between two cities to work.

- The parents could alter the living arrangements (and child support payments) so that the parent who wanted to move becomes the primary caretaker for the children.

Issue 21: If Our Homes Are Far Apart

If a parent moves a significant distance from the other, the parents face the challenge of helping the children maintain a close relationship with both. Transporting the children is covered in Issue 26, below.

ISSUE 21 CROSS-REFERENCES

Worksheet	Questions
Worksheet 1	3, 4, 5, 7, 8, 9
Worksheet 2	1, 2, 3, 7, 8, 9, 10
Worksheet 3	1, 3, 4, 6, 7, 8, 9, 14
Worksheet 4	1, 2, 3, 4, 5, 6, 7, 8, 9, 15, 18

a. School Year With One Parent, Summer With the Other

The most common solution parents choose when they live apart is for the children to spend the school year with one parent and the summer with the other. If your children's school district is on a year-round calendar, however, this option isn't very feasible.

b. Change Primary Residence With Change in Schools

Some parents consider alternating each school term—for example, third grade with one parent and fourth grade with the other. Few professionals would recommend it, however, because it provides little continuity in the children's education and social life. Here is a compromise: the children live with one parent during elementary school, the other parent during middle (or junior high) school and then choose where they live during high school. These transitions often involve minimal disruption because so many children change school districts at these times.

c. Children Attend Private Residential School

A few families send their children to a private residential school. The children alternate vacations with their parents according to a predetermined schedule. See Issue 22, Holidays, just below, for suggestions on alternating times with parents.

Issue 22: Holidays

Deciding who your children will spend holidays with can be difficult unless you can think beyond one year. Remember that every holiday comes around every year.

First, make a list of all holidays and other occasions important to your family, including extended school breaks and holidays you celebrate because of your faith, cultural heritage or family traditions. Then consider the following possible schedules:

- alternate on an odd-year and even-year basis
- split extended holidays in half
- celebrate certain holidays twice
- assign the same holidays to the same parent every year, or
- decide how your children will spend the holidays as each holiday approaches.

ISSUE 22 CROSS-REFERENCES

Worksheet	Questions
Worksheet 1	3, 5, 8, 9
Worksheet 2	1, 7, 8, 9, 10
Worksheet 3	1, 2, 3, 4, 5, 7, 9, 12, 13, 14
Worksheet 4	1, 2, 3, 5, 8, 9, 11, 13, 14, 15, 16, 17, 18

a.   Alternate on an Odd-Year/Even-Year Basis

This option assigns certain holidays to each parent in odd years, and then reverses the schedule in even years. For example, your children might spend Thanksgiving with you in 1996, and with their other parent in 1997. This plan is comforting because parents know they will never miss spending a holiday with their children more than one year in a row. By contrast, this schedule can be frustrating if a particular holiday is meaningful for only one parent.

b.   Divide Holiday Celebrations in Half

Some parents divide the actual holiday celebration (and associated vacation days) in half so that their children can spend part of the time with each parent. This option allows everyone to see each other on the "big day," but requires advance planning so that your children do not miss the main part of the celebration because of travel. Often parents use the odd-year/even-year plan to alternate who spends the first and second halves of the holiday with their children.

c.   Celebrate Important Holidays Twice

Some families celebrate their holidays twice. For example, one parent might celebrate Christmas with the children a week before the actual date, and the other celebrates it with the children on December 25th. This is certainly easier when one parent's family already celebrates a holiday one week before or one week after the actual date so that they can also fit in a "family reunion." Fortunately, few children complain about getting to celebrate twice!

d.   Develop a Fixed Holiday Schedule

If you and the other parent differ on which holidays are special, you can assign holiday time so that each of you celebrates the same holidays every year with your children. This option is ideal when, for example, one parent participates in religious celebrations and the other parent chooses nonreligious holiday times for vacations, trips or other activities.

e.   Make Decisions as Each Holiday Approaches

Some parents prefer not to be tied down to a holiday schedule. As long as you are communicating effectively and your ideas about a holiday schedule are similar, this plan works well. It means, however, that you must spend considerable amounts of time arranging every holiday. If you choose this option, decide how far in advance of each holiday you will make your plans.

Issue 23: Vacations

Vacationing can raise a multitude of questions. Among other things, you and the other parent should discuss:

- travel out of the area, out of the state or out of the country
- whether each parent must provide the other with an itinerary and contact information
- whether certain activities (such as hang gliding) will be permitted
- how long the children can be away, and
- whether you will schedule "make up" visits.

Informing the other parent well in advance of your intentions allows everyone to deal with schedule changes more easily. If you know how much vacation time you will have in a given year and how you'd like to spend it, you and the other parent can start early to figure out how the children will fit in.

ISSUE 23 CROSS-REFERENCES

Worksheet	Questions
Worksheet 1	3, 5, 9
Worksheet 2	1, 6, 7, 8, 9, 10
Worksheet 3	1, 3, 4, 7, 8, 9, 12, 13, 14
Worksheet 4	1, 4, 5, 7, 8, 11, 12, 13, 14, 15, 16, 17

Issue 24: Special Occasions and Family Events

Although you and the other parent have gone your separate ways, your children may want either or both of you to attend special events or ceremonies. By planning ahead, these decisions are considerably easier to make. With very little imagination you can expect this issue to come up over back-to-school night, a football game, a family picnic for your children's scout troop, graduation or a school play.

Although these events are meant to be fun and special for the participating families, they can also become frustrating and confusing. You, your children and the other parent need to develop a strategy for dealing with these invitations so that the event remains fun and are as simple to plan as possible.

Some parents alternate who attends each event ("You go to back-to-school night and I'll go to the open house"), others attend together, and still others attend the events that have the most meaning in their relationship with their child ("I'll do scouts if you do baseball").

ISSUE 24 CROSS-REFERENCES

Worksheet	Questions
Worksheet 1	5, 9
Worksheet 2	1, 6, 7, 8, 9, 10
Worksheet 3	1, 3, 4, 5, 7, 8, 9, 12, 13, 14
Worksheet 4	1, 2, 3, 4, 7, 8, 9, 10, 15, 16, 17

Issue 25: Grandparents, Relatives and Important Friends

After your separation or divorce, it is important to your children that you find ways for them to maintain relationships with other adults who are important to them—namely, grandparents, aunts, uncles, neighbors and family friends. Children need the security of familiar friends and relationships. These familiar people can help ease the transition for children when their parents no longer live together.

In your parenting agreement, you essentially have two options: simply list the other adults with whom you want your children to maintain contact, or list those adults and specify how and when visits will take place.

ISSUE 25 CROSS-REFERENCES

Worksheet	Questions
Worksheet 1	5, 9
Worksheet 2	6, 7, 10
Worksheet 3	7, 8, 9, 12, 13, 14
Worksheet 4	1, 4, 9, 11, 15, 16, 17

Issue 26: Transporting the Children

Transporting children for their time with each parent can be simple if you live near each other. Some children walk, ride their bicycles or take the city bus back and forth. For most parents, however, this subject is more troublesome. One way to ease your frustration is to agree on as many details as possible—how you will make exchanges, the time for pick-ups and drop-offs, how each parent will notify the other of last minute changes and who will pay for transportation costs.

Your options will depend on several factors, including how far apart you live, how often your children will see each parent, who has access to a car and the costs of transportation. If there has been violence between the parents, you may want to choose a busy public location for your exchanges. If weather is an issue in your area, you will want to choose a location that allows you, the other parent and your children to wait indoors—such as a shopping mall or museum—in the event of bad weather. If you or the other parent must use public transportation to make the exchanges, you will need to know the schedules and plan accordingly.

ISSUE 26 CROSS-REFERENCES

Worksheet	Questions
Worksheet 2	8, 9, 10
Worksheet 3	2, 3, 4, 6, 7, 9, 12
Worksheet 4	1, 9, 10, 11, 16, 17

a. Meet at a Mid-Point

This option lets the parents share the travel time by choosing a neutral location for making exchanges. It requires that each parent has access to a vehicle and arrives at the exchange point at approximately the same time.

b. Alternate Travel Responsibilities

In an effort to share the responsibility fairly equally, some parents alternate transporting the children over the entire distance. This option requires that each parent can obtain reliable transportation when it is his or her turn to drive, but allows more flexibility in setting a time for the exchange.

c. One Parent Transports

This option is ideal for parents who cannot absorb equally the time and vehicle maintenance necessary for transporting children. If one parent is without a vehicle, or cannot take the time to provide transportation, perhaps that parent can compensate by reimbursing the cost of gas or other expenses.

d. Parent Travels to Children

Some parents travel to the children and either rent an apartment or motel room, stay with a friend nearby or live with the children for the visit. This option allows parents to visit without otherwise disrupting their children's normal activities.

Parents often consider this option when the distant parent has more travel time available than do the children. Usually this happens during the school year when the recess is too short to allow the children to visit at their other parent's home. If you choose this arrangement, you will need to decide where the parent will stay, how travel expenses will be allocated and which parent will participate in the children's activities.

e. Parent Brings Children to Other Parent and Leaves

With this option, one parent takes the children to the other parent's home, and then vacations or visits friends before picking the children up at the end of the visit. This option probably won't work for other than occasional visits, but it can add variety or help one parent out if he or she has vehicle problems.

f. Children Travel by Themselves

Some parents let their children travel alone between homes—by train, bus or airplane—once they reach a certain age. Of course, the parents must still get the children to and from the stations, but this option can save a lot in time, money and aggravation.

Issue 27: Improving Transition Times

Many parents have difficulty handling the inevitable ups and downs that come when children travel between homes. This is especially true just after the separation or for a parent who hasn't seen the children in quite some time. Many parents have high expectations when their children are about to arrive, and get depressed when their children leave.

For children, the ups and downs are worse. Young children, especially, gear up when anticipating a visit with one parent and simultaneously crash because of the separation from the other. A child may be afraid of forgetting the schedule, particularly if it is new or irregular. Some children worry a good deal about going to the right home after school or getting in trouble for making a mistake.

ISSUE 27 CROSS-REFERENCES

Worksheet	Questions
Worksheet 1	1, 3, 4, 6, 7
Worksheet 2	7, 9, 10
Worksheet 3	2, 3, 4, 7, 8, 12, 14, 15
Worksheet 4	4, 5, 8, 9, 11, 18

a. Time the Exchange With Other Regular Transitions

By timing your exchange with a drop-off or pick-up at school, after a sporting event or before or after some other regular activity, the exchange won't feel artificial or forced.

b. Make Exchanges Simple and Quick

Children generally have an easier time of saying good-bye to one parent and taking up with the other if the actual exchange is quick and casual. One strategy is to carry out the exchange at a busy public place, such as a park, restaurant or shopping mall.

Another way to expedite the exchange is for parents to minimize their communication. Speak the day or evening before to discuss necessary information about the children's health, school and activities. Not only does this allow the exchange of the children to be brief, but also it helps parents exchange vital information without making the children sit around and wait. It is especially useful when tension is high.

c. Give Children Your Undivided Attention at the Start of the Visit

The start of any time with your children can be easier and more relaxing if you delay other activities, at least briefly, to give your children some time during which they have your undivided attention. This may be as simple as giving them uninterrupted time to tell you about their activities while with the other parent. If you have more than one child, taking them to a park or the zoo gives each child a chance to talk while the others play. This might be especially helpful if your children have half-siblings or step-siblings from your new relationship.

d. Give Your Children Some "Breathing Room"

Some children need quiet time at the start of a visit to get reacquainted with you and your household. For these chil-

dren, jumping right into a frenzy of activity will often backfire. You might give this child some pictures to look through, a book to read or some paper to color on, take this child on a short walk or find some other low-key activity to do together.

e. Be Patient When Your Children Ask Questions

Children have many questions after their parents go separate ways. Depending on their age and temperament, they may ask why you are no longer together, how decisions are being made, how they will be cared for, whether they will be able to form lasting intimate relationships as an adult or any number of other questions. You can best help your children by hearing and answering their questions patiently. Eventually, your children's questions will decrease and their comfort with the situation will increase.

Most mental health professionals agree that children don't really need, or necessarily want, to know the intimate details of your relationship. Be careful that in answering your children's questions you don't burden them with your frustration, anger or disappointment over your partner's sexual performance or compatibility. If they ask, don't ignore them, but redirect the conversation to a more appropriate topic.

f. Establish New Rituals

Children thrive on routines and love rituals. By setting aside a small amount of time at the beginning and end of each visit for a special activity or small ritual, you can ease the awkwardness of coming together and the discomfort of separation for both of you.

Issue 28: Treating Each Child as an Individual

Many parents assume that visits should always be the same for each child, and that children should always visit their parents together. Parents, however, can often do their children a great service by tailoring some visits to meet the needs, personalities and interests of only one child at a time.

In the book, *Divorce and Your Child*, (Yale University Press, 1984), the authors Sonja Goldstein and Albert Solnit observed that:

> *While it is generally preferable for brothers and sisters not to be separated by their parent's divorce, it does not follow that in a smoothly working joint custody situation ... all the children must spend the same day or parts of days with the same parent in the same manner. This is not the way it*

is for children whose parents live together; older and younger brothers and sisters do not have the same activities, and it would place an unwarranted burden on children of divorced parents if joint custody were to hamper them.

This is not to say that all visits should be separate, but only to suggest that parents consider occasional arrangements to allow each child time alone with each parent.

ISSUE 28 CROSS-REFERENCES

Worksheet	Questions
Worksheet 1	1, 2, 3, 4, 5, 7, 8, 9
Worksheet 2	1, 3, 4, 5, 7, 8, 9, 10
Worksheet 3	3, 4, 14
Worksheet 4	4, 5, 6, 7, 8, 9, 18

a.   Schedule Short, Separate Visits With Each Child

Scheduling a separate visit with each child allows you and each child to plan a special activity for just the two of you. It is a good strategy for smoothing over rough spots in the relationship, as well as providing a fun time that only the two of you have shared. To make the most of this kind of visit, have your child help plan the activities, and take pictures or collect mementos of your "adventure" for your child to keep.

b.   Children Take Turns Being the Center of Your Attention

You may not have the option of scheduling separate visits for each child. In this case, you can still carve out special time for each child by:

- setting aside a small amount of time for each child during each visit
- rotate having each child decide the activities that everyone will engage in during your visits, or
- staggering the arrival or departure times for each child (school or other activity schedules may facilitate this) to allow special time for each child.

Issue 29: When Parenting Styles and Values Are Very Different

Parents frequently differ in beliefs, values and expectations for themselves and their children. Children whose parents have substantially conflicting child-rearing rules and disciplinary styles sometimes feel as though they are two different people—one to please each parent. You can guard against this by not criticizing the other parent's style, and if possible, finding some common ground.

Differences are not necessarily bad—in fact, they are what make the world go 'round. While some children tolerate the variety, others find it overwhelming. You need to tailor your agreement on this issue to what best suits your children.

If the differences between you and the other parent come from differences in cultural backgrounds or religious beliefs, see Chapter 8 for more information. If your differences are because one of you recently came out as a lesbian or gay man, or have chosen a less than traditional way of living, read Chapter 9.

ISSUE 29 CROSS-REFERENCES

Worksheet	Questions
Worksheet 1	3, 4, 5, 8
Worksheet 2	3, 4, 5, 7, 9, 10
Worksheet 3	4, 5, 8, 9, 12, 13, 14
Worksheet 4	2, 3, 4, 5, 6, 8, 9, 10. 11, 17, 18

a. Focus on Your Child

Some parents can agree only that they both love their children. If this is true for you, use it as a starting point for a new partnership with the other parent. The key to making this option work is recognizing your children's skills, interests and personalities and finding ways to complement them.

Children's needs and interests depend a lot on their ages. Young children often find security in being with or near a close extended family. By contrast, teens often like to "hang" with their friends and need a parent who can supervise from a distance. For more information on how differences in parenting styles affect children of various ages, see Chapter 7.

If you and the other parent come from different cultural or religious backgrounds, teaching your children about who they are can give parents a way to focus on their children. In particular, consider having your children:

- hear stories from grandparents or other elders
- attend special religious or cultural functions
- learn skills unique to a particular culture, or
- attend special camps.

b. Structure the Living Arrangements or Transition Times to Reduce Conflict

If the lives your children lead are radically different in each parent's home, then you may find transition periods particularly difficult for your children. Several researchers have found that children adjust better to two homes with very different rules and standards than to open conflict between the parents.

Nevertheless, it may be very difficult for your children. To ease the contradictions, you have two options. One is to modify the living arrangements (Issue 14) so that your children go back and forth infrequently. For example, one parent can have the children during the school year and the other in the summer, again, with frequent communication but no physical exchanges.

Your other option is to improve transition times. For suggestions, see Issue 27.

c. Agree to Disagree

For some parents, the differences are so great that they do not try to bridge the gap. If you are in this situation, do your best to have some consistent standards for your children's conduct and to respect your children's right and desire to know, understand and love the other parent. Beyond that, each parent must be willing to let the other parent enforce his or her rules in his or her own home.

Issue 30: Consistency in Raising Children

Children need their parents to be as consistent as possible in approving or disapproving their conduct—whether the parents live together or apart. When parents separate or divorce, this is hard to achieve. As a start, you and the other parent might agree on certain daily routines, such as meal times, bed times and finishing homework before playing.

Children, as a rule, are remarkably flexible. They know that their parents are different people, and they can usually handle the variations in each home. Some of the differences between your two homes can be passed off rather simply by saying "Yes, at the other house you are allowed to do that, but I do things differently." Others cannot be dismissed so easily and require that the parents try to reach a common ground. If your parenting styles are vastly different, consider the additional options in Issue 29, above.

ISSUE 30 CROSS-REFERENCES

Worksheet	Questions
Worksheet 1	3, 4, 7, 8
Worksheet 2	3, 4, 5, 7, 9, 10
Worksheet 3	4, 5, 12, 13, 14
Worksheet 4	1, 4, 5, 7, 9, 16, 17, 18

a. Establish a Few Common Rules for Both Homes

Even when parents approach raising children differently, they can maintain a minimum level of consistency by agreeing on a few rules that will be enforced in both homes. Be creative—find issues that matter to you both and that you agree on. No two people disagree on absolutely everything. For example, you might agree on allowed snack foods, television shows (or the number of hours each day the children can watch television) or requiring the children to show respect for both parents.

b. Exchange Information About Behavior and Discipline

Parents can avoid problems by talking to each other about behavior and disciplinary issues. If you don't, your children will find the chinks in the unified front you may try to maintain, and will play one of you off the other.

With this option, each parent lets the other know about any behavior or discipline problems, and what actions the parent took to deal with the situation. In this way, you and the other parent can support each other, even if you might have handled the situation differently.

c. Acknowledge Your Differences

Along the lines of "variety is the spice of life," you can accept that you have different child-rearing styles. You must acknowledge, however, that this can be difficult for your children. Encourage them to describe exactly what bothers them and to talk to the other parent directly to work out a resolution. If you agree to this arrangement, you must also agree to let go—that is, to not try to tell the other how to handle situations in his or her own home.

Issue 31: Disparaging Remarks

You won't score any points with your children if you criticize the other parent, or his or her new partner or lifestyle. However critical children may be of their parents, most children love and revere them and don't want to hear the negative remarks.

A parent who makes disparaging remarks about the other in the children's hearing creates two serious problems. First, the critical parent weakens the children's relationship with their other parent. This can make it difficult for the children to live with and rely upon the other parent for care and companionship. Second, the critical parent conveys, quite clearly, that their children cannot express love or admiration for the other parent in that home. Children often grow to resent and distrust the critical parent for interfering in the children's other important relationships.

ISSUE 31 CROSS-REFERENCES

Worksheet	Questions
Worksheet 1	3, 4, 5, 9
Worksheet 2	5, 7, 8, 9
Worksheet 3	4, 9, 10, 11, 12, 13, 14, 15
Worksheet 4	4, 5, 6, 9, 10, 16, 18

Issue 32: Undermining the Parent/Child Relationship

Many parents are uncomfortable with their children's relationship with the other parent. Children seldom miss the message. When parents cry out in frustration "You are just like your (mother/father) when you do that," their children hear this as a warning that they possess a bad character trait or personality flaw that they will have to work to avoid.

Some parents are quite direct in trying to undermine their children's relationship with the other parent. Most commonly, a parent will force the children to sit through lectures on all of the other parent's faults. Less commonly, a parent will punish a child for talking about the other parent or asking to see that parent, or will bar the children from talking to, spending time with or accepting gifts from the other parent.

In some instances, a parent might physically inspect the children upon each return, looking for evidence of mistreatment. Unless you have real reasons for suspecting child abuse, do not examine your children in this way. You are likely to instill real, yet unwarranted, fear in your children that they must worry about their safety when they are with the other parent.

Whether your undermining efforts are indirect or direct, the effect on your children is the same. They will be torn between a desire to love both parents, and the need to earn approval by saying they love one parent and hate the other.

ISSUE 32 CROSS-REFERENCES

Worksheet	Questions
Worksheet 1	3, 4, 5, 8
Worksheet 2	4, 7, 8, 10
Worksheet 3	10, 11, 12, 13, 15
Worksheet 4	4, 5, 10, 11, 18

Issue 33: Denying Access to the Children

Some parents limit the relationship that their children have, or might have, with the other parent. It may be because of lingering anger or pain from the separation or divorce. More commonly, when communications break down and conflicts heat up, a parent stops adhering to the schedule governing when each parent is to spend time with the children. Difficult as it may be, your first responsibility when drafting and carrying out your parenting agreement is to look at the world through your children's eyes.

If you feel that your only recourse in a particularly troubling situation is to deny the other parent access to the children, you must obtain outside help. If you've already decided Issue 12—Resolving Disputes When Making Decisions Together—follow your agreement. If you haven't, consult Chapter 4 for information on negotiating, Chapter 6 for information on mediation and arbitration and Chapter 11 for ideas on finding appropriate resources.

ISSUE 33 CROSS-REFERENCES

Worksheet	Questions
Worksheet 1	3, 4
Worksheet 2	5, 6, 7, 10
Worksheet 3	4, 9, 10, 11, 12, 13, 14, 15
Worksheet 4	4, 5, 6, 7, 8, 9, 10, 11, 16, 17

Issue 34: When a Parent Needs to Develop Parenting Skills

Many parents need help with their role as a parent. For parents who were previously uninvolved in the day-to-day care and discipline of the children, having full responsibility for their children, even for relatively short periods of time, can be overwhelming. A parent who has abused or neglected his or her children in the past needs special help so that discipline and other child-rearing situations do not further harm the children. Fortunately, many agencies and other resources offer help in honing or developing parenting skills. See Chapter 11.

ISSUE 34 CROSS-REFERENCES

Worksheet	Questions
Worksheet 1	4, 5, 7, 8
Worksheet 2	3, 4, 5, 7, 10
Worksheet 3	4, 10, 11, 12, 13, 14
Worksheet 4	1, 3, 4, 5, 6, 7, 8, 9, 10, 17, 18

Issue 35: When Nonrelatives Live in the Home

Housing is expensive, especially on only one income. After a divorce or separation, you (or your ex) may need to share your home, especially if it means you can afford to live somewhere large enough to accommodate your children overnight.

You or the other parent may imagine the worst when you hear that one of you has roommates. Any concerns about roommates should be included in your parenting agreement. For example, you can:

- require the children to have separate sleeping quarters
- bar the roommates from having or using drugs in the home
- prohibit the roommates from disciplining the children, or
- restrict the number of outside visitors.

ISSUE 35 CROSS-REFERENCES

Worksheet	Questions
Worksheet 1	3, 4, 5, 9
Worksheet 2	4, 5, 7, 8, 9, 10
Worksheet 3	6, 7, 8, 9, 12, 13, 14
Worksheet 4	1, 2, 4, 5, 7, 8, 9, 10, 11, 12, 13, 14, 15, 16

Issue 36: When Parents Have New Partners

When a separated or divorced parent develops a new intimate relationship, both parents and the children are likely to have fairly intense feelings about the situation. The other parent may be jealous, even if he or she has no desire to get back together. That parent may also be afraid that the children will get attached to the new partner and lose their bond with their parent.

These feelings can be very powerful and can seriously disrupt your parenting relationship. Although you both know that you cannot tell the other whom to choose as a partner, you still must address certain issues, such as:

- how the children will relate to the new partner—in particular, whether that person will supersede the children's relationship with the other parent
- what the children will call the new partner
- ensuring that the children have their own sleeping quarters, and
- whether the new partner will make parenting decisions.

Even if neither of you has a new partner, you can include this provision in your parenting agreement in anticipation of that time. Or, you can skip this issue now and modify your agreement when necessary.

Additional information on new partners is in Chapter 7, Section A.4, and Chapter 9.

ISSUE 36 CROSS-REFERENCES

Worksheet	Questions
Worksheet 1	3, 4, 8, 9
Worksheet 2	2, 5, 7, 9, 10
Worksheet 3	1, 4, 5, 7, 8, 9, 12, 13, 14, 15
Worksheet 4	1, 3, 4, 5, 6, 7, 8, 9, 10, 11, 12, 15, 16, 17

Issue 37: Labeling the Custody Arrangement

Living arrangements and custody labels are two different issues. You described your children's actual living arrangement in Issue 14. Here you decide what these arrangements mean in terms of custody—the term used by the court in a divorce or legal separation.

Three custody labels are the most common:

- sole custody, which gives one parent authority for all decisions
- joint custody, which generally means that parents share child rearing, and
- split custody, which divides the children between parents.

In some states, custody is further defined as "legal" and "physical." Legal custody refers to making decisions regarding health, education and the child's best interests. Physical custody describes providing the majority of physical care for the children. A common arrangement in these states is for one parent to have sole physical custody, while the parents have joint legal custody. Chapter 10 indicates which states differentiate between legal and physical custody.

No matter what custody label(s) you use, you have tremendous latitude to spell out with whom your children will spend their time. For example, even with a sole custody arrangement, your children may live with the noncustodial parent every other weekend. Similarly, you can agree to joint custody, but have your children spend little time with one parent.

COURTS AND CUSTODY

In general, a judge will guarantee a parent's right to spend time with his or her children and a parent's obligation to care for and support his or her children. Furthermore, in most states, custody laws are gender-neutral. This means that neither parent is presumed to be more fit simply because that parent is a mother or a father. A few states retain one exception to this, called the "tender years" doctrine. In these states, a court may assume that very young children should live with their mothers whenever possible.

A parent could be denied contact with his or her children if the judge rules that:

- a parent is legally incompetent (even then, the court may permit supervised visitation)
- a parent is not related to the children by blood or legal adoption—such as a stepparent or same-sex co-parent (you can give that person the status of parent in your agreement, however), or
- the contact would be harmful to the children.

In extreme cases, a court can terminate a person's parental rights—usually after finding that the parent has abandoned the children or engages in behavior highly damaging to the children. If you are named in a hearing to terminate your parental rights, you will have the right to defend yourself—in many states, you will have to right to an appointed attorney if you cannot afford one yourself.

ISSUE 37 CROSS-REFERENCES

Worksheet	Questions
Worksheet 1	3
Worksheet 2	1, 2, 6, 7, 10
Worksheet 3	1, 7, 12, 14, 15
Worksheet 4	1, 2, 7, 8 ,10, 11, 12, 13, 14, 17, 18

a. Sole Custody

Parents frequently choose sole custody when distance, acrimony or other factors make it impossible for parents to collaborate on the decisions that affect their children. If your decision in Issue 11 (Making Decisions) is to have only one parent make decisions, you'll probably want to select sole custody.

A parent with sole custody cannot prevent the other parent from visiting the children. The sole custodian does have considerable discretion in scheduling visitation, however. The more specific you can be about your visitation schedule, the easier your plan will be to live with. The decisions you make here should also be consistent with the decisions you made in Issue 17.

Sole Custody and Child Support
A sole custody arrangement does not exempt the noncustodial parent from paying child support.

b. Joint Custody

Most parents who choose to make decisions together (Issue 11) choose joint custody or joint legal custody if their state differentiates between legal and physical custody. Joint legal custody can mean anything from consulting each other on every decision larger than the clothes to be worn to school, to consulting only on major issues, such as whether to allow underage children to marry, and everything in between.

Joint physical custody agreements may also vary widely. The most common joint physical custody awards specify that the children:

- spend equal time with each parent
- spend the school year with one parent and the summer with the other, or
- live primarily with one parent and spend weekly midweek visits or overnights, weekends and half of the holidays and summer vacation with the other parent.

For joint custody to succeed, you and the other parent must be willing to work together to make decisions, without using your children as either a weapon or an excuse. You can help your joint custody arrangements to succeed by being specific in your parenting agreement about how you will make decisions and how your children will share time with each of you.

All states allow parents to choose joint custody arrangements. A small number of states permit courts to order joint custody, even over the objections of a parent. Your state's rules on joint custody are spelled out in Chapter 10.

c. Split Custody

Splitting custody of the children between the parents is not recommended except under special circumstances. Such circumstances include:

- a history of irreconcilable conflict between a parent and one or more of the children
- incest or violence between the children, or
- children with different fathers or mothers.

Unfortunately, some parents split custody because it makes each of them feel as though they have "won." If this is your reason for considering it, be careful. Often, the bond between siblings is the only reliable support system children have after their parents split up. Eliminating it can have very serious consequences, even if the children have only one parent in common.

Consult a mental health professional before splitting custody of your children. If you still decide to opt for it, schedule a lot of time that your children can be together.

d. Third Party Custody

Some parents are unwilling or unable to care for their children. The parents may be children themselves, or may be undergoing psychiatric, substance abuse or physical rehabilitation. No matter what the reason, if you are in this situation you will have to choose a third person, such as a grandparent or other relative, to care for your children. You must also specify how you and the other parent will spend time with your children and how you will regain custody of your children.

Issue 38: Making Changes

You will need to make changes to your parenting arrangement in years to come, unless your children are about to move out on their own. All parents need to respond to their children's or their own changing lives. By anticipating the need to modify your agreement, you can minimize much of the conflict parents experience around change.

ISSUE 38 CROSS-REFERENCES

Worksheet	Questions
Worksheet 1	5, 8
Worksheet 2	2, 3, 8, 9,10
Worksheet 3	4, 7, 8, 14, 15
Worksheet 4	4, 6, 7, 8, 9, 11, 18

a. Set Up Regular Reviews

Consider reviewing your parenting agreement:
  • once a year
  • when your children change schools, or
  • as your children reach certain ages.

In the first few years after you separate or divorce, you might consider more frequent reviews (such as every six months) until you are sure you have settled upon a final agreement.

Give yourselves enough time to negotiate whatever changes are necessary. Scheduling the review approximately one month before the school year begins or about one month before the start of the summer break should give you plenty of time.

When you review your agreement, you may discover that you have already informally negotiated changes, or that certain aspects of the agreement no longer work. If you negotiate changes to the agreement, modify it in writing to reflect the changes.

b. Allow Your Children to Share in Decisions

You may want to give your children a role in deciding where they will live and how they will spend time with both parents. Some parents solicit their children no matter what their ages; others wait until the children are teenagers.

c. Consider Mediation

You may be willing to evaluate or renegotiate your parenting agreement only if a third party is present. In this situation, include an automatic mediation schedule for reviewing your agreement, or allow either parent to schedule mediation as necessary. More information on mediation is in Chapter 6.

Issue 39: Making Substantive Changes to This Agreement

If you make substantive changes to your parenting agreement, such as living arrangements, decision-making authority, or making a move, you will want to modify any existing and relevant court orders so that your agreement is enforceable. This may seem unnecessary if your relationship with the other parent is working well; if it deteriorates, however, you may not be able to enforce your agreement.

Issue 40: Explaining the Agreement to Our Children

You and the other parent must consider how you will tell your children about your parenting agreement. If possible, tell them together. If that won't work, decide who will tell them and what that person will say. You must also decide how your children's questions will be answered. You can agree that either parent will answer any question that the children have. Alternatively, you can select one parent to field most, if not all, questions.

Some children, especially younger children, have difficulty understanding that they will continue to be loved even though their parents no longer love each other. Many children fear that they were the cause of the separation or divorce, especially if you and the other parent argued frequently about child-rearing issues. To help your children, stress that the decision to separate or divorce was made because of the relationship between the parents, not because of anything that the children did or did not do. No matter what you say, find a way to ensure that your children know they are loved.

Pre-schoolers, especially, have little use for calendars, but do understand the sequence of familiar events. Try explaining when they will see you or the other parent again in relation to other events that they enjoy. For example, if your children attend pre-school, a play group or swimming lessons on Tuesdays and Thursdays, explain that you will see them after two more swimming lessons.

ISSUE 40 CROSS-REFERENCES

Worksheet	Questions
Worksheet 1	6, 7
Worksheet 3	4, 6

Making Mediation and Arbitration Work for You

Until recently, when parents could not agree on custody and visitation during or after a divorce, they would bring the case to court for a judge to decide. Now, many of these parents turn to a neutral third party who is trained to help people come to an agreement on their own. This process is called mediation, and the third party is known as a mediator.

Mediation has become such a well-accepted method of resolving custody and visitation disputes that most states encourage judges to order it in appropriate circumstances —indeed, a few states require it before a judge can even get involved. Even if a judge doesn't order mediation, you can voluntarily choose it if you need help in reaching an agreement. Although voluntary mediation usually requires that you pay the mediator, this cost is trivial compared to the cost of hiring lawyers to fight out custody and visitation issues in court.

You can use mediation in several different ways. Some parents use it to start the settlement process, and then stop mediation once they are able to negotiate on their own. Other parents use mediation now and then—an hour here, and an hour there—throughout the negotiation process to resolve various points of impasse. Still other parents mediate their entire parenting agreement. The point is this: view mediation as a flexible tool you can tailor to meet your family's needs as you design your agreement.

A. How Mediation Works

Mediators facilitate discussions so that parents can voice their concerns, identify important issues and focus their efforts on meeting their children's needs. Almost every mediation has the same characteristics listed below.

- **The mediator is neutral.** The mediator has no personal or business ties with either parent, has no past knowledge of the family, is not aware (in advance) of the specific issues to be mediated and has no preconceived ideas about what parenting plan would be best for that family.
- **The process is confidential.** The mediator will not disclose to a court or anyone else what either parent says during the mediation. Furthermore, no one will know about the mediation or its results unless the parents agree or submit their agreement to a court to be incorporated into a court order. In rare circumstances, a mediator may be subpoenaed by a court and com-

pelled to testify about the mediation if the mediator made a recommendation to the court and that recommendation is contested by a parent.
- **Mediation is focused on the future.** Most mediators ask parents to focus on what they'd like to happen in the future. This means that the mediator spends little time on who said or did what in the past, but significant time on what must be done to control or prevent these problems in the future. The mediator's goal is to help parents build agreements that are likely to succeed by avoiding past problems.
- **Agreements are voluntary.** An agreement is reached only when both parents say that the terms are acceptable.

B. Why Mediation Works

The reasons why mediation works and parents prefer mediation over litigation are many. Here are just a few:
- Mediation offers access to a trained neutral person who can help parents focus their attention on the issues to be resolved, as opposed to blaming each other for the problems they face.
- Mediation is confidential, which allows parents to freely discuss the issues and evaluate possible solutions without fear that the other parent can use the discussions or the mediator's statements to build a court case.
- Parents decide for themselves whether to accept or reject any particular agreement.
- Parents control the time, costs and acrimony associated with finding a resolution.
- Mediation helps parents improve their communication skills—an important part of successful separate parenting.

Mediators are especially skilled at generating ideas and helping parents overcome impasse. Mediators can also review a parenting agreement to point out such potential problems as:
- vague language—such as "reasonable visitation"
- vague action plans—for example, a plan that doesn't include specific pick-up and drop-off times for visits, vacations or holidays, and
- arrangements that might leave one parent feeling excluded from the children's lives—such as a sole custody arrangement with unspecified visitation.

Although mediators don't provide legal advice, they can often give general information about your state's custody and visitation laws, and suggest resources for information on child development and parenting theories. Especially if your mediator is also a family law attorney, you may be able to get the legal information you need if you want your agreement to best conform to what a court might want to see.

Even if your mediation sessions do not result in a complete parenting agreement, you probably will still benefit from the process. Partial agreements can narrow the issues to be negotiated or litigated later, and mediation can help open and improve lines of communication.

C. Proposing Mediation

For some families, the hardest task in mediation is getting it started. Many parents are reluctant to suggest to the other parent that they try mediation because they:

- are convinced the other parent will refuse, or
- fear they will appear weak to the other parent.

In fact, however, once you (or a mediator) explain mediation to the other parent, that parent is likely to see its obvious advantages over litigation and is likely to go along with it. And once mediation is underway, any suspicions of weakness in the position of the parent who initiated the mediation are usually rapidly dispelled.

Mediation can be suggested in several ways: by one parent, by a counselor, by a lawyer or by the mediator. Following are sample conversations that illustrate how each person's proposal for mediation might sound:

ONE PARENT PROPOSES MEDIATION:

I have heard about a process called mediation that might help us get these things resolved. From what I understand, the mediator would help us to talk about our parenting situation—without fighting—so that we could see whether we can make the decisions on our own. We wouldn't have to spend any more time than we need to cover the issues and reach agreements. We could choose whether or not to involve attorneys, we might be able to avoid a court hearing, and we wouldn't have to drag ourselves or the children through any more bitterness than is absolutely necessary. The mediator wouldn't tell us what to do, and each of us could decide for ourselves whether any particular agreement was fair before we agreed to, or signed, anything. If the mediation doesn't work, we can still try to negotiate

things on our own or we can go to court—but at least we will have tried one more way to make our own decisions about how our children will be raised.

A COUNSELOR OR ATTORNEY PROPOSES MEDIATION:

At this point, I'd like to suggest that you consider a process called mediation. Mediation can be very effective for starting the dialogue on some of these difficult issues, and may allow both of you to find things that you can agree on. The mediator cannot impose a settlement on you—you and the other parent will be the ones to make all of the decisions. What the mediator can do is to help you discuss your children's needs and how you plan to meet those needs— without allowing the discussion to deteriorate into an argument. When it works, and it works in the majority of cases, parents are in a better position to communicate and work together in the future. [Attorneys only:] After you reach an agreement, you can bring it back to me and I can review it. If mediation doesn't produce a full agreement, then you can go forward with negotiations on your own or through me, or you can take the matter to court.

THE PROSPECTIVE MEDIATOR PROPOSES MEDIATION:

_____ (name of parent, counselor or attorney) has asked me to contact you to discuss how mediation might help you and the other parent resolve custody and visitation decisions on behalf of your children. The focus of mediation is on your children, and making decisions in their best interests. If possible, we will work toward creating a comprehensive plan which describes all of the key elements of your parenting relationship. As a mediator, I am a neutral third party, meaning that I have no previous relationship with either of you, and that I have no preconceived ideas about what decisions you should make. Although I will be happy to offer general information about the legal process and child development, I will not be making any recommendations about which options you should choose, and I will not provide legal advice of any kind. I will help the discussion to remain civil, even when you or the other parent are describing difficult or angry feelings.

As you begin to develop your parenting plan, I will help you make sure that it is clear, detailed and easy to understand and live with. Because mediation is confidential you can be candid and don't need to worry that what you say will be repeated in court. Because an agreement results only when both parents say it is acceptable, mediated agreements generally last longer, and result in fewer arguments or court battles later, than nonmediated agreements.

D. Understanding Basic Mediation Techniques

One of the best ways to understand why mediation works is to look at a sample mediation session.

FAMILY PROFILE
Matthew and Brenda are parents who live in neighboring communities and want to renegotiate their parenting plan which has been in place for three years. Their children, Jason and Amy, are ages 9 and 7 respectively.

1. The Mediator's Introduction

In addition to introducing themselves, mediators help parents articulate their own needs, interests and concerns, and focus their attention on how to best meet their children's needs, interests and concerns. This is also the time when the mediator sets the ground rules for discussion, and answers any questions which the parents might have.

> MEDIATOR: *Now, I will ask each of you to describe your children, their needs, the current arrangements, any concerns which you have and your proposal for how you will share and divide your parenting responsibilities. As each of you speaks, I will ask that there be no interruptions, and that neither parent will make derogatory remarks about the other. Once we have done that, we will take each issue in turn, and discuss how it might be resolved so that you are meeting your children's needs. As you start discussing and evaluating your various options, I will be happy to offer information about some of the choices that other parents have considered, and will help you to generate ideas about solving difficult problems whenever it seems necessary. If either of you, or I, feel that discussion might be more productive if we meet separately, then I might take time to meet with each of you in private. Should either of you feel that you need advice from your attorney, just let me know and we will take a break.*

2. Parents' Opening Statements

The parents' opening statements offer an ideal opportunity for each parent to hear how the other views the issues, and what they propose as a solution to meet their children's needs. Mediators use this time to learn about a particular family and to get an idea of what an agreement will have to achieve in order to be acceptable to both parents. By using techniques such as "reflective listening" (verifying that the

listener has an accurate understanding of the speaker's meaning), mediators can be sure that they are developing a complete list of all the issues to be resolved.

> BRENDA: *Right now, the children live with me during the week and they see their father on alternating weekends. We split all of the big holidays, like Christmas and Easter breaks, and alternate who gets the shorter holidays such as Thanksgiving, President's Weekend and Memorial Day. I think that everything is working just fine. So do the kids. Matthew is the one who wants to change this.*

> MEDIATOR: *Can you tell me something about the children's activities, how they are doing in school and the things that you do together?*

> BRENDA: *Both children are doing fairly well in school, they are involved in after school sports, they do homework most days, and they have soccer games on the weekends. I try to carpool with some of the other parents to get them to practices and games. I help them with their homework each evening.*

> MEDIATOR: *Do both you and Matthew live in the same school district?*

> BRENDA: *No—and I don't particularly like the schools in Matthew's district.*

MEDIATOR: *Thank you Brenda. From what I understand, you and the children have developed some routines that accommodate their school work and sporting activities, and that you are basically happy with the overall arrangements. Additionally, you don't see any advantages in considering a change in schools. Is this correct?*

BRENDA: *Yes.*

MEDIATOR: *Do you have anything that you'd like to add at this point?*

BRENDA: *No.*

MEDIATOR: *Now, Matthew, can you give me the same kind of information from your point of view?*

MATTHEW: *I feel like I'm losing touch with the kids. I want more time with them and Brenda refuses. I am a good parent, but I gave in last time and let the kids live with her. Now it's my turn. I want them to live with me and they can see Brenda on alternating weekends. Jason says he wants to live with me, and Amy says that she doesn't care who she lives with, but I think that the kids should stay together.*

MEDIATOR: *Thank you Matthew. As I see it, you feel that you would like to play a greater role in both children's lives, and that Jason, at least, has expressed a preference for living with you. You also feel that it would be best if the children stayed together—regardless of the actual living arrangements. What do you know about the children's activities and school performance?*

MATTHEW: *Not enough. I often don't hear about their soccer games if it's not my weekend, and I almost never hear about their school activities or performance—except for getting a copy of their report cards. I'd like to know more about both things. Although our school district may not offer all of the same programs as the one the children are in now, it is still a good school. Jason will be transferring into the middle school in two years and the middle school in our area is just as good, if not better, than the one he would go to in his current district.*

MEDIATOR: *Clearly you would like to have more time to spend with Jason and Amy. Have you discussed this with them?*

MATTHEW: *Yes I have. Jason, especially, would like me to come to his games and practices. Amy has said that she'd like the same thing. If I at least knew something about the practice and game schedule, I could play a much bigger role in their lives—at least as far as sports goes. On the week-*

ends, they never bring home any school work, so I have very little information about how there're doing. I didn't want to sit in the same room as Brenda to have our parent/teacher conferences, so I missed out on that this year.

MEDIATOR: *Have you asked the children whether they want to change schools?*

MATTHEW: *Yes, and they're not happy about it, but they would do it as long as it happened over the summer.*

MEDIATOR: *O.K. Are their any other issues that you'd like to bring up at this time?*

MATTHEW: *No.*

3.   Negotiating the Agreement

Once a mediator has an idea of the issues each parent wants to address, he or she works with the parents to discuss each one to see whether it might be possible to find areas of agreement. From the conversation above, a list of issues might include:

- improving Matthew's access to information regarding school and sporting events
- increasing Matthew's time with the children
- evaluating how and when decisions should be made regarding which school the children will attend, and
- evaluating which should be the children's primary home during the week.

MEDIATOR: *Turning to one of the issues raised during your opening remarks, I am curious about what each of you thinks about finding ways that Matthew might increase the amount of time he spends with the children?*

BRENDA: *If Matthew wants to take over my turn in the carpool, he could get to know more of the children's friends and could attend some of the practices or games. In fact, I could give him a copy of the game schedule, and he could attend any of the games, whether I am there or not.*

MATTHEW: *I'd like to do that. What about school though? I should get a copy of their school calendar too, and maybe they should be bringing some of their work to me when they come to visit on the weekends.*

MEDIATOR: *Brenda, would you be willing to get this information to Matthew?*

BRENDA: *Sure.*

MEDIATOR: *Now how about parent/teacher conferences? How do each of you suggest that these be handled?*

BRENDA: *I think that Matthew should take the time to set up his own conferences. I don't want to have to have them together. All he has to do is to call the school and arrange to meet with each teacher.*

MEDIATOR: *Matthew, is this something that you'd be willing to do?*

MATTHEW: *Yes.*

4. Turning Negative Feelings Into Positive Actions

Mediators recognize that it is hard to express negative feelings positively, and so a big part of their job is looking for ways to take anger, fears or problems and transforming them into potential solutions. If mediators have a strong suit, it is turning "fighting words" into productive conversation.

> **EXAMPLE:** *A parent says something like: "He/She is such a flake that you can't expect him/her to follow through with any agreement." The mediator might help a parent to rephrase the objections as follows: "Do you mean that you don't trust him/her to follow through with agreements based on his/her past behavior? Can you describe the behavior that bothered you? What could he/she do to demonstrate trustworthiness in the future?"*

5. Joint Versus Separate Meetings

Usually, the parents and mediator are in the same room. This approach is favored by most mediators because it helps the parents communicate with each other about their children—a skill they will need to work together in the future. If, however, the mediator feels that holding separate sessions may lead to an agreement, the mediator places the parents in separate rooms and shuttles back and forth.

Many mediations consist of a blend of same-room and separate-room sessions, depending on how high tension is, and whether the mediator perceives that a parent might be more forthcoming about an issue if the other parent isn't present. If there's a history of violence between the parents, the mediation may consist entirely of separate meetings between the mediator and each parent. This can help prevent intimidation of one parent by the other.

6. Overcoming Impasse

Impasse, or seemingly unresolvable differences of opinion, need not bring mediation to a halt. Mediators have many

"tricks of the trade" that they can and do use to help parents over the rough spots. Many of the strategies that were described in Chapter 4 have their parallel in mediation. Additional strategies are outlined below.

a. Reframing Statements

When one parent makes a statement that seems to beg the other parent to respond aggressively, mediators can diffuse the tension by turning to the other parent and reframing the statement.

> **PARENT SAYS:** *If that is the way you are going to treat me, then you can just forget seeing the kids for half of the summer—we can just stick to the alternating weekend schedule all year long!*
>
> **MEDIATOR RESPONDS:** *It seems that _____ (parent's name) has a difficult time feeling cooperative about finding ways to expand the amount of time that you and the children spend together when you make statements such as _____. Are there any other ways you could get that point across without it leading to conflict?*

b. Focusing the Discussion on the Children

When the level of tension rises, mediators can try to diffuse it by asking the parents to focus less on themselves and more their children's best interests.

> **EXAMPLE:** *Matthew and Brenda are arguing heatedly over which home the children will live in during the school year. The mediator asks each parent to describe the school-aged child's interests, attachment to friends, activities and special needs. The mediator then suggests that the parents analyze the relative advantages of each school and choose a residence that provides access to the school which best meets the children's needs.*

c. Insisting on Clarity

If a parent makes blanket statements about the other (such as "He/she can't be trusted!"), the mediator can insist that this parent describe the events which led to a lack of trust, and ask what that parent could do to demonstrate trustworthiness in the future.

d. Balancing the Power

Sometimes impasse is the result of the power imbalance between the parents. The power imbalance may be for any number of reasons, but is often evident when one parent:

- is more articulate than the other
- has traditionally dominated the other in making decisions, or
- has more experience in caring for the children.

A mediator confronted with a power imbalance will try to "level the playing field" by:

- moderating one parent's dominating style and boosting the other parent's self-confidence
- allowing both parents equal time to speak, and
- insisting that parents take the time to be specific about their concerns and their proposals for the future.

Sometimes, the best way to balance power is to get outside help. A parent feeling at a disadvantage might turn to a counselor to improve self-esteem, consult a lawyer to understand his or her rights, speak with a child development specialist to understand the children's best interests or consult someone trained in domestic violence or child abuse to understand the impact of these events on all parties.

7. Recording the Agreement

When the parents reach agreement on a particular issue, the mediator takes careful notes. At the end of the sessions, the mediator will typically provide the parents with a summary of their entire agreement. It is each parent's responsibility to review that draft (with or without the help of an attorney) to make sure that it is accurate and complete.

E. Why Mediation Works in Very Difficult Cases

You still may be convinced that your conflicts with the other parent are unresolvable and that mediation will never work because:

- the conflicts are too intense
- each of you is entrenched in your positions, or
- the conflicts involve domestic violence, child abuse or substance abuse.

First, understand that all family law mediators assume there is substantial conflict between you and the other parent, and are prepared to use their facilitation skills to diffuse the tension and to refocus you on determining and protecting your children's best interests. Be encouraged by the fact that disputing parents reach agreement in approximately 70% of all cases that go to mediation. To understand

how serious conflict might be handled in mediation, consider a mediation between two divorcing parents, Joseph and Elizabeth.

FAMILY PROFILE

Joseph and Elizabeth are confronting the serious conflict, domestic violence, child abuse and substance abuse which were a part of their marriage and separation.

MEDIATOR: *Now that we have agreed that there will be no interruptions while one parent is speaking, and that each of you will focus on the issues rather than on making derogatory remarks about the other, I'd like each of you to help me understand the situation from each of your points of view. First, I will need you to describe your children and then I would like to hear how you propose to structure your parenting relationship to best meet your children's needs. Who would like to start?*

JOSEPH: *I'll start. Our kids have been through a lot. Joey and Mary are basically happy children, but this whole thing has been hard on them. Elizabeth's lifestyle has been so unstable. Her drinking problem ruined everything. First, she started hanging out at the bars, and had a few boyfriends. Then, she was upset at every little thing, and a few times she really took out after the kids. Once, the kids ran away to a neighbor's house because they were afraid that she was really going to hurt them. I think that the kids should live with me and see their mother one afternoon a week until she can prove that she can take care of them.*

ELIZABETH: *My drinking! Big Joe has been an alcoholic ever since I've known him! When I wanted to separate, he beat me in front of the kids. That's when I knew for sure that I couldn't live with him any more. Now, I have my own life, and no one to beat me, and I want them to live with me. I may have had my problems in the past, but that's all over now. I'm going back to school to get myself to a point where I can earn a good living and support myself and my kids. Pretty soon, I'll be able to afford my own place. He can be the one to see the kids one afternoon a week. The kids have told me that they want to live with me, and I said they could.*

MEDIATOR: *O.K. It sounds as though both you and your children have been through some tough times and have been dealing with some difficult issues. What do each of you think would be important for your children as you make plans for the future?*

JOSEPH: *For the future? Well, I suppose that the most important thing is to make sure that the children aren't around Elizabeth or her friends when they are drinking and partying. They do miss her, I know that, but I just don't know how I can trust her to take care of them given the way she is behaving.*

ELIZABETH: *I agree that they shouldn't be around in the wrong situations, especially the violence. I'd like to find some way that we could be sure that they'd be safe and cared for in both homes.*

As this mediation progressed, the mediator helped the parents explore the issues that they had raised, and began looking for available resolution options. After some discussion, Joseph and Elizabeth disclosed that they had never tried to get help with substance abuse, domestic violence or parenting skills, but that each was willing to try if the other agreed to do the same.

Elizabeth conceded that while Joseph might benefit by learning new parenting techniques for disciplining the children, he had never beaten or abused them in any way. Both Joseph and Elizabeth agreed that her few episodes of "taking it out on the children" happened after Joseph had beaten her during the separation and were not part of her normal parenting style. Neither parent feared for the children's safety while they were in either parent's care, but Joseph felt strongly that Elizabeth's new friends and frequent partying created an unhealthy environment for the children.

Joseph and Elizabeth acknowledged that they did not want their children exposed to the violence, alcohol, partying or anger that they had experienced in the past. Elizabeth acknowledged that although she had come a long way in establishing a new life for herself, she still had some work to do before she would feel confident about caring for the children for more than short periods of time. Joseph agreed that he needed to get help in learning how to control his anger, but both agreed that for the moment at least, he was probably better able to care for the children for longer periods of time. Both parents planned to remain in the same community.

MEDIATOR: *To re-cap what you have decided so far, you would like to make a temporary agreement that will carry you through the balance of the school year. Each of you agrees to meet together again at the start of the summer vacation to review this agreement and to negotiate any nec-essary changes. Either of you may request mediation for your next meeting, but it is not required.*

Here is the agreement as I understand it: Elizabeth and Joseph agree to seek independent counseling or other support to deal with alcohol abuse. Each of you will continue with this counseling or support until such time as both you and your counselors agree that you can handle these issues on your own. Joseph agrees to seek counseling and support for dealing with anger. He will continue with this counseling until he and the counselor agree that he no longer needs this assistance. When his counseling has concluded, his counselor will write a letter to Elizabeth explaining the general issues covered in the counseling and that those issues have been dealt with or resolved. The children will be offered a chance to talk to a counselor, and may choose to continue counseling if they so desire. Both parents agree to identify at least one adult that the children can contact if they ever fear for their safety, or are concerned that their parent is too inebriated to provide adequate care. Neither child will be punished for contacting this "safe" adult— even if they misjudge the situation.

The children will live with Joseph during the week, and with Elizabeth two weekends out of the month. Elizabeth will arrange to take the children after school at least one afternoon a week, and will return them to Joseph's home by 7:00 p.m. Joseph will call Elizabeth each Monday evening between 4 and 6 p.m. to arrange for her midweek time with the children, a weekend visit, if appropriate, and to discuss the children's activities so that she can decide whether she will attend or otherwise participate. Each parent will be responsible to handle day-to-day decisions for the children when they are the primary caretakers, and each agrees to consult the other if important decisions are needed, and there is some lead time before the decision must be made. In the event of an emergency, either parent may seek whatever emergency attention is required, and will inform the other parent of the steps taken at the earliest practical time thereafter.

F.   What Mediators Don't Do

There are some things mediators won't do. First and foremost, mediators won't make decisions for you. A mediator's sole mission is to help you and the other parent build your own agreement about how you will meet your children's needs. Sometimes, you may want to give in and have someone else decide an issue for you. To get an outsider to make these decisions, however, you must choose a forum other than mediation. This usually means an expensive and divisive court hearing.

Mediators can offer general information, but they don't provide legal advice or counseling—even when they are also attorneys or mental health professionals. Legal advice can be offered by an attorney to only one parent, so each parent needs his or her own attorney. This is because each parent has his or her own separate legal interests, and one attorney cannot counsel a separating or divorcing couple on what is legally best for each of them.

If parents want to know what their legal rights are, they will have to consult with a good self-help law reference, do some legal research in a law library or pay for a consultation with an attorney.

⚠ BE CAREFUL ABOUT TURNING YOUR CASE OVER TO A LAWYER

While each spouse can often benefit from talking to an attorney for an hour or two to get some advice and information, once one spouse is represented, the other spouse usually finds it necessary to also obtain representation. Once two attorneys are involved in the case, you run a high risk of a costly and adversarial process.

G. Choosing Between Court-Ordered and Private Mediation

Increasingly, parents cannot simply ask the court to resolve their custody or visitation dispute. Instead, a court orders a custody or visitation dispute to be mediated. Most states authorize, but don't require, their courts to order mediation. But a few states, including California, require it.

STATES IN WHICH A COURT MAY ORDER MEDIATION IN A CUSTODY OR VISITATION DISPUTE

Alabama	Kentucky	North Dakota
Alaska	Louisiana	Ohio
Arizona	Maine	Oregon
California	Maryland	Pennsylvania
Colorado	Michigan	Rhode Island
Connecticut	Minnesota	South Carolina
Delaware	Mississippi	South Dakota
Florida	Missouri	Texas
Idaho	Montana	Utah
Illinois	Nevada	Virginia
Indiana	New Jersey	Washington
Iowa	New Mexico	West Virginia
Kansas	North Carolina	Wisconsin

If you live in a state that authorizes or requires mediation, you have a choice. You can present the dispute to the court and accept what mediation the court orders, or hire a private mediator to help you reach agreement, thereby avoiding going to court in the first place.

The advantage to court-ordered mediation is that it is likely to be free or nominally priced. Private mediators, on the other hand, must earn a living and will probably charge a significantly higher fee. The advantages to using a private mediator, however, are many:

- You can shop for a mediator who suits both parents.
- You will have greater flexibility in scheduling.
- You can take as much time as you can afford.
- You can focus your full attention on the mediation without worrying about what the mediator will recommend to the court (see Section H below).

As a general rule, if you are using mediation as a backup to negotiating your own parenting plan in Chapter 5, you will most likely want to use a private mediator. This is because most court mediation services are designed to settle only the basic custody and visitation questions that arise during a divorce or modification request, rather than help parents draft a detailed parenting agreement.

If you want to first try court-ordered mediation and you live in a state where it is available, you must first file the appropriate legal papers setting out your dispute and asking that it be resolved by the court. (See Chapter 11 for how to find an attorney or paralegal to help you do this.) You will then be informed of your requirement to participate in mediation, and may even be given a person to contact, or a date and time for your mediation hearing.

Mediators in court-based programs generally have a mental health, social service or probation department background. They are usually trained in the art and science of facilitating negotiations, and have general knowledge of family law and the principles of child development.

Court appointed mediators are often limited to spending from one to six hours on any one case, depending on their caseload. Whenever possible, court-appointed mediators try to help parents find areas of agreement, and report that agreement to the court. If the parents are unable to reach an agreement through mediation, however, the court may ask the mediator, or a separate custody evaluator (see Section I, below), to assess the family's situation and make a recommendation about how the custody and visitation issues should be decided. When this happens, the mediator or evaluator's recommendations are often the most important factor influencing the court's decision.

➡️ For more information about court-ordered mediation and evaluation, read Sections H and I. If you want more information about private mediation, skip ahead to Section J.

H. When the Mediator Makes a Recommendation to the Court

Most states that authorize court-ordered mediation do not ask the mediator to file a recommendation regarding custody or visitation with the court in the event the parents can't reach agreement. Instead, the court will make its own decision, perhaps based on an independent evaluation that the court orders to be conducted.

Alaska, California and Delaware are exceptions to this rule. In these states, judges may ask their court-appointed mediators to make a recommendation in the absence of an agreement between the parents. Regardless of your state, if you use court-ordered mediation, ask the mediator whether he or she will make a recommendation to the court if you and the other parent fail to reach agreement.

If your mediator will make a recommendation to the court, your strategy and focus during mediation will change. In this setting, you have two audiences—the other parent and the mediator who can influence a later court proceeding. Not only must you try to reach an agreement

with the other parent, but also you must try to make a favorable impression on the mediator. Many mediators are impressed by parents who demonstrate the following qualities:

- a primary concern for understanding and protecting their children's best interests
- a willingness to consider a variety of settlement options, and
- a desire to facilitate contact between the children and their other parent.

To prepare for mediation that involves the possibility of a recommendation to the court by the mediator, you will want to research the factors your mediator will use in reaching a decision about what to recommend to the court and how the mediator's report will be treated by the court. You can get this information by talking to a person in the mediation program or by asking a knowledgeable attorney. (See Chapter 11.)

I. Custody Evaluations

Many states allow judges to appoint a custody evaluator if the parents cannot reach an agreement on their own or through mediation. You may or may not be charged for this service. The evaluator, generally a mental health professional, spends time with the children and the parents to understand how the family currently functions, and to gain insights about what future arrangements might be in the children's best interests. Custody evaluations are often ordered when the parents disagree about custody and visitation, and:

- there is a history of domestic violence
- there is a history of child abuse or neglect
- there are allegations of substance abuse, or
- someone other than the biological or adoptive parents perhaps should be granted custody or visitation.

If an evaluation is conducted in your case, you will want to convince the evaluator that you have:

- a primary concern for understanding and protecting your children's best interests
- a willingness to consider a variety of settlement options, and
- a desire to facilitate contact between the children and their other parent.

As a general rule, a judge who orders an evaluation is very likely to adopt the evaluator's recommendation.

J. Selecting a Mediator

As mentioned, mediators generally fall into two groups: court-connected and private practice.

1. Court-Connected Mediators

If your state requires mediation whenever parents dispute custody and visitation issues, then the court will have a list of mediators or an in-house mediation program. You will have little, if any, choice over who actually conducts your mediation. If you need help in finding your local family conciliation or mediation court service, you can contact the court, ask an attorney or paralegal, or contact one of the organizations listed in Chapter 11.

2. Private Mediators

If you have a choice of mediators, because either the court gives you a choice or you are seeking private mediation, narrow your list of potential mediators to two or three candidates, and have each parent interview them. Ideally, the person you should choose is the one you agree is most likely to:

- be neutral—he or she has no preconceived ideas about how you should decide custody and visitation issues
- have expertise—he or she has had training and experience in dealing with custody and visitation issues

- focus on children—he or she understands general child development principles and knows how to identify children's interests, and
- have facilitation skills—he or she knows how to structure a mediation session so that each parent is heard and conflict is addressed and diffused, and he or she can assist you in overcoming impasse and planning for the long term.

When interviewing a mediator, you might ask questions such as:

- *What kind of training have you had?*
- *What subjects or skills did your training emphasize?*
- *How much experience have you had in working with individuals or families going through divorce or separation?*
- *How much do you know about childhood development?*
- *How well versed are you in the effects of divorce and separation on children?*
- *Do you have any biases about how parenting issues should be settled, such as favoring custody with the mother or joint custody?*
- *What is your fee?*
- *How long do you think our mediation will take?*
- *What can I do to make mediation more productive?*

Although you may feel awkward in asking these questions, you should be able to get a good sense of whether you can trust the mediator simply by monitoring your reaction to the answers the mediator provides. That is, the answers themselves are not as important as how you feel about the mediators.

3. Finding a Private Mediator

If you need help in finding your local family conciliation or mediation court service, you can contact the court, ask an attorney or paralegal, or contact the Association of Family and Conciliation Courts. The AFCC can be reached as follows:

Association of Family and Conciliation Courts
329 West Wilson
Madison WI 53703-3612
Voice: (608) 251-0604
FAX: (608) 251-2231

If you want to find a mediator in private practice, you can check your telephone directory under "Mediation" or "Divorce Assistance," or you can contact:

- a community meditation program
- the court

- a paralegal
- a legal forms preparation service
- a public mental health agency, or
- the local Bar Association.

If none of these efforts generate a sufficient list of mediators, you can contact one of the following national organizations for a referral in your area:

- Conflict Resolution Center, Inc. publishes a directory of all kinds of ADR (Alternative or Appropriate Dispute Resolution) service providers. They can provide a list of mediators in your area and are available as follows:

  Conflict Resolution Center, Inc.
  2205 E. Carson Street
  Pittsburgh, PA 15203-2107
  Voice: (412) 481-5559
  FAX: (412) 481-5601
  e-mail: crcii@igc.apc.org

- The Academy of Family Mediators has approximately 2,000 members, requires that members meet certain basic training standards and complete a certain amount of continuing education each year. The Academy will give you a list of their members in your area and can be contacted as follows:

  Academy of Family Mediators
  4 Militia Drive
  Lexington, MA 02173
  Voice: (617) 674-2663
  Fax: (617) 674-2690
  email: afmoffice@igc.apc.org

- The Society of Professionals In Dispute Resolution (SPIDR) is an association of all kinds of ADR service providers, including family and custody mediators throughout the country. They have chapters in each state and can give you a list of providers in your area. You can reach SPIDR through your state's local chapter (consult a telephone directory) or by contacting the national headquarters at:

  Society of Professionals In Dispute Resolution
  815 15th Street NW, Suite 530
  Washington DC 20005
  Voice: (202) 783-7277
  FAX: (202) 783-7281

- The American Arbitration Association has begun developing its own panels of mediators. They have local area offices in most states (consult your telephone directory) and will give you local area information

about their mediation services, or you can reach the national headquarters as follows:

  American Arbitration Association
  140 West 51st Street
  New York, NY 10020-1203
  Voice: (212) 484-4100
  FAX: (212) 307-4387

K. Preparing for Mediation

To prepare for mediation, complete the worksheets in Chapter 3. By doing so, you and the other parent will have written down your individual views on your children and separate parenting, and will have some idea of the issues to be addressed during mediation. These worksheets can provide your mediator with a wealth of information.

Prior to your first mediation session, you should ask your court-appointed or private mediator about the availability of:

- informational brochures explaining the mediation process
- informational classes or video tapes on mediation or custody disputes, or
- materials that might be available in your public library to help you prepare for mediation. (Chapter 11 has titles of books or articles that might be helpful.)

As you prepare for mediation, keep in mind the following five points:

1. **Focus on your children.** The best preparation for mediation is to think about how you can meet your children's needs for high quality care and meaningful ongoing relationships with both parents. This step is especially important if your mediation is with a court-appointed mediator who will make a recommendation to the court if you and the other parent can't agree. (See Section H, above.) You will want the mediator to know that your positions reflect your children's—not your—needs and interests.

2. **Minimize conflict.** Your ability to work with the other parent with a minimum of conflict is crucial to a successful separate parenting relationship. Ongoing conflict between parents can be one of the most destructive forces in a child's life. In particular, explore ways to minimize the conflict by minimizing the contact you have, while maintaining the best possible relationship with your children. Issues to focus on in Chapter 5 are:

- 11, Making Decisions
- 13, Exchanging Information
- 14, Where Our Children Will Live
- 17, Maintaining Contact When the Children Are With the Other Parent
- 24, Special Occasions and Family Events, and
- 27, Improving Transition Times.

3. **Handle your anger**. Angry feelings and poor communication are common when parents separate or divorce. For some parents, the anger is so intense that they will go to great lengths to avoid reaching any agreement. Others will take great pains to make sure that their agreement inflicts humiliation, loss or significant inconvenience on the other parent. If this situation continues over time, you may need professional help to put your feelings into perspective so that you can focus on making decisions for your children.

   If you and the other parent cannot make these decisions on your own, through mediation or with the help of a counselor or attorneys, resolution will probably come via a court order. This is likely to cost a considerable amount of time, money and grief for everyone involved.

4. **Be positive**. Positive thinking reflects confidence in yourself, both in what you want to achieve and in your determination to find an acceptable solution. For some, this attitude comes naturally. For others—it requires a commitment to sort out their own thoughts and feelings so that they are certain of what they want. In either case, take a deep breath, put your "best foot forward" and see what happens!

5. **Be informed**. If you want to know your legal rights and obligations in a separation or divorce, you can consult with an attorney or hire one to represent you. Various attorney-client relationships are described in Section M.2, below.

L. If You Can't Reach an Agreement

If you cannot reach an agreement resolving all parenting issues, you can:

- continue discussions on your own
- schedule further mediation sessions
- seek an independent evaluation and recommendation
- submit the matter to arbitration, or
- litigate the issues in court.

M. Alternatives to Mediation

Many parents, attorneys and courts are confused about how mediation differs from counseling, attorney advocacy or arbitration. Following are some of the characteristics of each process. As you will see, counseling, legal advocacy and arbitration can be complementary to, but are fundamentally different from mediation.

1. Counseling

The focus in counseling or other forms of therapy is on helping one or both parents explore, understand and resolve the personal and emotional aspects of a situation. Many parents use counseling to reduce or remove the anger, jealousy, bitterness and other feelings they have about the separation or divorce. This can help improve the working relationship with the other parent. In short, counseling explores "inner" space while mediation helps parents develop detailed plans for how they will parent separately.

Occasionally, a counselor who has worked with one or both parents may then attempt to mediate the parenting disputes. This practice is problematic. During therapy, patients disclose their thoughts, feelings and motivations to the therapist. Having this information makes it difficult, if not impossible, for the counselor to be a truly neutral facilitator.

2. Attorney Representation

Although many parents consider that divorce and attorneys go hand in hand, recent studies show that in nearly one-half of all divorces, at least one party is proceeding without a lawyer. Some go it alone because of the high cost of legal representation. Others choose to represent themselves to retain full control over their case. When parents complain about involving attorneys, it is usually because they feel that they have lost too much control over their cases, the decisions and the costs of finding a resolution.

You can use an attorney in one of two ways. First, an attorney can be a resource for legal information and ideas about how the law might affect your decisions. Attorneys can also negotiate on your behalf, examine your rights, represent your interests or advocate your position in court or during arbitration. (Arbitration is covered in Section 3, below.)

Lawyers, without representing either party, can serve as mediators. If a lawyer represents either parent, however, the lawyer must advocate for that parent. The lawyer can work to facilitate negotiations between the parents, but the lawyer cannot serve as a neutral mediator.

3.   Arbitration

The process and results of arbitration are very similar to a court case, but less formal. You and the other parent (or, more likely, your attorneys) present your positions and requests for particular decisions to the arbitrator, who decides the dispute. Most parents choose to be represented by an attorney during arbitration.

There are two types of arbitration:

• **Binding arbitration** means you cannot appeal the arbitrator's decision to a court, unless you prove that the arbitrator abused the process.

• **Nonbinding arbitration** means that you can appeal the arbitrator's decision to a court, but may have to pay the other parent's court costs if you do not get a better result in court than you did in arbitration.

Only a few states specifically offer arbitration as an acceptable dispute resolution method in custody and visitation cases. Chapter 10, Section C, contains a list of states that permit, prohibit or are silent on the subject of arbitrating custody and visitation disputes.

a.   Choosing an Arbitrator

In almost all cases, parents use a single arbitrator to settle their differences, and the arbitrator is generally an attorney. Occasionally, the arbitrator will be a mental health professional, but generally this happens only when the issues in dispute involve an assessment of the children's mental health. More information about arbitrators is in Chapter 11.

b.   Arbitration Shouldn't Rise to a Court Trial

One of the dangers of arbitration is that it can turn into a miniature court trial. When this happens, arbitration becomes just as time consuming and costly as a court trial, and the proceedings become just as adversarial. Discovery, the process by which each side finds out the other's evidence, can be just as extensive for arbitration as for a court trial.

Once way to keep arbitration from turning into a court trial is to set limits in advance. For example, the parents can agree to share information rather than conduct extensive discovery. ■

Understanding Your Children's Needs

Understanding and meeting your children's needs following a separation or divorce can be challenging, but it is certainly not impossible. To help you meet the challenge, this chapter includes the following:

- strategies for dealing with children of all ages and both sexes
- strategies for dealing with children at different ages and developmental stages (although your children may react differently at the ages and developmental stages described, the information may still help you to understand your children as time goes along), and
- strategies for dealing with children who have special needs.

The suggestions in this chapter refer to specific issue/option sets from Chapter 5 without duplicating the information contained in other parts of the book. Use the references to help you focus on your children.

A. Strategies for Your Children at Any Age

Children of all ages and both sexes usually share these three reactions to their parents' separation or divorce:

- they maintain a passionate desire to see their parents reunited
- they feel sad and angry, and
- they want their parents to stop fighting.

Therapist-researcher, Linda Bird Francke, author of *Growing Up Divorced* (Linden Press/Simon & Schuster, 1983) estimates that children need three years to get used to their parents' separation or divorce, and that the first year is the most difficult for them. During that time, children almost universally experience shock, depression, denial, anger, low self esteem, shame, and (especially among younger children) guilt—they think that they caused the divorce.

First and foremost, children need to know that their basic physical needs will be met. Despite the fact that in many households one parent provides considerably more child care than the other, most children feel cared for by both. A separation or divorce brings on feelings of loss, knowing that they will be cared for by only one parent at a time, and fear that their needs won't be met.

Second, children want the conflict between their parents to lessen, if not end altogether. However difficult it may seem now, you and the other parent must find ways to work together without having your discussions deteriorate into arguments.

The seven strategies in this section suggest ways to reassure your children that they will continue to be loved and cared for. Each strategy identifies specific issue/option sets which apply in Chapter 5.

1. Reduce Conflict Between Parents

Ongoing conflict can be devastating for children of any age. Children burdened by ongoing conflict often have problems performing in school and relating to their friends, parents and other relatives. You will take an enormous amount of pressure off of your children if you can work with the other parent without arguing regularly.

Managing conflict is difficult, but can be done. Chapter 4 suggests ways to manage conflict during your negotiations with the other parent. Chapter 11 has information on resources beyond the book which can help you understand, manage and resolve conflict.

RELEVANT ISSUES IN CHAPTER 5

Making Decisions	11
Resolving Disputes When Making Decisions Together	12
Exchanging Information	13
Improving Transition Times	27
When Parenting Styles and Values Are Very Different	29
Disparaging Remarks	31
Undermining the Parent/Child Relationship	32
Denying Access to the Children	33

2. Help Children Maintain Good Relationships With Both Parents

Almost all children whose parents separate or divorce struggle at one time or another with how to be loyal to both parents. Some children have trouble showing that they love each parent equally. Others are pressured by one parent (directly or subtly) to love that parent more than the other. Parents who demand this of their children are putting them in an almost impossible situation. Dr. Isolina Ricci (*Mom's House, Dad's House*, Macmillan Publishing, 1980) offers an important insight into the tension that these feelings produce:

If we think of ourselves as part our mother and part our father, it may be easier to see how conflicting and frighten-

ing it can be to have one part inside of us hate the other part that is also inside.

To minimize any "loyalty" issues for your children, try to:

- balance the time that your children spend in each home
- be aware of what your children's lives are like in each home
- strengthen your children's relationship with each parent, and
- reduce your children's exposure to the conflict between you and the other parent.

RELEVANT ISSUES IN CHAPTER 5

3.　Establish a Sense of Family With Each Parent

It is common for both adults and children to worry about how parents and children will get along after the adults separate or divorce. Whether the parents remain single or have new partners, each parent must develop new ways to establish a consistent family environment for the children. Here are some suggestions that might work for you:

- establish a "normal" schedule with regular routines and special traditions that your children can share
- do not raise false hopes of reconciliation
- find a secure spot for your children to leave their things, and
- explore your new neighborhood with your children, if you moved away from the family home.

RELEVANT ISSUES IN CHAPTER 5

4.　If a Parent Has a New Partner

Managing your life as a single parent will be quite challenging. It will be even more complex if you form a new relationship, especially when your children are living in your home.

Here are some ways to deal with a new partner:

Keep the relationship separate from your children until it becomes serious. Your children may develop a close attachment to your new partner and may have difficulty dealing with any break-up. One way to safeguard your children's feelings is to minimize contact between your new partner and your children. When your children and new partner do meet, keep it brief and casual until the relationship becomes serious. When your partner does stay over, be sure your children know there will be a guest at breakfast.

Be honest, but selective, in what you tell your children. Many parents are so pleased to have a new love interest that they are tempted to talk to their children as if they were adults. While your children may be flattered if you take them into your confidence, information about adult relationships can be overwhelming for children. For these reasons, openly acknowledge your new relationship and feelings when it becomes serious, but keep the details to yourself.

Decide what relationship your new partner will have with your children. If your relationship with a new partner becomes serious, you must consider what role your partner will have with your children. This subject will certainly be of interest to your children, and may cause some conflict between you and the other parent.

This decision may best be made after everyone involved is consulted. Among the questions you'll want to consider are your partner's role in:

- administering discipline
- providing child care
- sharing in household responsibilities

- participating in family events
- traveling on vacations, and
- making parenting decisions.

RELEVANT ISSUES IN CHAPTER 5

5. Keep Your Children From Growing Up Too Soon

Although everyone must assume new responsibilities after a separation or divorce, you must be careful not to overload your children. While most children are pleased to help when times get tough, some parents take this to an inappropriate extreme. For example, older children are sometimes asked to assume nearly all responsibilities for younger siblings, cooking and cleaning. Although you may not feel you have many options, your goal is to avoid turning your child into a full time housekeeper and baby-sitter.

In addition, many parents experience intense emotional pressures from the changes that come after separation or

divorce. The need to make more decisions, respond to your children's questions and support your children during their own adjustment period can leave you feeling overwhelmed. Although parents and children are natural sources of support for each other, parents should not rely heavily on their children for this support. Taking on the quasi-adult roles of confidante and comforter can cause serious psychological problems for your children later in life. Find another adult in which to confide and relieve your own stresses so you are ready and able to support your children.

You can address these concerns by including counseling or other emotional support in your parenting agreement, and by sharing more evenly the physical tasks of child rearing.

RELEVANT ISSUES IN CHAPTER 5

6. Help Children Who Are Having Difficulty Adjusting

Separation and divorce present difficulties for all children, but some have an unusually difficult time adjusting. Boys especially tend to become more aggressive, and girls often become depressed and withdrawn. No one expects children or parents to be happy with all aspects of a parenting arrangement; but children should be able to develop a generally positive attitude over time. If your children are having problems adjusting, you will need to intervene.

First, you need to know what's "normal" and what's not. Several resources can help you understand how children generally react to separation and divorce and how to recognize the symptoms of a truly troubled child.

Ask your librarian or public mental health department for a list of books, magazines and videos containing information on these issues. Three excellent books are:
- *Divorce and Your Child*, by Sonja Goldstein and Albert Solnit (Yale University Press, 1984)
- *How It Feels When Parents Divorce*, by Jill Krementz (Alfred A. Knopf, 1984), and
- *Mom's House, Dad's House*, by Isolina Ricci (Macmillan Publishing, 1980).

Chapter 11 and the bibliography include additional resources which might help you assess your children.

RELEVANT ISSUES IN CHAPTER 5

7. Be Ready for Change

Parents commonly forget that their children grow up, and perhaps will change dramatically over the years. When you negotiate your initial parenting agreement, you'll be tempted to assume that it will stand, unchanged, until your children reach adulthood. While it is possible that your first agreement will be your last, it's highly unlikely.

RELEVANT ISSUES IN CHAPTER 5

B. Strategies for Your Children at Different Ages and Developmental Stages

Children seldom fall exactly into the age categories that psychiatrists, psychologists and other counselors use to describe them. Nevertheless, these categories are very useful because they describe the sequence of developmental changes most children follow. Furthermore, boys and girls may grow and develop somewhat differently, and these gender-related characteristics are noted as well.

Judith Wallerstein and Joan Kelly were the first researchers to systematically evaluate and document children's responses to divorce by age. Linda Bird Francke reaffirmed this research during interviews with 100 children of varying ages. In *Growing Up Divorced* (Linden Press/ Simon & Schuster, 1983), she concluded that:

- initially, both boys and girls experience high levels of stress and depression after the actual separation or divorce, and boys typically have more long-term adjustment problems following the separation or divorce
- girls whose fathers leave when they are very young and remain relatively uninvolved with the family are more likely than their counterparts whose fathers remain home to become sexually precocious
- single mothers often have more difficult relationships with their sons than they do with their daughters, and
- children between the ages of 9 and 15 have more difficulty handling a parent's remarriage than do children who are either younger or older.

1. Children Under Age Two

Infants and children under the age of two must rely upon their parents and other care providers for almost all of their needs. Food, clothing, toilet training, entertainment, physical protection and emotional comfort are the most obvious.

In addition, children this age have fairly limited memory capabilities, and seldom understand that people and objects exist even though they cannot be seen and touched. Researchers know that children under two can form a number of relationships (or attachments) to their care providers, but suffer when there are too many differences in the way that care is provided and in the routines that are followed.

If your children are under two years old when you separate or divorce, consider the bird nesting option described in Issue 14, Where Our Children Will Live. If this isn't feasible, seriously consider designating one parent as the primary caretaker, while providing the other parent with frequent, if brief, visits.

If neither parent can provide the constant, demanding care required by very young children, you might turn to a relative or close friend to be your child's primary care taker.

Your children may feel somewhat insecure about what is happening, but it is preferable to your children receiving inconsistent care or being neglected.

2.   Children Ages Two to Six

Pre-schoolers can, and do, accomplish some tasks on their own, but still rely heavily on care providers for most of their necessities. Children this age understand that people continue to exist even when they are not physically present. Because most pre-schoolers are used to viewing their parents as a unified team, separation from one often introduces a fear that the child will lose the other parent as well. Children this age can easily persuade themselves that the separation or divorce would not have happened if they had only behaved better, so you will need to pay attention and reassure them that this is not true.

In general, boys of this age with one mother and one father tend to go through a period when they hate all women. Boys also tend to have more trouble than girls dealing with the realities of a separation or divorce after their parents have parted company. Some speculate that this is because many parents provide their sons with minimal physical and emotional comfort. Parents may also expect their sons to get over their anger or pain—or at least hide them. These responses to sons may help your child handle a situation like a "little man," but are likely to lead to an inability to face and resolve painful emotional issues.

Children often formulate their sexual identities and preferences during this age period. For this reason, finding ways in which parents or other adults of both sexes can have a significant and ongoing relationship to your children is especially important.

As you plan for your pre-schooler's living arrangements, keep in mind the following:

- overnight visits can be started or increased at these ages
- parents should expand communication and cooperation between the households
- children should be encouraged to keep pictures of both parents at both homes

- children should have frequent contact with both parents, and
- parents need to explain their parenting agreement in terms that the children can easily understand.

RELEVANT ISSUES IN CHAPTER 5

3.   Children Ages Six to 12

Grade schoolers are better able than younger children to deal with most parenting arrangements. They understand and can usually follow schedules in a parenting agreement, although transitions between homes can present a problem. In general, calm children tend to handle the transitions better than irritable children.

Children in these middle years are busy forming their own identities and value systems, and lean heavily on their parents for guidance. Children need active participation by both parents in their daily lives, school and outside activities.

These children are also especially sensitive to both parents' feelings, and would do almost anything to avoid hurting either parent. As a result, some children are afraid to let their parents know if they are dissatisfied or angry. You may not know that your children are hurting unless you look hard. Here are some signs:

- inconsolable grief over their parents' breakup
- unhappiness, no matter where they are or what they are doing, and
- behavior that seems to be "too good to be true."

One ten-year-old who didn't want to hurt his parents, but was thoroughly unhappy with the arrangements, summed up all of his frustrations by saying "I just wish I could grow up faster. It's better than being a kid."

Experts and parents alike recommend that you strive to achieve the following goals for separately parenting your elementary-school-aged children:

- tailor the schedule to meet your child's personality
- stick to the schedules you establish
- don't put children in the middle by asking them to carry messages to the other parent
- offer counseling or other emotional support, and
- support your children's participation in outside activities.

RELEVANT ISSUES IN CHAPTER 5

4. Adolescents

Adolescence is a turbulent time for both boys and girls. In addition to the hormonal changes their bodies experience, adolescents increasingly become dependent on their peer group, have more activities independent of their parents and siblings and are trying to distinguish their values and attitudes from those of their parents.

A separation or divorce is difficult for most teens. As one 15-year-old said during mediation, "I wish that they (his parents) would just remember that they aren't the only ones going through this."

A teen's concerns can run the gamut. Some panic at the idea that they have to give their friends two phone numbers to call for social engagements. Others struggle with constant conflict with one parent and little or no contact with the other. The parenting arrangements that once worked may now be unrealistic given your teen's activities and preferences. Although adolescents are not yet legally capable of making all of their own decisions, parents should allow their teens more and more input into the decisions that shape the parenting agreement.

When you adjust your parenting agreement to meet your teen's interests and needs, consider:

- letting your teen decide where he or she wants to live
- strengthening your teen's relationship with one parent or another important adult if the teen and the other parent fight constantly
- involving your teen in identifying problems and developing solutions
- participating in parent-teen mediation, and
- guarding against forcing your teen(s) to grow up too soon.

RELEVANT ISSUES IN CHAPTER 5

C. Strategies for Children With Special Needs

Children with special educational, physical or emotional care needs require equally special consideration in your parenting agreement. Your needs for child care, ongoing medical or educational assessment and support will be substantial. Also, your agreement may have to stay in place longer than for other children. Rather than ending your parenting agreement when your children become adults or graduate from college, you may find that your separate parenting relationship lasts indefinitely.

As you consider each issue/option set in Chapter 5, you may have to add your own agreements to make sure you are meeting your child's needs. Here are some issue/option sets which may require your special attention, and some suggestions that go beyond what is in Chapter 5.

Issue 1:   Medical, Dental and Vision Care

• Keep the number of health care providers down so there is consistency in your children's care.
• Any and all health care providers should be kept informed of your children's condition and progress.

• Be explicit about the kinds of ongoing assessment, therapy, medications or other treatment which may be necessary.
• Identify who will meet with doctors, therapists or other personnel to insure that your children's ongoing care needs are met.

Issue 2:   Psychiatric and Other Mental Health Care

• Plan for how mental health support or assessment may be offered to your children.
• Plan for how mental health or emotional support may be provided to other family members.

Issue 3:   Education

• Be explicit about how any special education needs will be met.
• Identify who will be involved in meetings with teachers, administration or other school personnel to insure that your children's ongoing educational needs are met.

Issue 10: Insurance

• Decide how your child's ongoing needs for health or other kinds of insurance will be met.
• Make sure that you incorporate your decisions into any agreements which provide for your children's financial future, such as a child support agreement.

Issue 11: Making Decisions

If your special-needs child will not be able to make his or her own decisions upon reaching legal adulthood, you may need to establish an adult guardianship and add language to that effect here.

Issue 14: Where Our Children Will Live

Because some special-needs children require intense, long term care, consider including provisions which give the primary caretaker periodic breaks.

Issue 18: Reinvolving a Previously Absent Parent

A parent who has been uninvolved with a special-needs child because of the costs, time or special care required may need training, counseling or other support before providing any care.

Issue 19: Child Care

- Make sure the number of child care providers is kept down to provide consistency.
- Insure that any child care providers are capable of caring for your special-needs children.

Issue 30: Consistency in Raising Children

- Make an effort to keep your expectations and standards for behavior consistent between both parent's homes.

- Make sure that any discipline is consistently applied in type and manner in both homes.

Issue 34: When a Parent Needs to Develop Parenting Skills

A parent who is not used to providing full time care for a special-needs child may need training. ■

Multiracial, Multicultural and International Families

V irtually all parents who separate or divorce experience conflict over some, if not many, childrearing issues. Parents whose cultural, religious, ethnic or national identities differ often find that separate parenting presents even greater challenges. For example, you may have been attracted to your partner—at least in part—because of your cultural, religious, ethnic or national differences. These once-intriguing differences, however, may now be a source of conflict concerning your children.

Fortunately, diversity within a family need not be the source of unresolvable problems. Many parents find that by first acknowledging their different viewpoints on certain issues, they are able to address the following common concerns:

- accommodating differences in child rearing practices
- encouraging the children to celebrate the traditions of both parents
- sorting out the role of power within the family
- accommodating religious differences
- working within the American legal system, and
- deciding if another country has authority over parenting (custody) issues.

A. Accommodating Differences in Child Rearing Practices

In the United States, we have developed increasingly clear standards regarding how children must be raised and cared for, and the kinds of discipline which are, and are not, acceptable. These standards may conflict with the practices of other cultures or some religions, and may lead to serious disagreements. Sometimes the practices are so different from the generally accepted American "norm" that a parent is accused of child abuse or neglect.

Most frequently, practices acceptable in a particular culture which clash with American standards pertain to discipline in general and corporal punishment (such as spanking, caning or striking with an object) in particular. Some cultures and religions consider corporal punishment essential to properly mold a child's behavior. A nation's legal code or a religious doctrine may spell out the methods for inflicting this kind of punishment.

By contrast, corporal punishment is rarely acceptable in the U.S., especially in public schools and other public institutions. In fact, in some states, all forms of corporal punishment are illegal. Other states prohibit it after a certain age, such as 12.

Another area in which certain cultures or religions don't follow the dominant American norm is medical care. For example, parents of certain cultures or religions will refuse specific kinds of medical intervention on behalf of their children. Other parents distrust or reject Western medicine and instead follow Eastern practices such as acupuncture. Still other parents prefer holistic healing or other alternative medicines.

Don't Agree to Break the Law

If you and the other parent are divorcing or legally separating, a court will probably review your parenting agreement. If any provision violates a state or federal law which governs the treatment of children, the court will reject your proposed parenting plan. It will probably also order a social worker to investigate both parents' homes and submit an evaluation to the court. The court will make whatever orders it deems necessary to protect your children's best interests, which always will be interpreted in accordance with the U.S. legal system.

B. Encouraging Children to Celebrate the Traditions of Both Parents

One way to minimize the childrearing conflicts you experience because of cultural, religious, ethnic or national differences is to instill in your children a sense of "specialness." Often children feel lost, angry and rejected after their parents separate or divorce, and the children's low feelings exacerbate the parental conflicts. You can help your children adjust to the separation or divorce, and therefore lessen your conflict with the other parent, by doing any of the following:

- teaching them who they are
- celebrating special traditions, and
- teaching them to respect (and embrace, if relevant) the ceremonies, rituals and traditions of their other parent.

For some parents, the core of their disagreement is over whose culture or religion is "better" or represents the "truth." You can hold firmly to your beliefs, but always remember that your children have two parents. Rather than trying to prove which culture or religion is better, try to find ways to equip your children to make their own decisions about both. One way to do this is to raise your children in both cultures or religions.

If those cultures or religions differ to the point that you cannot fully integrate your children into both, you can minimize your conflict—and differences—by finding a common principle, such as a commitment to family, and working from there. Perhaps mediators, elders or leaders within your particular communities can offer suggestions on living together peacefully.

Another suggestion is to teach your children about both cultures or religions, but to withhold certain ceremonies, rituals or traditions, such as initiations into a church or congregation, participation in funerals, undergoing religious communion or administering certain medical care. You might set limits because your children are not considered full members of the culture or group, or because certain functions might frighten or overwhelm your children.

C. Sorting Out the Role of Power Within the Family

One feature of certain cultures, religions and ethnicities is that near absolute power is given to men, who make most of the substantive decisions that affect all family members. In such a situation, the bargaining power between the parents may be highly unequal, and you may seek certain specifics with your dispute resolution method. For example, in a culture in which men issue orders, fathers will seldom accept information or direction unless it comes from another male. These parents might purposely select a male mediator, and the mother might hire a male attorney to negotiate with the father or his attorney.

D. Working Within the American Legal System

The way that a culture describes conflict often indicates how that culture prefers to resolve it as well. In American society, conflict usually means there are two or more competing interests—one will win while the other(s) lose. For the most part, divorce or matrimonial litigation in our current legal system encourages each parent to confront the other and prove who will uphold the best interests of the children. Although litigation may be appropriate when a parent with a history of abuse, neglect or serious instability insists on significant unsupervised time with the children, litigation is usually unnecessarily costly and bitter. And to parents from outside of the U.S., American litigation can be bewildering.

In some cultures, conflict is thought to result from in-harmonious relationships. Once a relationship is found to be inharmonious, it is the community's responsibility to help the individual rediscover and fulfill his or her proper role. In many of these cultures, the best interests of the child are synonymous with the best interests of the group. The role which any one individual is therefore expected to fulfill within these communities is generally a function of his or her age, sex, social standing and economic resources.

Many of these communities are fairly cohesive, and the elders within the community or within the extended family are well-regarded for their wisdom and leadership. When facilitators are needed to resolve conflict, elders are called upon because their status allows them to be persuasive problem solvers. Given this view of conflict and resolution, it is understandable why some parents are mystified when told that their decisions must hinge on the child's best in-terests as determined by state legislatures, the mental health profession and the courts.

Even mediation, which often is a versatile tool for resolving disputes, can be culturally biased. For example, selecting a mediator in the U.S. typically means finding someone totally neutral and unknown. In many cultures, however, parties are willing to participate in the process and reach agreement because the facilitator is well known to them. Additionally, the predominant mediation model in the U.S. today presumes that the parties will come to an agreement. In some other cultures, mediation is most effec-tive when the facilitator suggests the solution and then per-suades the parties to agree.

If you or the other parent comes from a background that is substantially different from the dominant Anglo-American culture, you may need to find attorneys, media-tors, counselors or others sensitive to the issues and cultural differences. If you feel at a disadvantage because of lan-guage, either because you recently arrived in this country or because you don't understand the American legal system, you need to find knowledgeable support people from within your community who do.

To resolve your conflicts, look for people who can con-nect the priorities of each culture with the issues of dis-agreement.

RELEVANT ISSUES IN CHAPTER 5

Psychiatric and Other Mental Health Care	2
Making Decisions	11
Resolving Disputes When Making Decisions Together	12
When Parenting Styles and Values Are Very Different	29

E. Deciding if Another Country Has Authority Over Parenting (Custody) Issues

If one or both parents are not U.S. citizens, your separate parenting may involve additional issues related to interna-tional borders. You—or the other parent—may justifiably fear that your children will be taken out of the U.S. without your knowledge or consent. Although protecting your chil-dren from a parent who truly wants to kidnap and hide his or her own children can be hard, laws do exist to help. Chapter 10, Section F, has information on laws which can help you if your children are taken out of the country.

RELEVANT ISSUES IN CHAPTER 5

International Travel and Passports	6
Making Decisions (If there is any question over which country actually has jurisdiction, consider adding specific language)	11

Although not located on foreign soil, American Indian nations have a special legal standing within the United States. Section 1911 (a) of the Indian Child Welfare Act states:

An Indian tribe shall have jurisdiction exclusive as to any state over any child custody proceeding involving an Indian child who resides on or is domiciled within the reservation of such tribe, except where such jurisdiction is otherwise vested in the State by existing Federal law. Where an Indian child is a ward of a tribal court, the Indian tribe shall retain exclusive jurisdiction, notwithstanding the resi-dence or domicile of the child.

This Act covers the termination of parental rights, foster care and adoptive placements as well as custody proceed-ings. If you are unsure whether or not you must resolve your differences within a tribal court, see an attorney. ■

CHAPTER

9

Nontraditional Families

The traditional image of a family is a mother, father and their children. Millions of American families, however, look very different, and are often referred to as "nontraditional families." Some of these families consist of childless couples—married or unmarried, gay or straight, although most include children. Nontraditional families—as we define them below—make up the substantial majority of U.S. families.

A.   What Are Nontraditional Families?

Nontraditional families fall into one of the following categories.

Step families. In a step family, a single parent establishes, usually by marriage, a new long-term relationship. The children usually refer to the new partner as a stepmother or stepfather. The partner calls the children his or her stepchildren.

Blended families. A blended family consists of at least two, and as many as four, step families. At its core, it's a former couple, their children, the new relationships entered into by the members of the former couple and the children of those new relationships. Dr. Constance Ahrons describes these families as binuclear families in her book *The Good Divorce* (Harper Collins, 1994). Here is an example of a blended or binuclear family: Mark and Evelyn marry and have a daughter Lisa. They get a divorce, sharing custody of Lisa. Mark remarries Shauna, who is divorced herself with a child from her previous marriage. Mark and Shauna have a son Rueben. Evelyn comes out as a lesbian after divorcing Mark, and forms a relationship with Cindy. Together they adopt a child.

Single parents. Many people—through circumstance or choice—are single parents. Obviously, the separate parenting issues in this book are not relevant, unless the single parent has involved another adult in raising the children. For example, a single mother may get help from her own parents or from a close friend in raising her children.

Grandparent-headed families. Some parents go beyond "getting help" from their own parents in raising children. In many families, especially those torn apart by violence or drugs, the grandparents have custody of, or guardianship over, their children—either formally (by court order) or informally (by agreement of the parents).

Unmarried couples. Many unmarried heterosexual couples have children together.

Same-sex parent-headed families. Current estimates indicate that more than 15,000 lesbians and gay men have had or adopted children during the lesbian and gay "baby boom" of the 1980s and 1990s. Many, if not the majority, of these children are being raised by two mothers or two fathers.

Open-adoptive families. In general, a legally married husband and wife who adopt a child do not fall into the category of a nontraditional family. This changes, however, if the couple maintains a relationship with the birth mother—meaning the child is raised by the adoptive parents but has visits with the birth mother.

B.   The Legal Relationship of a Nontraditional Parent and His or Her Children

Probably the greatest challenge faced by nontraditional families is the lack of societal and legal recognition. Despite the fact that fewer and fewer American families consist of the traditional mother, father and their children, the institutions—including the legal system—that deal with families are still geared for the traditional family model. Nontraditional families often feel left out, ignored and unsupported. And the problems are exacerbated when the adults in that family divorce or separate. Sometimes, a person who has spent years raising children now finds himself or herself shut off because he or she is not considered a legal parent.

In a nontraditional family, it is imperative that when the adults raising the children split up, they continue to look out for the best interests of their children. If that means maintaining contact with all the adults involved in raising the children, then the parenting agreement must explicitly provide for this. Don't expect a court to do it—a court will order continuing contact usually only when the adult is a recognized "legal parent." (Some courts will order contact between children and a "psychological" parent, but often only if the legal parent doesn't object.)

Parents generally fall into one of four categories:
• legal parents
• biological, nonlegal parents
• psychological parents, and
• legal guardians.

Depending on the category, a parent may or may not have the legal right to custody or visitation with, or the legal responsibility to care for or support, the children.

As you read about the various categories of legally recognized and unrecognized parents, remember that you are not obligated to follow the strict letter of the law. As mentioned, if it's in the best interests of your children for them to maintain contact with the adults who have been raising them, then by all means continue that contact.

1. Legal (Biological and Adoptive) Parents

Legal parents have both the authority and the obligation to provide basic care and comfort for their children. They are charged with making the decisions that affect their children's health, education and welfare. They are further charged with providing for their children's financial support. Recognizing a child's legal parent can differ for men and women.

The legal mother is usually, but not always, the woman who conceives and gives birth to the child (see Section 2, below) or who legally adopts the child.

The legal father is a man who legally adopts a child, or was married to the mother when the child was conceived or born, or declared the father in a paternity action. In addition, a man may be presumed to be the legal father if he:

- attempted to marry the mother (even if the marriage wasn't valid) and the child was conceived or born after the attempt
- married the mother after the birth and agreed either to have his name on the birth certificate or to support the child, or
- welcomed the child into his home and openly held the child out as his.

A legal parent's obligations and rights end *only* if a court issues an order terminating parental rights. If you are the biological father of a child you have not seen for a while,

you are still considered a parent unless a court says otherwise. This means you have the right to seek custody of or visitation with your child and you can be sued to pay child support.

2. Biological, Nonlegal Parents

In a number of situations, a person is biologically related to a child but nevertheless is not considered the child's legal parent.

a.   Birth Mothers

The most common biological, nonlegal parent is a birth mother who gives up her child for adoption. A birth mother traditionally severs all ties (if she had any) with the child—and adoptive parent(s)—following an adoption.

In recent years, however, a number of adoptive parents have chosen to retain an ongoing relationship with their child's birth mother. This arrangement is usually called an open adoption. In some families, the relationship is little more than an exchange of holiday and birthday cards. In others, it includes regular visits and attendance at family celebrations.

b.   Surrogate Mothers

A surrogate mother is a woman who bears a child for someone else. Most surrogate mothers become pregnant with the semen of a man wishing to become a father. A few others have an already-fertilized egg of another woman implanted in their uterus, in which case the surrogate mother is not genetically related to the child. In either case, upon the birth of the child, the surrogate mother relinquishes all rights and responsibilities for the child and either turns the child over to the man (in the former situation) or the man and/or woman (in the latter situation).

Surrogate mothers offer infertile and gay male couples a way to become parents. The process is not without risk, however. Surrogacy carries with it a risk that the surrogate mother will change her mind and refuse to relinquish the child. Some states have passed laws regulating surrogacy contracts. For example, they are prohibited in Arizona, Michigan, New York and a few other states. Only two states expressly authorize their use—Iowa and New Hampshire. Most states are silent on the issue.

A few highly-publicized cases in which the surrogate mother changed her mind have drawn attention to the issue. In general, courts have ruled that a surrogate mother has the rights of a legal parent if she contributed genetic material to the child—that is, she became pregnant with the semen of a man wanting to become a father. If, however, an already-fertilized egg of another woman is implanted in her uterus, the donor generally has no parental rights.

Robin Leonard and Stephen Elias, in *Nolo's Pocket Guide to Family Law* (Nolo Press, 1994), summarize the New Jersey Supreme Court's holding in the first, and most famous surrogacy case, the *Matter of Baby M.* (537 A.2d 1227):

> *The surrogate mother changed her mind after the baby was born and decided that she wanted to keep the baby. The baby's father and his wife sued the surrogate mother to enforce the contract. The trial court declared the contract valid, terminated the surrogate mother's parental rights, and allowed the father's wife to adopt the baby. The New Jersey Supreme Court reversed that decision, ruled that surrogate motherhood contracts are unenforceable, and then treated the case like any other disputed custody case, awarding custody to the father and visitation rights to the surrogate mother.*

Some parents who have obtained their children through a surrogacy arrangement have chosen to retain an ongoing relationship with the surrogate mother, similar to the open adoption described above.

c. Semen Donors

Artificial insemination (also called alternative insemination) is the process in which a woman is inseminated by a means other than sexual intercourse. If the semen comes from the woman's husband, the man is considered the legal father of the child.

In the majority of cases, the semen comes from someone other than the woman's husband. This type of artificial insemination offers infertile and lesbian couples a way to become parents. The process is not without risk, however, because a semen donor who is known to the couple might change his mind and sue for paternity.

If the woman is married when the insemination and birth occur, her husband, not the donor, is considered the legal parent. If the woman is unmarried when the insemination and birth occur, whether the donor is considered the legal father depends on a number of factors, including the procedure and the state. In Oregon and New Jersey, for example, the woman and the donor may enter an agreement spelling out their intentions, including that the donor not be considered the legal father. In California, if the insemination of a married woman is performed by a doctor, the donor is not considered the legal father. If no doctor is used, the donor may be considered the legal father.

As with open adoptions and some surrogacy arrangements, a few legal parents maintain an ongoing relationship between the semen donor and the child.

d. Ova Donors

In one of the newest reproductive techniques, a woman donates an egg, which is fertilized in vitro and then implanted in the uterus of a different woman who wishes to become a mother. Usually, the egg is fertilized with the semen of the husband of the woman into whom the egg is implanted.

This is such a new procedure that the legal relationship of the ova donor and the child is unknown. In the long run, the donor will probably not be considered a legal parent, based on two analogies. First, the ova donor is similar to a surrogate mother who shares no genetic material with the child. Second, the ova donor can be equated to a semen donor, who usually is not considered a legal father.

3. Psychological Parents

"Psychological parent" is a general description of an adult who has formed a significant emotional bond with a child by contributing substantially to the child's care and upbringing. Psychological parents are not legally responsible for the care or support of a child; nor are they automatically entitled to custody of, or visitation with, the child.

In some situations, a court will grant visitation between a child and a psychological parent if the court believes it would be detrimental to the child for the relationship to end.

a. Stepparents

A stepparent is the new spouse of a legal parent. In general, the stepparent and stepchild have no legal relationship. This means that unless the stepparent legally adopted the child, the stepparent is not obligated to care for or support the child and is not entitled to seek custody or visitation. Of course, many stepparents are instrumental in the upbringing and support of their stepchildren.

In a few states, including Michigan and Wisconsin, some stepparents have been granted the status of "equitable" parent. Most often, this occurs when the stepparent and child consider themselves to be parent and child, or when the legal parent has encouraged the relationship.

Equitable parents are often granted shared custody of, or visitation with, the children, and are ordered to pay child support.

b.   Co-Parents

A co-parent is the unmarried partner of a biological or adoptive parent. The concept of co-parent has become extremely important for lesbian and gay couples. Because no state allows same-sex couples to legally marry, the partner of a lesbian mother or gay father cannot adopt the parent's child under a state's traditional stepparent adoption statute. This means that when a lesbian or gay couple raise a child together, usually only one partner (the biological or adoptive parent) is recognized as the legal parent.

In such a situation, the co-parent has few legal rights if the couple splits up. Tragically, the co-parent is not entitled to visitation or custody; nor is the co-parent obligated to provide financial support. In a few states, a lesbian co-parent has sued for visitation after the couple separated and the legal parent barred the co-parent from seeing the child. In only one state—New Mexico—did the court grant the co-parent visitation, based on an agreement the couple had giving the co-parent visitation. The court said that a parent "may enter into an agreement with another person concerning the custody of a child" and that "sexual orientation, standing alone, is not a permissible basis for the denial of shared custody or visitation."

CO-PARENTS WHO ARE ALSO LEGAL PARENTS

Until 1985, gay and lesbian couples (and their lawyers) assumed that state laws were written so that adoptions were available only to married couples and single people. If a "single" person—such as the partner of a biological parent—sought to adopt, the biological parents' rights would first have to be terminated, hardly the result a lesbian or gay couple wanted.

Then the lawyers got smart and began reading the text of the state adoption statutes. Most laws, they realized, authorized adoptions by married couples and single people, but didn't expressly exclude unmarried couples. Similarly, the stepparent adoption statutes expressly authorized adoptions by the new spouse of a legal parent if the other legal parent was dead, had his parental rights terminated, abandoned the child or consented to the adoption, but didn't forbid an unmarried partner from becoming a stepparent.

Now, joint adoptions by gay and lesbian couples or second-parent (the equivalent of stepparent) adoptions have been granted in the District of Columbia and several states including Alaska, California, Illinois, Massachusetts, Michigan, Minnesota, New Jersey, Oregon, Pennsylvania, Texas, Vermont and Washington. In New York, the courts are split—some have granted the adoptions while others have denied them. When a court grants a joint or second-parent adoption, both mothers or fathers are considered legal parents.

c. Other Important Adults

Grandparents, aunts and uncles, and adult friends of legal parents often form significant emotional bonds with children. In all states, grandparents (and in some states, aunts and uncles) can ask the court to grant them visitation with their grandchildren following a divorce or separation. It's up to the court whether or not to grant the visitation, but many will, recognizing the special relationship children often have with their grandparents.

4. Legal Guardians

A legal guardian is an adult given the legal right—either by the parents or by a court—to care for and control a minor child. Formal legal guardianships (those ordered by a court) tend to be set up for children who lack stable parenting. For instance, grandparents (or aunts and uncles) are often appointed legal guardians of their grandchildren (or nieces and nephews) when the parents are unable to care for the children because of drug abuse, imprisonment or lack of basic parenting skills. A legal guardian often needs a court order so that schools, hospitals and other institutions have an adult to turn to when a decision about the child needs to be made.

If the legal guardian has completely taken over the parenting role, a court may grant custody of the children to the guardian. The court may also order that the legal guardian allow the parents to visit with the children. Some legal guardians have a more limited role because they are only asked to care for a child who is away at school. When this happens, the legal guardian is there to make quick decisions in the event of an emergency.

C. Recognizing the Nontraditional Parent's Role

If your children have a close relationship with a biological, nonlegal parent, a psychological parent or a legal guardian, you will want to provide for the continuation of that relationship in your parenting agreement unless you believe your children are being harmed.

You have several ways to handle this, depending on your children's relationship with the adult. If your children haven't been living with the adult, as might be the case with a close friend or nearby relative, you can either incorporate a regular visitation schedule or allow your children to initiate contact in your parenting agreement.

If, however, your children have been living with the adult and for all intents and purposes that adult is another parent to your children, do what you can to minimize the harm to them. You may be angry and want that person out of your life. And that person may have no legal standing whatsoever to claim "parenthood." But if your children know that person as a parent, put your anger and the legal labels aside and fill out the parenting agreement in Chapter 5 as if you were a legally married couple getting a divorce, both entitled to continuing contact with your children.

RELEVANT ISSUES IN CHAPTER 5

Making Decisions	11
Grandparents, Relatives and Important Friends	25
When Parents Have New Partners	36

D. Resolving Conflict in a Way That Meets Your Family's Needs

Most nontraditional families need to find ways to resolve disputes outside of the courtroom. The court system is geared to working with traditional families. This does not necessarily mean that nontraditional families suffer discrimination within the court system, although lesbian and gay couples often justifiably feel that way.

In most situations, however, the dynamics of nontraditional families require more effort and understanding than the legal system can give. Court calendars are overcrowded and court personnel are overworked; judges cannot take the time to thoroughly investigate your children's relationship with their step-siblings, their grandparents, your partner and all the other important people in their lives.

When adults who have raised (or at least lived) together with children in a nontraditional family decide to live apart, they often find mediation helpful for defining the role the nonlegal parent will have in the children's lives and developing a plan to carry it out. If mediation isn't an option or doesn't work, consider arbitration—where you can obtain a resolution without having to negotiate with the other person. Chapter 6, *Making Mediation and Arbitration Work for You*, has information on how each process works and how to select a mediator or arbitrator.

No matter which process you use, it is imperative that the facilitator understands the issues that are important to you and structures the process so that it will meet your needs. You may need to go beyond the suggestions in Chapter 6 for finding the right facilitator. For example, if you're a lesbian couple splitting up, consider contacting a gay community center, support group, religious organization or other gay or lesbian institution for help in finding someone to mediate your parenting issues.

E. Creating New Relationships After the Divorce or Separation

You may be reading this chapter because while your traditional family divorced or separated a while ago, you or your children's other parent have formed a new relationship, creating a nontraditional family. A new relationship can bring joy to the new couple and anguish for the still single parent. Depending on who is now coupled and who is still single, you or your ex may be jealous or suspicious of the new partner. Or, you or your ex may be scared that your children will want to live in the other household, especially if the new mate has children of similar ages to yours.

Similarly, your children might feel awkward when a parent has a new partner. If you form a new relationship, you must find ways to maintain the existing parent-child relationship while creating and cementing new bonds. One highly effective way to do this is to find times when just you and your children can spend time with each other. Don't use the excuse that "everyone is too busy." If you don't spend quality time with your children, they may begin to feel left out, especially if your new partner has children or you and your new partner have a child together. Occasional lunch dates, trips to the park or video parlor, or other one-on-one activities can make all the difference in the world.

With your new family in place, you often have the perfect excuse to start building some new family traditions that can give your children a sense of belonging to your new family. These rituals can be simple or elaborate, but must happen consistently to become routine. If your new family has established a family activity night, then setting aside one night a week or month will be a priority. If your new tradition is a holiday (either real or invented), then be sure to celebrate it annually.

Finally, remember that language is powerful and finding names or descriptions for new relatives can be challenging. Some children call a parent's new partner something like Mom or Dad (or Mother or Father); other children use the new partner's first name. Still others invent a name, or use a word from a language other than English. Describing step-siblings can present similar problems and solutions (such as inventing a name or using a non-English word). Other children simply describe the step-siblings as "new" brothers or sisters in order to avoid a lengthy explanation.

RELEVANT ISSUES IN CHAPTER 5

State and Federal Laws Affecting Child Custody

This chapter summarizes state and federal laws applicable to certain child custody and visitation issues. It is not intended to be a treatise on child custody law, or definitive legal advice upon which you should rely. Statutes are often repealed or amended, or are vague or confusing. Also, courts interpret statutes (in cases) in ways that are difficult to understand and keep track of. For complete, accurate and up-to-date information on a specific law, either do your own research or consult with an attorney. (See Chapter 11, *Help Beyond the Book.*)

As the specific information in this chapter indicates, a few basic similarities exist in states regarding the upbringing of children whose parents divorce or separate, and the methods used to help parents resolve disputes about custody and visitation. Unless a court has convincing evidence of harm to the children or either parent, most states:

- prefer that the parents share in parenting their children
- place a value on children maintaining frequent and continuing contact with both parents
- insist that both parents have access to medical, school, religious and other relevant information about their children
- recommend or order mediation before deciding custody and visitation disputes in court
- presume that mediation sessions should be confidential and not examined in any later court proceeding, as long as both parents expressly do not waive that confidentiality
- expect mediators who accept referrals from the court to meet certain state-specific qualification standards, and
- believe that custody decisions should be based on an evaluation of the children's best interests rather than on biases based upon a parent's gender.

A. Custody and Visitation

Custody generally refers to:

- the legal authority to make decisions about a child (sometimes called legal custody), and
- maintaining physical control over a child (sometimes called physical custody).

These terms are explained in Chapter 2.

DIFFERENTIATION BETWEEN LEGAL AND PHYSICAL CUSTODY

In the states listed below, a court may make different awards for legal and physical custody. In all other states, a custody award encompasses both legal and physical custody.

Arizona	Iowa	Pennsylvania
California	Minnesota	Texas
Colorado	Mississippi	Utah
Connecticut	Missouri	Virginia
Georgia	New Hampshire	West Virginia
Idaho	New Jersey	Wisconsin
Indiana	Ohio	

Depending on the state and the situation, a court can award sole custody (to just one parent) or joint custody (to both parents). A joint custody award can be for legal and physical custody or for legal custody only. Rarely, if ever,

will a court authorize parents to share only physical custody of their children.

JOINT CUSTODY

Only Arkansas, North Dakota, Rhode Island and Virginia have no statutes relating to joint custody. In these states, joint custody may be allowed under court decisions.		
Joint custody required unless the children's best interests— or a parent's health or safety—would be compromised:		
Idaho	New Mexico	New Hampshire
Joint custody permitted even when one parent objects to the arrangement:		
Alaska	Iowa	Nebraska
Arizona	Massachusetts	New Jersey
California	Michigan	Ohio
Colorado	Minnesota	Oklahoma
Florida	Mississippi	South Dakota (possibly)
Illinois	Missouri	Utah (possibly)
Indiana	Montana	Wisconsin
Joint custody available if both parents agree:		
Alabama	Louisiana	South Carolina
Connecticut	Maine	Tennessee
Delaware	Maryland	Texas
District of Columbia	Nevada	Vermont
Georgia	New York	Washington
Hawaii	North Carolina	West Virginia
Kansas	Oregon	Wyoming
Kentucky	Pennsylvania	

A few states expressly discourage judges from splitting children between their parents homes.

SPLIT CUSTODY

Except in unusual situations, a court should not grant custody of one or more children to one parent and grant custody of different children to the other parent.		
Alaska	Texas	Washington (possibly)

A number of states have specific laws regarding awarding custody of very young children to their mother.

AUTOMATICALLY AWARDING CUSTODY TO MOTHERS

Judges are permitted to award custody to a mother solely because a child is of tender years.		
South Carolina	Tennessee	
Judges are prohibited from awarding custody to a mother solely because a child is of tender years.		
Alaska	District of Columbia	Kansas
California	Florida	Missouri
Delaware (possibly)	Hawaii (possibly)	Utah

Visitation describes the time that a noncustodial parent, grandparent or other important person spends with a child.

GRANDPARENT VISITATION

All states specifically provide grandparents the right to ask for visitation as part of a court order.

SEXUAL ORIENTATION AND CUSTODY OR VISITATION

Only the two jurisdictions listed below have enacted laws stating that a parent's sexual orientation cannot be a factor in a custody or visitation award.	
District of Columbia	New Mexico

Only two states have laws stating that a parent's sexual orientation cannot be a factor in a custody or visitation award. In a few other states, including Alaska, California and Pennsylvania, courts have ruled that a parent's homosexuality, in and of itself, cannot be grounds for an automatic denial of custody. In truth, a lesbian or gay parent faces a difficult struggle trying to gain custody in most American courtrooms, especially if that parent lives with a partner. It is fair to say that many, if not most, judges are ignorant about, prejudiced against, or suspicious of, gay and lesbian parents. Only a few judges understand that a parent's sexual orientation, alone, does not affect the best interests of the children. But judges often use the best interests standard to deny a gay or lesbian parent custody.

B. Defining the Best Interest of the Child

Courts place a higher value on protecting a child's best interests than upon any other factor when deciding custody and visitation. You will find discussion of the best interests standards in Chapters 2 and 7.

Most states have laws listing factors that a court should consider when assessing the best interests of the children. Below are the most common factors and the states that include them. You would be mistaken to conclude that a judge won't consider a factor just because the state isn't listed under it. In fact, you are safer to assume that all of the factors below are important to a judge who is deciding who gets custody.

PARENT'S ABILITY TO MEET THE CHILDREN'S NEEDS

Alabama	Maine	Ohio
Alaska	Maryland	Oregon
Arizona	Michigan	South Dakota
Colorado	Minnesota	Texas
Connecticut	Mississippi	Utah
Florida	Missouri	Vermont
Georgia	Nebraska	Washington
Illinois	New Jersey	Wisconsin
Iowa	New Mexico	
Louisiana	North Dakota	

INSURING THAT CHILDREN WILL NOT BE EXPOSED TO THE THREAT OF VIOLENCE OR ABUSE

Alabama	Kentucky	Oklahoma
Alaska	Louisiana	Oregon
Arizona	Maine	Pennsylvania
California	Massachusetts	Rhode Island
Colorado	Minnesota	Texas
Delaware	Missouri	Utah
Florida	Montana	Vermont
Hawaii	Nebraska	Virginia
Idaho	Nevada	Washington
Illinois	New Jersey	Wisconsin
Indiana	New York	Wyoming
Iowa	North Dakota	
Kansas	Ohio	

QUALITY OF THE PARENT-CHILD AND OTHER FAMILY RELATIONSHIPS

Alaska	Kansas	New Mexico
Arizona	Kentucky	North Dakota
Colorado	Louisiana	Ohio
Delaware	Maine	Oregon
District of Columbia	Michigan	Utah
Florida	Minnesota	Vermont
Hawaii	Missouri	Washington
Illinois	Montana	Wisconsin
Indiana	Nebraska	
Iowa	New Jersey	

CHILD'S PREFERENCES

If the child is considered old enough to reasonably assess his or her own feelings—the older the child is, the more weight is given.

Alaska	Indiana (age 14)	Nevada
Arizona	Iowa	New Hampshire
California	Kansas	New Mexico
Colorado	Kentucky	North Dakota
Connecticut	Louisiana	Ohio
Delaware	Maine	Oklahoma
District of Columbia	Michigan	South Dakota
Florida	Minnesota	Texas (age 12)
Georgia (age 14)	Missouri	Utah
Hawaii	Montana	Wisconsin
Illinois	Nebraska	

GEOGRAPHIC DISTANCE BETWEEN PARENT'S HOMES

Alaska	Missouri	Texas
Arizona	Nevada	Utah
Colorado	New Jersey	Washington
Indiana	New Mexico	
Louisiana	Ohio	

MOVING COULD RESULT IN A CHANGED CUSTODY ORDER

A parent's move may constitute a changed circumstance that gives the court justification to modify a custody or visitation order to accommodate the needs of the noncustodial parent. Some courts switch custody from one parent to the other. Other courts require that the relocating parent pay transportation costs for visits with the noncustodial parent.

MORAL FITNESS AND CONDUCT OF THE PARENTS

Alabama	Louisiana	New Jersey
Colorado	Michigan	North Dakota
Delaware	Mississippi	Pennsylvania
Florida	Nebraska	Rhode Island

HOUSEHOLD STABILITY AND CONTINUITY OF CARE

Alaska	Kansas	New Jersey
California	Kentucky	North Dakota
Colorado	Louisiana	Ohio
Delaware	Maine	Oklahoma
District of Columbia	Michigan	Oregon
Florida	Minnesota	Texas
Hawaii	Mississippi	Utah
Illinois	Missouri	Washington
Indiana	Montana	Wisconsin
Iowa	Nevada	

HOSTILITY OF A PARENT AND WHETHER A PARENT IS UNDERMINING THE RELATIONSHIP BETWEEN THE OTHER PARENT AND THE CHILDREN

Alaska	Louisiana	Texas
California	Maine	Utah
Colorado	Michigan	Vermont
Florida	Missouri	Washington
Illinois	New Jersey	Wisconsin
Iowa	New Mexico	
Kansas	Ohio	

EFFECT OF LIFESTYLE CHANGES

Changes in custody or visitation orders may be obtained if substantial changes in a parent's lifestyle threaten or harm the child. If, for example, a custodial parent begins working at night and leaving a nine-year-old child alone, the other parent may request a change in custody. Similarly, if a noncustodial parent begins drinking heavily or taking drugs, the custodial parent may file a request for modification of the visitation order (asking, for example, that visits occur when the parent is sober, or in the presence of another adult). Determining what constitutes a lifestyle sufficiently detrimental to warrant a change in custody or visitation rights varies tremendously depending on the state and the particular judge deciding the case. For instance, cohabitation by a parent may be ignored in one place, but not another.

CAN RACE PLAY A ROLE IN CUSTODY DECISIONS?

Palmore v. Sidoti, 466 U.S. 429 (1984) is a U.S. Supreme Court decision in which the court ruled that it was unconstitutional for a court to consider race when a noncustodial parent petitions a court for a change of custody. In the case, a white couple had divorced, and the mother had been awarded custody of their son. She remarried an African-American man and moved to a predominantly African-American neighborhood. The father filed a request for modification of custody based on the changed circumstance that the boy was now living with an African-American man in an African-American neighborhood. A Florida court granted the modification. The U.S. Supreme Court reversed, ruling that societal stigma, especially a racial one, cannot be the basis for a custody decision.

C. Mediation and Arbitration

Mediation is a nonadversarial process in which a neutral person (called a mediator) meets with disputing persons to help them settle a dispute. It is discussed in Chapter 6.

PARENTS CAN BE ORDERED TO PARTICIPATE IN MEDIATION BEFORE BRINGING A CUSTODY OR VISITATION DISPUTE TO COURT

Alabama	Kentucky	North Dakota
Alaska	Louisiana	Ohio
Arizona	Maine	Oregon
California	Maryland	Pennsylvania
Colorado	Michigan	Rhode Island
Connecticut	Minnesota	South Carolina
Delaware	Mississippi	South Dakota
Florida	Missouri	Texas
Idaho	Montana	Utah
Illinois	Nevada	Virginia
Indiana	New Jersey	Washington
Iowa	New Mexico	West Virginia
Kansas	North Carolina	Wisconsin

PARENTS CAN BE EXCUSED FROM COURT-ORDERED MEDIATION IF IT IS FOUND TO BE INAPPROPRIATE UNDER THE CIRCUMSTANCES

Colorado	Michigan	Oregon
Georgia	Minnesota	Texas
Idaho	Nebraska	Utah
Indiana	Nevada	Virginia
Kansas	New Jersey	Washington
Maine	North Carolina	Wisconsin
Maryland	Ohio	

JUDGES CAN ASK A MEDIATOR FOR A RECOMMENDATION ON CUSTODY AND VISITATION IF THE PARENTS CAN'T SETTLE THE ISSUES DURING MEDIATION

Alaska	California	Delaware
New Mexico (possibly)		

PARENTS CAN BE EXCUSED FROM COURT-ORDERED MEDIATION IF THERE IS A HISTORY OF DOMESTIC VIOLENCE

Alaska	Maryland	North Dakota
Colorado	Minnesota	Ohio
Delaware	Montana	Utah
Florida	Nebraska	Virginia
Hawaii	New Jersey	Washington
Idaho	New Mexico	Wisconsin
Louisiana	North Carolina	

MEDIATION IS CONSIDERED CONFIDENTIAL— THE MEDIATOR CANNOT TESTIFY IN COURT ABOUT ANYTHING SAID DURING MEDIATION

If both parents expressly waive this or let the mediator conduct a subsequent investigation or evaluation regarding custody, the mediator may testify in court.

Alabama	Kansas	North Carolina
Alaska	Louisiana	North Dakota
Arizona	Maryland	Ohio
California	Massachusetts	Oklahoma
Colorado	Michigan	Oregon
Connecticut	Minnesota	Rhode Island
Delaware	Mississippi	Tennessee
Florida	Missouri	Utah
Georgia	Montana	Virginia
Idaho	Nebraska	Washington
Illinois	Nevada	Wisconsin
Indiana	New Hampshire	Wyoming
Iowa	New Jersey	

PARENTS CAN BE EXCUSED FROM COURT-ORDERED MEDIATION IF THERE IS A HISTORY OF CHILD ABUSE

Delaware	Nebraska	Ohio
Florida	Nevada	Utah
Idaho	New Hampshire	Virginia
Louisiana	New Jersey	Washington
Maryland	New Mexico	Wisconsin
Minnesota	North Carolina	
Montana	North Dakota	

A Court Can Order a Custody Investigation or Evaluation to Help It Make a Decision

California	Michigan	Ohio
Delaware	Minnesota	Pennsylvania
Georgia	Missouri	South Dakota
Hawaii	Nebraska	Utah
Illinois	Nevada	Virginia
Kansas	New Jersey	Washington
Kentucky	New Mexico	Wisconsin
Maryland	North Dakota	

Child Custody Mediators Must Possess Certain Educational, Training and Experience Qualifications

California	Michigan	Ohio
Colorado	Minnesota	Oklahoma
Florida	Mississippi	Oregon
Georgia	Missouri	Texas
Idaho	Montana	Utah
Indiana	Nebraska	Virginia
Iowa	Nevada	Washington
Kansas	New Hampshire	West Virginia
Kentucky	New Jersey	Wisconsin
Maine	North Carolina	
Maryland	North Dakota	

Arbitration Is Specifically Permitted to Resolve Custody and Visitation Disputes

Arbitration is a process similar to court because the parties, or more likely their attorneys, present a "case" and the arbitrator resolves the issues. Arbitration is discussed in Chapter 6.

Georgia	New Mexico	Texas
Indiana	North Dakota	Washington
Michigan	Oklahoma	
Minnesota	South Carolina	

D. Interference With Custody or Visitation

Custodial interference occurs when a parent (or guardian) keeps a child away from a person who has a legal right to custody. In most states, it is a crime to take a child from his or her parent or guardian intending to deprive that person of custody. In many states, depriving a parent or guardian of custody is a felony if the child is taken out of state. Also, in most states, the parent or guardian deprived of custody may sue the person who took the child for damages.

Many states recognize good-cause defenses to custodial interference, as outlined below. In most cases, a defense negates the charge; in others, it reduces the charge from a felony to a misdemeanor.

Defense to Custodial Interference: Taker Has or Seeks Legal Custody

Alabama	Iowa	Oregon
Alaska	Kentucky	Pennsylvania
Arizona	Louisiana	Rhode Island
Arkansas	Maine	South Carolina
California	Maryland	South Dakota
Connecticut	Minnesota	Tennessee
District of Columbia	Mississippi	Texas
Florida	Nebraska	Vermont
Georgia	New Hampshire	Virginia
Hawaii	New Jersey	West Virginia
Idaho	New Mexico	Wisconsin
Illinois	New York	

Defense to Custodial Interference: Guardian or Child Over a Certain Age Consented

Colorado (age 14)	Ohio (age 12)
District of Columbia (age 12)	Pennsylvania (age 12)
Florida (age 12)	Rhode Island (age 12)
Idaho (age 12)	South Dakota (age 12)
Minnesota (age 12)	Washington (age 15)
Nevada (age 12)	Wyoming (age 12)
New Jersey (age 12)	

DEFENSE TO CUSTODIAL INTERFERENCE: PROTECTING CHILD OR SELF FROM BODILY HARM

California	Minnesota	Rhode Island
Colorado	Missouri	Utah
District of Columbia	Nevada	Vermont
Florida	New Hampshire	Washington
Idaho	New Jersey	West Virginia
Illinois	New Mexico	Wisconsin
Louisiana	New York	Wyoming
Maryland	Ohio	
Michigan	Pennsylvania	

DEFENSE TO CUSTODIAL INTERFERENCE: REPORTED TO POLICE OR PARENT; CHILD RETURNED PROMPTLY

Arizona	Missouri	Pennsylvania
California	Montana	Rhode Island
District of Columbia	New Jersey	South Carolina
Idaho	New Mexico	Tennessee
Illinois	North Carolina	Texas
Indiana	North Dakota	Washington
Kentucky	Ohio	West Virginia
Minnesota	Oregon	

E. When a Child Has Been Taken Out of State

All states and the District of Columbia have enacted a statute called the Uniform Child Custody Jurisdiction Act, which sets standards for when a court may make a custody determination and when a court must defer to an existing determination from another state. In general, a state may make a custody decision about a child if (in order of preference):

1. The state is the child's home state—this means the child has resided in the state for the six previous months, or was residing in the state but is absent because a parent has removed the child from or retained the child outside of the state.

2. There are significant connections with people—such as teachers, doctors and grandparents—and substantial evidence in the state, concerning the child's care, protection, training and personal relationships.

3. The child is in the state and either has been abandoned or is in danger of being abused or neglected if sent back to the other state.

4. No other state can meet one of the above three tests, or a state can meet at least one of the tests but has declined to make a custody decision.

If a state cannot meet one of these tests, even if the child is present in the state, the courts of that state cannot make a custody award. Also, a parent who has wrongfully removed or retained a child in order to create a home state jurisdiction or significant connections will be denied custody. In the event more than one state meets the above standards, the law requires that only one state award custody. This means that once the first state makes a custody award, another state can neither make another "initial" award nor modify the existing order.

Having the same law in all states helps achieve consistency in the treatment of custody decrees. It also helps solve many of the problems created by kidnapping or disagreements over custody between parents living in different states.

BOARDING GATE 221
DEPARTURES ⇨

EXAMPLE: *Sam and Diane met and married in Missouri. They moved to Delaware where their child (Sam Jr.) was born. Sam, Diane and Junior lived in Delaware until Junior was ten. At that time, Sam took Junior to Missouri in an effort to divorce Diane and raise Junior himself. When Sam went to court in Missouri and requested custody, his request was denied because Delaware is Junior's home state, the state with which he has significant connections, and Sam removed Junior from Delaware in an effort to create home state jurisdiction in Missouri. (Diane should go to court in Delaware and request custody, even though Junior is in Missouri.)*

The Parental Kidnapping Prevention Act (28 U.S.C. §1738A and 42 U.S.C. §§654, 663) is a federal statute enacted in 1980 to address kidnapping by noncustodial parents and inconsistent child custody decisions made by state courts. The law provides for penalties for kidnapping and requires states to recognize and enforce the custody decisions of courts in other states, rather than make a second, and possibly inconsistent, decision.

F. When a Child Has Been Taken Out of the Country

"Comity" is a legal doctrine under which countries recognize and enforce each others' legal decrees. Under the Uniform Child Custody Jurisdiction Act (see Section E, above), courts in the U.S. must recognize properly-entered-into custody decrees of other nations. In turn, many other countries now recognize U.S. custody orders.

The International Child Abduction Remedies Act (12 U.S.C. §§601 through 610) is a federal U.S. law that enables the Hague Convention on the Civil Aspects of International Child Abduction to be followed in the U.S. This Hague Convention is an international agreement among the U.S. and about 30 other nations. Its purpose is to provide the prompt return of children wrongfully removed or retained in any participating country, and to ensure that the rights of custody and access under the law of one country are effectively respected in another. It addresses jurisdictional questions and provides common rules and procedures to determine child custody in a dispute that crosses international borders.

The Convention on the Rights of the Child has been signed by more than 170 nations, including the United States (although the U.S. Senate has not yet ratified it). This Convention describes an international commitment to children, and is relevant for children of divorced parents of different nationalities. Specifically, this convention provides that:

- both parents have responsibilities, rights and duties in common for the upbringing and development of their children (this concept is also supported by the Convention to End All Forms of Discrimination Against Women)
- all signatory nations have an obligation to support parents in providing their children the necessary protection and care to sustain a minimum quality of life
- children have the right to regular and sustained contact with both parents even across national borders
- decisions affecting children should preserve the best interests of the child, and
- children should be given a voice in the legal decisions which affect them.

Also, you can contact the U.S. State Department Office of Citizen and Counselor Services for help if a child is abducted from the U.S. to another country or a child is abducted from another country and brought to the U.S.

Finally, to prevent a child from being taken out of the U.S. without the custodial parent's consent, that parent can do the following:

- provide the State Department with a copy of a custody order showing who is the custodial parent, and
- request that the State Department withhold a child's passport unless it is requested by the custodial parent.

G. Custody and the IRS

The following tax benefits are available to parents to offset the cost of raising children:

- the earned income credit
- the child care credit
- medical expense deductions, and
- the head of household filing status.

Only a custodial parent is entitled to claim the child care tax credit. In general, employed custodial parents of a dependent child under the age of 13 are eligible for the credit for child care expenses incurred so that the parent can earn an income. As the custodial parent's income increases, however, the credit phases out.

Both parents can claim a deduction for medical expenses actually paid, but only if those medical expenses exceed 7.5% of their adjusted gross income. If your total medical expenses are high enough, you may want to allocate them to the lower wage earner so that that parent can take the deduction.

Only a parent with physical custody (meaning custody more than half of the time) can file as head of household. If the parents have joint legal and physical custody (and physical custody is divided 50-50), neither can file as head of household because the dependent child resides with neither parent for more than 50% of the year. If you have more than one minor child and share physical custody, you can specify your arrangement as 51% for one child with one parent and 51% for the other child with the other parent. Because each parent has a dependent child in the home more than 50% of the year, each parent can file as head of household. ∎

CHAPTER

11

Help Beyond the Book

Understanding and resolving child custody and parenting issues can be a challenge, but by reading this book and completing the various worksheets, you and the other parent have gone a long way toward building a successful separate parenting relationship. You now have more information, problem solving skills and insights than most parents who separate or divorce—and your children are the lucky beneficiaries of your efforts!

Many parents find that child custody and separate parenting issues are too difficult, emotional or technical to handle completely on their own. If this is true for you, consider taking any of following courses of action:

• do some legal research
• research nonlegal issues, or
• work with any number of professionals, including mediators, counselors, attorneys, arbitrators, paralegals or child custody evaluators.

A. Researching Legal Issues

This brief discussion tells you how to use a reference from this book to look up a state or federal statute or court decision.

1. Finding a Law Library

To look up state or federal statutes or court decisions, go to your county law library (usually in the county courthouse) or the library of a law school that is open to the public. (Most law school libraries open to the public are ones at state universities. A private university law library must let members of the public in, too, if that library is a "federal depository." This means that it houses all federal government documents.) Some, but not all, large public libraries also have collections of state or federal statutes; call before you go.

2. Finding Background Materials

Before turning to statutes and cases to answer a legal question on child custody, it is often helpful to use a background resource. This not only will help you narrow your question, but will also, more often than not, get you to the right statute and case as well.

Three excellent books for researching state laws on child custody and visitation are:

• *Handling Child Custody, Abuse, and Adoption Cases,* by Ann M. Haralambie (Shepard's/McGraw-Hill).
• *Child Custody and Visitation Law and Practice* (Matthew Bender).
• *Joint Custody and Shared Parenting,* edited by Jay Folberg (Guildford Press).

3. Finding Statutes

When you go to look up a statute, try to use what is called an "annotated" version of the statutes. Annotated statutes include not only the text of the statutes themselves, but also brief summaries of court cases and legal articles that have discussed each statute. After you look up a statute, you may well want to read the cases listed, too, to see how courts have construed the language of the statute.

Federal statutes. Federal statutes are organized by subject in a set of books called the United States Code (U.S.C.), which is available in probably every law library. Libraries often have one of both annotated versions of the U.S.C.— either United States Code Service (U.S.C.S.) or United States Code Annotated (U.S.C.A.). If you know the statute's common name or its citation, you should be able to find it easily.

EXAMPLE: You want to read some of the provisions of the International Child Abduction Remedies Act, 12 U.S.C. §601 and following. You would look in Title 12 of the U.S.C., U.S.C.S. or U.S.C.A. (the numbers are on the spine of the book) and find section 601. The statute begins with section 601 and includes many sections.

State statutes. State statutes, which fill many volumes, are often organized into "codes." Each code covers a separate area of law, such as Marriage and Divorce or Husbands and Wives. Although you probably won't have a citation from this book, you can look up the subject of the law you want to read in the index to the code or statutes.

4. Making Sure You Have the Most Recent Version of the Statute

Each year, state legislatures and Congress pass hundreds of new laws and change (amend) lots of existing ones. When you look up a statute, it's crucial that you get the most recent version.

To do that, always look for a pamphlet that is inserted in the back of the hardcover volume of statutes. It's called a pocket part, and it contains any changes made to the statute

in the hardcover book since the hardcover was printed. Pocket parts are updated and replaced every year—it's much cheaper than producing a whole new hardcover volume every year.

Look up the statute again in the pocket part. If there's no entry, that means the statute hasn't been changed as of the date the pocket part was printed. If there is an entry, it will tell you what language in the statute has been changed.

To check for changes that are even more recent—made since the pocket part was printed—you can check something called the Advance Legislative Service. It's a series of paperback pamphlets that contain the very latest statutory changes.

5. Finding Cases

If you want to look up a case (court decision) and have the citation, all you need to do is decipher those strange numbers and abbreviations.

The proper citation for the case holding that it is unconstitutional for a court to consider race in a custody dispute is *Palmore v. Sidoti*, 466 U.S. 429 (1984).

The name of the case includes the name of the plaintiff (Palmore) followed by a v. (meaning versus) followed by the defendant's name (Sidoti). 466 is the volume number where the case is found in the series called United States Reports (abbreviated by U.S.) at page 133. The case was decided in 1984.

Only cases decided by the U.S. Supreme Court are published in the United States Reports. (They are also published in the Supreme Court Reports.) Most of the cases you'll want to read will have been decided by courts within your state, and published in volumes entitled something like [name of your state] Reports or [name of your state] Appellate Reports, or possibly in a reporter for a region of the U.S., such as the Atlantic Reporter. A law librarian can help you figure out exactly which series of reports contain the case you are looking for.

6. Making Sure the Case Is Still Good Law

Judges don't go back and change the words of earlier decisions, like legislatures amend old statutes, but cases can still be profoundly affected by later court decisions. For example, any state's highest court, usually called the Supreme Court, has the power to overrule a decision of a trial court or an appellate court. If it does, the trial court or an appellate court's written decision no longer has any legal effect.

There are several ways to check to make sure a case you're relying on still represents valid law. The most common is to use a collection of books called *Shepard's*, which lets you compile a list of all later cases that mention the case you're interested in. Unfortunately, the *Shepard's* system is too complicated to explain here. If it's important to you, consult one of the legal research tools mentioned below.

7. More Legal Research

Legal research is a subject that can (and does) easily fill a whole book of its own. Here are some good resources if you want to delve further into the subject:

- For a thorough, how-to approach to finding answers to your legal questions, see *Legal Research: How to Find and Understand the Law*, by Stephen Elias and Susan Levinkind (Nolo Press, 1995).
- For an entertaining and informative video presentation of the basics of legal research, take a look at *Legal*

Research Made Easy: A Roadmap Through the Law Library, by Professor Robert Berring of the University of California-Berkeley (Nolo Press/LegalStar).

B. Researching Nonlegal Issues

The bibliography at the end of this chapter (Section E) lists a wide range of books and articles that discuss both the legal and nonlegal aspects of separate parenting. What follows are citations to books and articles that are particularly strong in certain areas. To find additional possible titles, browse in your public library or local bookstore.

1. Children and Divorce

• *Boys and Girls Book About Divorce,* by Richard A. Gardner, M.D. (Jason Aronson, Inc.)
• *Divorce and Your Child: Practical Suggestions for Parents,* by Sonja Goldstein, LL.B., & Albert Solnit, M.D. (Yale University Press)
• *Growing Up Divorced,* by Linda Bird Francke (Linden Press/Simon & Schuster)
• *How It Feels When Parents Divorce,* by Jill Krementz (Alfred A. Knopf)
• *Mediation and the Special-Child Family,* by Jeff Davidson (Jossey-Bass), particularly pages 79-83.
• *My Parents are Divorced Too,* by Bonnie Robson, M.D. (Everest House)

2. Conflict Resolution

• *Divorce and Decision Making: A Woman's Guide,* by Christina Robertson (Follett Publishing Company)
• *The Eight Essential Steps to Conflict Resolution,* by Dudley Weeks, Ph.D. (Jeremy Tarcher, Inc.)
• *Fighting Fair,* by Robert Coulson (The Free Press)
• *Getting To Yes: Negotiating Agreement Without Giving In,* by Roger Fisher & William Ury (Harvard Negotiation Project/Penguin Books)
• *A Guide To Divorce Mediation,* by Gary Friedman, J.D. (Workman Publishing)
• *You and Divorce Mediation,* by Richard H. Millen (Richard H. Millen)

3. Shared Custody

• *The Joint Custody Handbook: Creating Arrangements That Work,* by Miriam Galper Cohen (Running Press)

• *Mom's House, Dad's House: Making Shared Custody Work,* by Isolina Ricci, Ph.D. (Macmillan Publishing Co.)

4. Parenting Skills

• *Divorce and Your Child: Practical Suggestions for Parents,* by Sonja Goldstein, LL.B. & Albert Solnit, M.D. (Yale University Press)
• *Mom's House, Dad's House: Making Shared Custody Work,* by Isolina Ricci, Ph.D. (Macmillan Publishing Co.)

5. General Information About Divorce and Related Topics

• *Divorce and Child Custody,* by Deanna Peters & Richard L. Strohm (Layman's Law Guides)
• *Divorce and Decision Making: A Woman's Guide,* by Christina Robertson (Follett Publishing Company)
• *Effects of Divorce on the Visiting Father-Child Relationship,* by Judith S. Wallerstein, Ph.D., & Joan B. Kelly, Ph.D. (American Journal of Psychiatry, 1980)
• *Nolo's Pocket Guide to Family Law,* by Robin Leonard & Stephen Elias (Nolo Press)
• *Uncoupling: Turning Points in Intimate Relationships,* by Diane Vaughan (Oxford University Press)
• *You and Divorce Mediation,* by Richard H. Millen (Richard H. Millen)

C. Finding Professionals Who Can Help

Often, a human being can be great help if you hit a roadblock in negotiating or carrying out your parenting arrangements. Below are some suggestions on finding professionals who can help and what to expect of them. Because your relationship with any helping professional will be a deeply personal one, whenever possible, meet with two or three different people to see whose education, experience and style best match your needs.

Each section below (except Section 1 on mediators, which refers you to Chapter 6 for possible questions) includes a few questions you might use to structure your initial meeting with a professional. Use these questions only as one tool as you make a decision. More important in making your decision is your instinct, the professional's answers and any personal referrals you've received. The key is feeling comfortable working with the person. This means that you want someone who can:

- understand and identify with your general situation
- learn about your particular circumstances, and
- communicate effectively so you can make appropriate decisions.

1. Mediators

Mediators can help parents resolve separate parenting issues. The goal of mediation is for you and the other parent to develop an agreement which protects your children's best interests and is acceptable to both of you. Parents can use mediation to resolve some or all of their parenting issues or as a tool for reopening lines of communication and improving information exchanges. Detailed discussion on mediation and mediators is in Chapter 6.

2. Counselors, Therapists and Other Mental Health Professionals

Counseling, therapy or other mental health assistance can be an important part of dealing with separation, divorce and separate parenting issues—for parents and children. For example, if parents find that they cannot discuss any issue without arguing, dealing with the underlying feelings about themselves, each other or the end of the relationship can help. Information about the role of counseling is in Chapter 6.

Mental health professionals are fairly easy to find. You may be able to get referrals from friends or relatives, the local mental health department, a battered women's shelter, a school counselor, your religious advisor or your family physician. If none of those lead to possible candidates, you can look in your Yellow Pages directory under:

- Counseling
- Mental health
- Psychiatrists
- Psychologists
- Psychotherapists, or
- Social Workers.

When interviewing a mental health professional, you might ask questions such as the following:

- What kind of training have you had?
- What subjects or skills did your training emphasize?
- How much experience have you had in working with individuals or families going through divorce or separation?
- How much do you know about childhood development?

- How well versed are you in the effects of divorce and separation on children?
- Do you have any biases about how parenting issues should be settled, such as favoring custody with the mother or joint custody?
- What is your fee?
- How long do you think I will need to spend with you to resolve the issues we've talked about?

3. Child Custody Evaluators

Most child custody evaluators are mental health professionals, but may not advertise these evaluation services. To get a list of potential evaluators, you can contact your court, court-connected mediation program, local mental health department, a family law or matrimonial law attorney or the local bar association.

When interviewing a child custody evaluator, you might ask all but the last question listed in Section 2, above, for counselors, therapists and other mental health professionals, as well as the following:

- How long does a child custody evaluation take?
- What kind of information will you be looking for from me, the other parent and our children?
- How can I help make the evaluation process go smoothly?

4. Professionals With Training in Domestic Violence

Not every mental health professional or health care worker has the training and experience to understand and effectively deal with domestic violence issues. To find someone who does, be specific about what you are looking for. Many public mental health departments and all battered women's shelters have access to volunteer or paid staff members who know how to recognize and respond to families who have experienced domestic violence. Additional resources may be available through local police departments, hospitals and schools (especially in larger cities and metropolitan areas).

5. Professionals With Expertise in Dealing With Child Abuse

Assessing the nature and extent of child abuse or neglect, often requires special training and expertise. Depending on the type of abuse which is suspected, doctors can help detect physical assaults, and psychologists or pediatric psychiatrists can help to discover and document emotional, sexual or other forms of abuse.

To find a professional with training in these areas, contact:

- the child protection division of your local welfare department
- your local police department
- your doctor
- a hospital
- your religious advisor,
- the school your children attend, or
- a battered women's shelter.

6. Attorneys

If you choose to work with an attorney and you have read some or all of this book, you will probably want someone who is willing to work with you rather than take over your case. More and more family and matrimonial law attorneys offer their clients a large role in shaping their own cases. Nevertheless, choosing the right attorney for your particular case is critically important.

Traditional lawyering tends to be highly adversarial. But only a handful of cases merit this kind of attention. Most separate parenting issues need a cooperative problem-solving approach rather than a contest to assign blame, guilt and declare a "better" parent.

If you decide that you need an attorney's advice, you will be happier in that relationship if you first decide exactly what kind of help you need. For example, you may want:

- general information on certain issues of law
- information on how courts in your area tend to decide certain questions, or
- an analysis of what might happen if you took your case to trial.

Each question defines a slightly different role for your attorney. Shopping for legal assistance in this way can be discouraging, because many attorneys hesitate to give any advice without full authority over all aspects of the case. If you persevere, however, you'll find an attorney willing to work with you in the way you have defined, and you'll be very happy with the overall results.

Attorneys are very easy to find. You may be able to get referrals from friends or relatives, a battered women's shelter or a paralegal. If you are gay or lesbian, are from another country, a member of a religious or ethnic minority, have a physical disability or are in some other way considered a

minority, you need a lawyer particularly sensitive to your needs. Try contacting a local support group or legal organization for your community for names of possible attorneys. If none of those lead to candidates, you can contact your local bar association or look in your Yellow Pages directory.

Most important is that you find an attorney whose skills and experience are adequate, whose style is compatible with the job you want performed, and who will let you keep control over your case. Finding someone with a lot of family or matrimonial law experience will be attractive, but keep looking if that person opposes mediation (if you want to use it) or wants to take over your case entirely.

To find the right attorney for your situation, make a list of exactly what kind of help you want from an attorney, figure out how much you can afford and then interview two or three possible candidates. Start your initial meeting by explaining your needs and then by asking the following questions:

- Do you have any specialized training other than your legal education? (Some attorneys have advanced legal degrees, such as in tax law, which can be very helpful

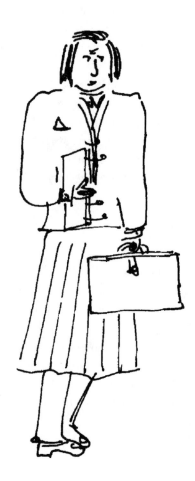

if you are going through a divorce; other attorneys are considered specialists in particular fields; still others have mediation training.)

- How many custody cases have you handled?
- How much do you know about childhood development?
- How well versed are you in the effects of divorce and separation on children?
- Do you have any biases about how parenting issues should be settled, such as favoring custody with the mother or joint custody?
- What legal issues do you anticipate will need resolving?
- How do you feel about resolving parenting disputes outside of court, such as through mediation or arbitration?
- How long do you think it will take to settle the issues we've discussed?
- What is your fee?

7. Legal Typing Services (Independent Paralegals)

Thirty years ago, people who didn't want to hire a lawyer to help with a legal problem had two choices: handle the problem themselves or don't handle it at all. Now, businesses known as "typing services" or "independent paralegals" exist in many places to assist people in filling out the forms necessary to complete their own legal work. Independent paralegals often can help in routine family law matters, including the preparation and filing of a separate parenting agreement in the appropriate court on the appropriate form.

Independent paralegals are very different from lawyers. They cannot give legal advice or represent you in court—by law, only lawyers can do those things. When you consult an independent paralegal, it will still be up to you to decide what steps to take in your case, and to gather the information needed to complete necessary court forms. Independent paralegals can, however:

- steer you to appropriate written instructions and legal information you need to do your own legal work
- provide the appropriate court forms, and
- type your papers in a format acceptable to a court.

The following statement, posted in Divorce Centers of California, a prominent typing service near San Francisco, summarizes its services well:

WE ARE NOT ATTORNEYS

We are pro per assistants. Attorneys represent people. We assist people to represent themselves. If you want someone to represent you, you will need to hire an attorney. If you want to "do it yourself," we can help. We believe that representing yourself is the only way to gain, and keep, control over your own life and your own legal problems. You don't need legal training to use the courts or manage your own legal affairs. You have a constitutional right to represent yourself without an attorney. Let us assist you!

A recommendation from someone who has used an independent paralegal is the best way to find a reputable one in your area. Failing that, services often advertise in classified sections of newspapers under Referral Services, usually immediately following attorneys. Also check the Yellow Pages under "divorce assistance" or "legal help." A local legal aid office may provide a reference, as will the occasional court clerk. Also, many offices advertise in local throwaway papers.

8. Arbitrators

Arbitration is fairly uncommon in custody and visitation cases, but might be considered to obtain access to specialized expertise. For example, parents with a special-needs child might ask a specialist to evaluate and decide (which is what an arbitrator does) a particularly difficult legal or physical custody issue. Arbitration is discussed in Chapter 6.

Several organizations offer arbitration services. Perhaps the best known is the American Arbitration Association. You can find a local chapter in the telephone directory, or you contact the national headquarters, listed below, for referrals to local providers.

American Arbitration Association
140 West 51st Street
New York, NY 10020-1203
Voice: (212) 484-4100
FAX: (212) 307-4387

The Conflict Resolution Center, listed below, publishes a directory of all kinds of ADR (Alternative or Appropriate Dispute Resolution) service providers, including arbitrators.

Conflict Resolution Center, Inc.
2205 E. Carson Street
Pittsburgh, PA 15203-2107
Voice: (412) 481-5559
FAX: (412) 481-5601
e-mail: crcii@igc.apc.org

The Society of Professionals In Dispute Resolution (SPIDR) is a national association of ADR service providers, including arbitrators. SPIDR has chapters in every state. You can contact a state or local chapter (look in a telephone directory) or the national headquarters:

Society of Professionals In Dispute Resolution
815 15th Street NW, Suite 530
Washington DC 20005
Voice: (202) 783-7277
FAX: (202) 783-7281

In addition to these national organizations, arbitrators are listed in the Yellow Pages directory under "Arbitration." You might also get referrals to arbitrators from a community mediation program, your court, your local mental health agency or the local bar association.

D. Additional Resources

Bill of Rights for Children of Divorce, by Vance Packard, 87 Mill Road, New Canaan, CT 06840. Vance Packard is a severe critic of the effects of divorce on children, and a staunch advocate of the child's right to remain whole in spite of his or her parent's divorce. His views are contained in his "Bill of Rights for Children of Divorce," which is printed below. Mr. Packard has given permission for parents to tear this out and keep it for their own use.

BILL OF RIGHTS FOR CHILDREN OF DIVORCE

1. Children of divorce are entitled to parents who set aside at least 20 minutes every month to discuss, in person or on the phone, the progress and problems of the children—and only the children. There should be no recriminations about any other topic, such as money. The children's schoolwork, health, mental state, activities, and apparent reaction to the divorce should be the focus of such talks.

2. Children of divorce are entitled to parents who go out to dinner together with them, if desired by the child, on their birthdays or other important holidays. The parents should also both go to school events important to the children.

3. Children are entitled to have separated parents who do not belittle the other parent in front of the children.

4. Children of divorce are entitled to have parents who refrain from any action that would seem to force the children to take sides.

5. Children of divorce are entitled to be free from any sense of pressure from either parent to serve as informants about the ex-partner's spending, dating, or other activities. If children freely choose to chat about the other parent, that is another matter.

6. Children of divorce are entitled to have complete freedom to phone either parent. If distances are involved, the calls will be collect. The children's parents will also agree that it is permissible for the noncustodial parent to call his or her children at least once a week.

7. Children of divorce are entitled to have parents who agree to notify each other in all emergencies or important events involving the children.

8. Children of divorce are entitled to have parents who by agreement are civil and avoid recriminations when they are in the presence of the child.

1. National Support Organizations

Step Family Foundation
(Assists step families)
333 West End Ave
New York, NY 10023
Voice: (212) 877-3244
FAX: (212) 362-7030

ABA Center on Children and the Law
(Studies how courts deal with children and children's issues)
1800 M Street NW, Suite 200 South
Washington DC 20036
Voice: (202) 331-2250
FAX: (202) 331-2225

National Center for Youth and the Law
(Studies how courts and legislatures deal with children's issues)
114 Sansome St., Suite #900
San Francisco, CA 94104
Voice: (415) 543-3307
FAX: (415) 956-9024

Fathers for Equal Rights of America
(Advocacy for fathers as involved and custodial parents)
General information message tape: (810) 354-3080
Telephone Counseling: (900) 225-3080

Joint Custody Association
(Advocacy for joint custody arrangements and assistance to joint custodial parents)
10606 Wilkins Ave.
Los Angeles, CA 90024
Voice:(310) 475-5352

Equality Nationwide for Unwed Fathers
(Advocacy and assistance for unwed fathers)
10606 Wilkins Ave.
Los Angeles, Ca 90024
Voice:(310) 475-5352

Kayama
(Assistance with obtaining a Jewish divorce)
1202 Avenue J
Brooklyn, NY 11230
Voice: (718) 692-1876
FAX: (718) 258-7042

Childfind Mediation Program
(Assistance for parents who have taken or are considering taking their child in violation of existing court orders)
P.O. Box 277
New Paltz, NY 12561
Voice: 1 (800) AWAYOUT
FAX: (914) 255-5706
and
11 Park Place
New York, NY 10007
Voice: (212) 766-4030
Voice to receive FAX information: (818) 791-0578 Box 777

Lambda Legal Defense and Education Fund
(Legal informational and referral for gay and lesbian parents)
666 Broadway
New York, NY 10012
Voice: (212) 995-8585
FAX: (212) 995-2306
and
606 South Olive Street, Suite 580
Los Angeles, CA 90014
Voice: (213) 629-2728
FAX: (213) 629-9022
and
17 E. Monroe Street, Suite 212
Chicago, IL 60603
Voice: (312) 759-8112

Custody Action for Lesbian Mothers
P.O. Box 281
Narbeth, PA 19072
(215) 667-7508

Gay & Lesbian Advocates & Defenders
(Legal informational and referral for gay and lesbian parents)
P.O. Box 218
Boston, MA 02112
Voice: (617) 426-1350

Lesbian Mother's National Defense Fund
(Fundraising and advocacy for lesbian mothers)
P.O. Box 21567
Seattle, WA 98111
Voice: (206) 325-2643

National Center for Lesbian Rights
(Legal informational and referral for gay and lesbian parents)
870 Market Street, Suite 570
San Francisco, CA 94102
Voice: (415) 392-6257
and
462 Broadway, Suite 500A
New York, NY 10013
Voice: (212) 343-9589

2. Domestic Violence Resources

Domestic violence tends to carry forward from one generation to the next. Do yourselves and your children a favor—get help now and try to break the cycle.

You can get a referral to professionals with experience in domestic violence from many sources, including the following:

- battered women's shelters
- local mental health departments
- hospitals
- doctors
- school counselors
- religious institutions
- police departments
- social service agencies
- women's groups, and
- community organizations.

Many books and videos provide real and practical insights into managing anger and frustration more productively. A librarian, local mental health department or private practice counselor, psychologist or psychiatrist may be able to suggest materials or offer information about how to help your children deal with the issues.

3. Alcohol or Drug Abuse Organizations

Perhaps the best-known programs for alcohol and drug abuse are Alcoholics Anonymous, Al-Anon and Narcotics Anonymous. To find a local group, contact one of the national organizations as follows:

Alcoholics Anonymous
Box 459 Grand Central Station
New York, NY 10163
Voice: (212) 870-3400
FAX: (212) 870-3003

Al-Anon Family Groups
(For friends and families of alcoholics)
1372 Broadway
New York, NY 10018
Voice: (212) 302-7240
FAX: (212) 869-3757

Narcotics Anonymous
16155 Wyandotte St.
Van Nuys, CA 91406
Voice: (818) 359-0084
FAX: (818) 785-0123

Other ways to find alcohol or drug treatment programs or support groups include contacting your local mental health department, police department, hospital, family physician or library or consulting your Yellow Pages directory under the following headings:

- Alcoholism information and treatment, or
- Drug abuse and addiction.

E. Bibliography

- Ahrons, Constance R., Ph.D., *The Good Divorce*, Harper Collins Publishers, 1994.
- Brown, Neil D., Samis, Michelle D.C., "The Application of Structural Family Therapy in Developing the Binuclear Family," Mediation Quarterly, 1987, pp. 51–69.
- Bryant, Suzanne, "Mediation for Lesbian and Gay Families," *Mediation Quarterly*, 1992, pp. 391–395.
- Burbano, Maria Elena, Cordona, Ray, *Cross-cultural Issues In Mediation, Mediation Quarterly*, 1992.
- Campbell, Linda E.G., Johnston, Janet R., "Multifamily Mediation: The Use of Groups to Resolve Child Custody Disputes, *Mediation Quarterly*," 1987, pp. 137-162.
- Charlesworth, Stephanie, "The Acceptance of Family Mediation in Australia," *Mediation Quarterly*, 1991.
- Cloke, Kenneth, "Shared Custody: A Case Study in Mediation, *Mediation Quarterly*," 1988, pp. 31–35.

- Cohen, Miriam Galper, *The Joint Custody Handbook: Creating Arrangements That Work,* Running Press, 1991.
- Corcoran, Kathleen O'Connell, Melamed, James C., "From Coercion to Empowerment: Spousal Abuse and Mediation," *Mediation Quarterly,* 1990, pp. 303–316.
- Coulson, Robert, *Fighting Fair,* The Free Press, 1983.
- Davidson, Jeff, *Mediation and the Special-Child Family, Mediation Quarterly,* 1987, pp. 79–83.
- Davis, Albie M., Salem, Richard A., "Dealing With Power Imbalances in the Mediation of Interpersonal Disputes," *Mediation Quarterly,* 1984, pp. 17–26.
- Edelman, Joel, Crain, Mary Beth, *The Tao of Negotiation,* Harper Business Press, 1993.
- Emery, Robert E., Jackson, Joanne A., "The Charlottesville Mediation Project: Mediated and Litigated Child Custody Disputes," *Mediation Quarterly,* 1989, pp. 3–18.
- Erickson, Stephen K., Erickson, Marilyn S. McKnight, "Dan and Linda: A Typical Divorce Mediation Case" *Mediation Quarterly,* 1988, pp. 3–21.
- Fisher, Roger, Ury, William, *Getting To Yes: Negotiating Agreement Without Giving In,* Harvard Negotiation Project, Penguin Books, 1981.
- Francke, Linda Bird, *Growing Up Divorced,* Linden Press/Simon & Schuster, 1983.
- Friedman, Gary J., J.D., *A Guide To Divorce Mediation,* Workman Publishing, 1993.
- Gadlin, Howard, Ouellette, Patricia A., "Mediation Milanese: An Application of Systemic Family Therapy Approach to Family Mediation," *Mediation Quarterly,* 1987, pp. 101–118.
- Gardner, Richard A., M.D., *Boys and Girls Book About Divorce,* Jason Aronson, Inc., 1983.
- Garwood, Fiona, "Divorce and Conciliation In Sweden and Scotland," *Mediation Quarterly,* 1991, pp. 293–301.
- Goldstein, Sonja, LL.B., Solnit, Albert, M.D., *Divorce and Your Child: Practical Suggestions for Parents,* Yale University Press, 1984.
- Haynes, John M., "John and Mary: Sharing Parenting After Divorce," *Mediation Quarterly,* 1988, pp. 23–29.
- Haynes, John M., "The Process of Negotiations," *Mediation Quarterly,* 1983, pp. 75–92.
- Heitler, Susan M., Ph.D., *From Conflict to Resolution: Strategies for Diagnosis and Treatment of Distressed Individuals, Couples and Families,* W.W. Norton & Co., 1990.
- Hurt, Barbara J., "Gentle Jeopardy: The Further Endangerment of Battered Women and Children in Custody Mediation," *Mediation Quarterly,* 1990, pp. 317–330.
- Ihara, Toni, Warner, Ralph, *The Living Together Kit,* Nolo Press, 1990.
- Kaplan, Nancy M., The Development and Operation of the Northwest Mediation Service, *Mediation Quarterly,* 1984, pp. 47–58.
- Kelly, Joan B., "Mediation and Psychotherapy: Distinguishing the Differences," *Mediation Quarterly,* 1983, pp. 33–44.
- Kirkpatrick, Gary, "The Good, The Bad, The Indifferent," *Mediation Quarterly,* 1988, pp. 37–45.
- Kirkpatrick, Martha, M.D., Smith, Catherine, Roy, Ron, M.D., *Lesbian Mothers and Their Children: A Comparative Survey,* American Orthopsychiatric Association, Inc., 1981.
- Krementz, Jill, *How It Feels When Parents Divorce,* Alfred A. Knopf, 1984.
- Leitch, M. Laurie, "The Politics Of Compromise: A Feminist Perspective On Mediation," *Mediation Quarterly,* 1987, pp. 163–175.
- Lemmon, John Allen, Ed.D., "Dimensions and Practice of Divorce Mediation," *Mediation Quarterly,* 1983.
- Leonard, Robin, Elias, Stephen, *Nolo's Pocket Guide to Family Law,* Nolo Press, 1994.
- LeResche, Diane, "Comparison of the American Mediation Process With A Korean-American Harmony Restoration Process," *Mediation Quarterly,* 1992, pp. 323–339.
- Levy, Bert, *Trust—The Main Ingredient for a Successful Mediation,* Bancroft Whitney, 1993.
- Lutker, Eric R., Ph.D., Wand, Carl F., Esq., *Do It Yourself Divorce,* The Forms Man, 1992.
- Maccoby, Eleanor E., Mnookin, Robert H., *Dividing the Child: Social and Legal Dilemmas of Custody,* Harvard Press, 1992.
- Maxwell, David, "Gender Differences in Mediation Style and Their Impact on Mediator Effectiveness," *Mediation Quarterly,* 1992, pp. 353–364.
- Mayer, Bernard, "Mediation in Child Protection Cases: The Impact of Third-Party Intervention on Parental Compliance Attitudes," *Mediation Quarterly,* 1989, pp. 89–106.
- McIsaac, Hugh, *Toward a Classification of Child Custody Disputes: An Application of Family Systems Theory, Mediation Quarterly,* 1987, pp. 39–50.
- Mehren, Elizabeth, "Lesbian Mothers: Two New Studies Shatter Stereotypes," *Los Angeles Times,* June 1, 1983.
- Melton, Gary, "Families and the Courts in the Twenty-first Century," University of Nebraska, 1992.

- Millen, Richard H., *You and Divorce Mediation*, Richard H. Millen, 1991.
- Miller, Brian, "Gay Fathers and Their Children," *The Family Coordinator*, 1979.
- National Center for State Courts, *National Symposium on Court-Connected Dispute Resolution Research*, State Justice Institute, 1994.
- Oshiro, Donna A., O'Donnell, Clifford R., *A Culturally Competent Legal System: Cultural Factors in Family Court Cases in Hawaii*, University of Hawaii, 1992.
- O'Toole, Kathleen, "Joint Custody Can Work," *Academy of Family Mediation News* #10.4, 1992.
- Pagelow, Mildred Daley, "Effects of Domestic Violence on Children and Their Consequences for Custody and Visitation Agreements," *Mediation Quarterly*, 1990, pp. 347–363.
- Peters, Deanna, Strohm, Richard L., *Divorce and Child Custody*, Layman's Law Guides, 1993.
- Plesent, Emanuel, "Mediation for Reconciliation," *Mediation Quarterly*, 1988, pp. 47–50.
- Ricci, Isolina, Ph.D., *Mom's House, Dad's House: Making Shared Custody Work*, Macmillan Publishing Co., 1980.
- Robertson, Christina, *Divorce and Decision Making: A Woman's Guide*, Follett Publishing Company, 1980.
- Robson, Bonnie, M.D., *My Parents Are Divorced Too*, Everest House, 1980.
- Rogers, Susan J., "The Dynamics of Conflict Behavior in a Mediated Dispute," *Mediation Quarterly*, 1987, pp. 61–71.
- Samis, Michelle D.C., Saposnek, Donald T., "Parent-Child Relationships in Family Mediation: A Synthesis of Views," *Mediation Quarterly*, 1987.
- Saposnek, Donald T., "Aikido: A Systems Model for Maneuvering in Mediation," *Mediation Quarterly*, 1987, pp. 119–136.
- Saposnek, Donald T., "Strategies in Child Custody Mediation: A Family Systems Approach," *Mediation Quarterly*, 1983, pp. 29–54.
- Saposnek, Donald T., "The Value of Children in Mediation: A Cross-Cultural Perspective," *Mediation Quarterly*, 1991, pp. 325–342.
- Sargent, George, Moss, Bleema, "Eriksonian Approaches in Family Therapy and Mediation," *Mediation Quarterly*, 1987, pp. 87–100.
- Sherman, Ed, *Practical Divorce Solutions*, Nolo Press Occidental, 1994.
- Stern, Marilyn, Van Slyck, Michael R., Newland, Lori M, "Adolescent Development and Family Dynamics: Delineating a Knowledge Base for Family Mediation," *Mediation Quarterly*, pp. 307–322.
- Stuart, Richard B., Jacobson, Barbara, "Principles of Divorce Mediation: A Social Learning Theory Approach," *Mediation Quarterly*, 1987.
- Vaughan, Diane, *Uncoupling: Turning Points in Intimate Relationships*, Oxford University Press, 1986.
- Walker, Janet A., *"Family Mediation in England: Strategies for Gaining Acceptance," Mediation Quarterly*, 1991.
- Wallerstein, Judith S., Ph.D., "Psychodynamic Perspectives on Family Mediation," *Mediation Quarterly*, 1987, pp. 7–21.
- Wallerstein, Judith S., Ph.D., "The Impact of Divorce on Children," *Psychiatric Clinics of North America*, 1980.
- Wallerstein, Judith S., Ph.D., "Children and Divorce," *Pediatrics in Review*, 1980.
- Wallerstein, Judith S., Ph.D., Kelly, Joan B., Ph.D., "Effects of Divorce on the Visiting Father-Child Relationship," *American Journal of Psychiatry*, 1980.
- Weeks, Dudley, Ph.D., *The Eight Essential Steps to Conflict Resolution*, Jeremy Tarcher, Inc., 1992.
- Yahm, Howard, "Divorce Mediation: A Psychoanalytic Perspective," *Mediation Quarterly*, 1984, pp. 59–63.
- Zaidel, Susan, "Challenges Facing the Development of Family Mediation in Israel," *Mediation Quarterly*, 1991, pp. 281–292. ■

Appendix: Tear-Out Forms

Worksheet 1: Describe Your Child

Worksheet 2: Describe Your Relationship With Your Child

Workshhet 3: Adding the Details

Worksheet 4: Checklist of Issues for Your Parenting Agreement

Parenting Agreement

WORKSHEET 1: DESCRIBE YOUR CHILD

Child's name: _____

1. What kind of person is this child?

   _____

   _____

2. What makes this child special?

   _____

   _____

3. How does this child like the current parenting arrangements?

   _____

   _____

   _____

   _____

4. How has this child's behavior changed since the separation or divorce?

   _____

   _____

   _____

   _____

5. Has this child expressed any preferences regarding the future?

   _____

   _____

   _____

6. How does this child react to change?

   _____

   _____

7. What makes change easier for this child to accept?

   _____

   _____

8. How does this child let you know that something is wrong?

   _____

   _____

   _____

9. Who else is important in this child's life?

   _____

   _____

WORKSHEET 2: DESCRIBE YOUR RELATIONSHIP WITH YOUR CHILD

Child's name: _____

1. What do you and this child like to do together?

   _____

   _____

   _____

2. What are your plans and wishes for this child's future?

   _____

   _____

   _____

3. What do you think are the most important things for this child to achieve?

   _____

   _____

   _____

4. How do you and this child handle and resolve conflict?

   _____

   _____

   _____

5. How do you handle discipline with this child?

   _____

   _____

   _____

6. How did you share parenting responsibilities and time with this child during the time you were married or living together?

   _____

   _____

   _____

7. How do you and the other parent share parenting responsibilities and time with this child now?

   _____

   _____

   _____

   _____

8. Are you happy with the current arrangements? (Please explain)

   _____

   _____

   _____

   _____

9. Is this child happy with the current arrangements? (Please explain)

_____

_____

_____

10. If changes are in order, what would you suggest?

_____

_____

_____

_____

_____

_____

WORKSHEET 3: ADDING THE DETAILS

1. List of existing court documents, orders or agreements: (Note that the terms listed here might be different in your state. See Chapter 11 for the terms used in your state.)

   _____

   _____

   _____

   _____

2. Parent's name, occupation and work schedule.

   _____

   _____

3. Schedule of children's activities (such as school, religious training and after-school activities).

   _____

   _____

   _____

   _____

4. Children's special needs or interests.

   _____

   _____

   _____

5. Religion.

   _____   _____

   _____   _____

6. Where do you live now?

   _____

   _____

7. Do you have any plans to relocate from the area? (Please explain)

   _____

   _____

   _____

8. Do you have any plans for remarriage?

   _____

   _____

9. Are there any adult relatives or friends with whom the children should or should not have close contact?

   _____

   _____

   _____

10. Counseling for children.

_____
_____
_____

11. Counseling for parents.

_____
_____
_____

12. Do you want to address domestic violence issues in your Parenting Agreement? If yes, why?

_____
_____
_____
_____

13. Do you want to address the use or abuse of drugs or alcohol in your Parenting Agreement? If yes, how do you think these issues should be handled in your parenting agreement?

_____
_____
_____
_____

14. Do you have any special concerns about your parenting arrangements?

_____
_____
_____

15. Do you have any special concerns about your relationship with the other parent?

_____
_____
_____
_____

WORKSHEET 4: CHECKLIST OF ISSUES FOR YOUR PARENTING AGREEMENT

1. Existing court documents, orders or agreements which must be changed to accommodate your parenting agreement.

   _____
   _____
   _____
   _____

2. Existing agreements to consider while negotiating this parenting agreement.

   _____
   _____

3. Steps you will have to take to resolve legal or religious issues such as divorce, legal separation, annulment, etc.

   _____
   _____
   _____

4. Any concerns or recommendations made by a counselor, school, therapist or other interested adult regarding your children's emotional, spiritual or physical well-being.

   _____
   _____
   _____
   _____

5. Each child's current relationship with each parent.

   _____
   _____
   _____
   _____
   _____
   _____
   _____

6. Each child's feelings, reactions or concerns about separation or divorce.

   _____
   _____
   _____
   _____
   _____
   _____
   _____

7. Changes you think would be good in each child's current relationship with each parent.

_____

_____

_____

_____

_____

_____

8. Changes that may be necessary in each child's current relationship with each parent.

_____

_____

_____

_____

_____

9. Current problem areas for children.

_____

_____

_____

_____

_____

10. Current areas of conflict between the parents.

_____

_____

_____

_____

_____

11. Changes either parent would like to see in current parenting relationship.

_____

_____

_____

_____

12. Times when either parent is available to care for children: _____

_____

13. Times when only _____ is available to care for children: _____

14. Times when only _____ is available to care for children: _____

15. Other adults children will be spending time with.

_____

_____

16. Adults or minors the children should not spend time with (or be alone with).

_____

_____

17. Any problems with violence, abuse or neglect that would have to be accommodated.

_____

_____

_____

_____

_____

_____

_____

18. Other comments or issues to be included.

_____

_____

_____

_____

_____

_____

_____

_____

_____

_____

_____

PARENTING AGREEMENT

A. Parties. The following is a mutually acceptable agreement between _____ _____ and _____ _____ regarding how we will share parenting responsibilities for our children [list names]:

_____   _____

_____   _____

_____   _____

_____

B. How Long this Agreement Lasts. The term of this agreement is _____ [period of time].

If this is a temporary agreement, we will negotiate a new agreement on or before _____ [date].

C. Terms of the Agreement.

#_____   **Medical, Dental and Vision Care**

_____ Our children's medical, dental, and vision care providers will be [choose one]:

_____ We will use only the following health care providers:

_____ [medical].

_____ [dental].

_____ [vision].

_____ We will each choose health care providers. We will exchange names, addresses, phone numbers and releases so that our providers can share records and information.

_____ _____ [parent] will see to it that our children receive their routine care.

_____ Our children's special health care needs will be met as follows [specify]:

_____

_____

_____

_____ In a medical emergency [choose one]:

_____ Either parent may seek medical treatment and must inform the other parent as soon as possible thereafter.

_____ Either parent may seek medical treatment, except for the following procedures or interventions:

_____

_____

_____ _____ [parent] is the only person who may seek medical treatment.

_____ If our children develop an on-going medical condition or have other special health care concerns, we will assure consistency in their care as follows [choose all that apply]:

_____ We will share all medical records.

_____ We will include the medications with our children as they travel between our homes.

_____ We will each fill all prescriptions and dispense the medications when caring for our children.

_____ We will exchange written instructions on needed care.

_____ We will each keep whatever physical supports or enhancements our children need in our home.

_____ Our children will receive the following dental care [specify]:

_____

_____

_____

_____ Our children will receive the following vision care [specify]:

_____

_____

_____

_____ We further agree that [specify]:

_____

_____

_____

_____

#_____ **Psychiatric and Other Mental Health Care**

_____ Our children may undergo psychiatric or other mental health care as follows [choose all that apply]:

    _____ If either parent feels it is necessary.

    _____ If it is recommended by a school counselor or other health care provider.

    _____ Only if we agree.

    _____ Only if it is made available through the school.

    _____ Only if it is available at low or no cost to us.

_____ Either of us may undergo psychiatric or other mental health care as follows [choose all that apply]:

    _____ If either parent feels it is necessary.

    _____ If it is recommended by a school counselor or other health care provider.

    _____ Only if we agree.

    _____ Only if it is made available through the school.

    _____ Only if it is available at low or no cost to us.

_____ Our children's other mental health issues, such as _____ [specify], will be addressed as follows [specify]:

_____

_____

_____

_____

#_____ **Education**

_____ Our children will attend [choose one]:

    _____ public school.

    _____ private school.

    _____ home school.

_____ We will pay for any private or home school as follows [specify]:

_____

_____

_____

_____ Any decision to change schools will be made as follows [choose all that apply]:

    _____ If we agree.

    _____ After consulting our children.

    _____ After consulting with _____ [parent].

    _____ Only _____ [parent] may change our children's enrollment in a particular school.

_____ Any decisions to support our children's special educational needs or talents will be made as follows [choose all that apply]:

    _____ If we agree.

    _____ After consulting our children.

    _____ After consulting with _____ [parent].

    _____ Only _____ [parent] may change our children's enrollment in a particular school.

_____ We will participate in parent associations as follows [choose one]:

    _____ Either parent may participate.

    _____ Only one parent may participate at a time.

    _____ _____ [parent] will participate.

_____ We will participate in the classroom as follows [choose one]:
    _____ Either parent may participate.
    _____ Only one parent may participate at a time.
    _____ _____ [parent] will participate.

_____ We will participate in parent-chaperoned events as follows [choose one]:
    _____ Either parent may participate.
    _____ Only one parent may participate at a time.
    _____ _____ [parent] will participate.

_____ We will attend parent-teacher or other school conferences as follows [choose one]:
    _____ Both will attend.
    _____ Each will schedule a meeting with the teacher or other school official.
    _____ _____ [parent] will attend and will inform the other of the matters discussed.
    _____ _____ [parent] will attend and will not inform the other of the matters discussed.

_____ Any emergency contact information needed by a school will be completed as follows [choose one]:
    _____ We both will be listed in the following order:
    _____
    _____
    _____ Only _____ [parent] will be listed.
    _____ Others to be listed will be [list names]:
    _____
    _____

_____ Good school performance means:
_____

We will encourage good school performance as follows [choose all that apply]:
    _____ After discussion and agreement.
    _____ After consultation with our children.
    _____ With the following rewards:
    _____
    _____

_____ Poor school performance means:
_____

We will discourage poor school performance by [specify]:
_____
_____
_____

_____ Our children [check one] ☐ may ☐ may not attend sex education classes at school.
    _____ _____ [parent] will to notify the school of this decision.
_____ Our children's post-secondary education will be paid for as follows [specify]:
_____
_____

_____ Any decisions regarding our children's options for post-secondary education will be made as follows
[choose all that apply]:
    _____ By agreement between parents and children.
    _____ Based on the children's interest and ability to be accepted at a particular school.
    _____ Based on what we can afford.
    _____ Other [specify]:
    _____
    _____

_____ We further agree that [specify]:
_____
_____

#_____ **Surname**

_____ Our children's surname is _____

Any decision to change that surname will be made as follows [choose all that apply]:

_____ Our children will keep this surname until they become legal adults.

_____ Our children may choose their surname.

_____ Our children may choose their surname after age _____.

_____ We will discuss and agree on any change of surname.

_____ _____ [parent] has the authority to change our children's surname.

_____ We further agree that [specify]:

_____

_____

_____

_____

#_____ **Religious Training**

_____ Our children's religious beliefs and training will be as follows [choose all that apply]:

_____ Our children will be raised _____ [specify].

_____ Our children will be taught about both of our religions: _____

and _____

_____ Our children may choose their religious training as long as it generally conforms to the principles of the

_____ religion.

_____ Our children may choose their religious training. _____ [parent]

will supervise such training.

_____ We further agree that [specify]:

_____

_____

_____

_____

#_____ **International Travel and Passports**

_____ Our children may obtain a passport under the following conditions [choose one]:

_____ Either parent may obtain a passport if it is necessary for travel.

_____ Either parent may obtain a passport, but our children may travel out of the country only if the other parent approves of the itinerary and the dates of the trip.

_____ Either parent may obtain a passport, but our children may not travel out of the country unless _____ [adult's name] travels with them.

_____ A passport may not be issued to our children under any circumstances.

_____ Only _____ may obtain a passport for the children.

_____ We further agree that [specify]:

_____

_____

_____

_____

#_____ **Driving and Owning a Car, Motorcycle or Off-Road Vehicle**

_____ We will permit our children to own a car.

_____ We will not permit our children to own a car.

_____ We will permit our children to drive a car under the following conditions [choose all that apply]:

_____ After completing a certified training course.

_____ With the consent of _____ [one or both parents].

_____ With adult supervision.

_____ Driving only on unpaved roads.

_____ Using a family car.

_____ After buying a car.

_____ After being given a car.

_____ After paying their own car insurance.

_____ They must pay for any tickets received while operating the car.

_____ We will permit our children to own a motorcycle.

_____ We will not permit our children to own a motorcycle.

_____ We will permit our children to drive a motorcycle under the following conditions [choose all that apply]:

    _____ After completing a certified training course.

    _____ With the consent of _____ [one or both parents].

    _____ With adult supervision.

    _____ Driving only on unpaved roads.

    _____ Using a family motorcycle.

    _____ After buying a motorcycle.

    _____ After being given a motorcycle.

    _____ After paying their own motorcycle insurance.

    _____ They must pay for any tickets received while operating the motorcycle.

_____ We will permit our children to own an off-road vehicle.

_____ We will not permit our children to own an off-road vehicle.

_____ We will permit our children to drive an off-road vehicle under the following conditions [choose all that apply]:

    _____ After completing a certified training course.

    _____ With the consent of _____ [one or both parents].

    _____ With adult supervision.

    _____ Driving only on unpaved roads.

    _____ Using a family off-road vehicle.

    _____ After buying an off-road vehicle.

    _____ After being given an off-road vehicle.

    _____ After paying their own off-road vehicle insurance.

    _____ They must pay for any tickets received while operating the off-road vehicle.

_____ We further agree that [specify]:

_____

_____

_____

#_____ **Military Service**

_____ Our children may enter military service if they are under the legal age as follows [choose all that apply]:

    _____ If they so choose.

    _____ In the event of a war.

    _____ If they are at least age _____ .

    _____ If we both agree.

    _____ If _____ [parent] consents.

    _____ Never.

_____ We further agree that [specify]:

_____

_____

_____

#_____ **Allowing Underage Marriage**

_____ Our children may marry if they are under the legal age as follows [choose all that apply]:

    _____ If they so choose.

    _____ In the event of a pregnancy.

    _____ If they are at least age _____ .

    _____ If we both agree.

    _____ If _____ [parent] consents.

    _____ Never.

_____ We further agree that [specify]:

_____
_____
_____

#_____ **Insurance**

_____ Our children's medical insurance will be provided as follows [choose all that apply]:

    _____ We both will obtain coverage if it is available through an employer at low or no cost.

    _____ We will share the costs of any uncovered expenses as follows [specify]:

_____
_____

_____ _____ [parent]

will obtain coverage up to $ _____ under the following conditions [choose all that apply]:

    _____ Type of coverage: _____

    _____ Named beneficiaries: _____

    _____ Insurance claims submitted by: _____ [parent].

_____ Our children's dental insurance will be provided as follows [choose all that apply]:

    _____ We both will obtain coverage if it is available through an employer at low or no cost.

    _____ We will share the costs of any uncovered expenses as follows [specify]:

_____
_____

_____ _____ [parent]

will obtain coverage up to $ _____ under the following conditions [choose all that apply]:

    _____ Type of coverage: _____

    _____ Named beneficiaries: _____

    _____ Insurance claims submitted by: _____ [parent].

_____ Our children's vision care will be provided as follows [choose all that apply]:

    _____ We both will obtain coverage if it is available through an employer at low or no cost.

    _____ We will share the costs of any uncovered expenses as follows [specify]:

_____
_____

_____ _____ [parent]

will obtain coverage up to $ _____ under the following conditions [choose all that apply]:

    _____ Type of coverage: _____

    _____ Named beneficiaries: _____

    _____ Insurance claims submitted by: _____ [parent].

_____ We will obtain life insurance coverage as follows [choose all that apply]:

    _____ We both will obtain coverage if it is available through an employer at low or no cost.

    _____ We will share the costs of any uncovered expenses as follows [specify]:

_____
_____

_____ _____ [parent]

will obtain coverage up to $ _____ under the following conditions [choose all that apply]:

    _____ Type of coverage: _____

    _____ Named beneficiaries: _____

    _____ Insurance claims submitted by: _____ [parent].

_____ We will obtain _____ insurance as follows [choose all that apply]:

    _____ We both will obtain coverage if it is available through an employer at low or no cost.

_____ We will share the costs of any uncovered expenses as follows [specify]:

_____

_____

_____ _____ [parent]

will obtain coverage up to $ _____ under the following conditions [choose all that apply]:

_____ Type of coverage: _____

_____ Named beneficiaries: _____

_____

_____ Insurance claims submitted by: _____ [parent].

#_____ **Making Decisions**

_____ Choose all that apply:

_____ Whenever possible, we will discuss the issues and attempt to reach an agreement.

_____ We both will make an effort to remain aware of our children's interests, activities, school performance and overall health.

_____ _____ [parent] will make an effort to keep _____ [other parent] aware of our children's interests, activities, school performance and overall health.

_____ _____ [parent], as the primary caretaker will be responsible to make [most/all] of the decisions on behalf of our children and will inform _____ [other parent] as soon as possible thereafter.

_____ _____ [parent], as the primary caretaker, will be responsible to make all of the decisions on behalf of our children and need not inform _____ the other parent of these decisions.

_____ _____ [other adult] will be given authority to make decisions on behalf of our children.

_____ We further agree that [specify]:

_____

_____

_____

#_____ **Resolving Disputes When Making Decisions Together**

_____ If disagreements arise regarding this Parenting Agreement or our general parenting arrangements, we agree as follows [choose all that apply]:

_____ _____ [parent] has authority to make final decisions when we can't agree.

_____ Before this parent makes a final decision which resolves a disagreement, he/she will consult with _____ [other adult] for advice first.

_____ _____[parent] has authority to make final decisions regarding _____ [specify] and_____ [other parent] has authority to make final decisions regarding _____ [specify].

_____ We will participate in the following, at either parent's request [choose all that apply]:

_____ counseling

_____ mediation

_____ arbitration

_____ meeting with attorney[s]

_____ other: _____ [specify]

_____ We further agree that [specify]:

_____

_____

_____

#_____ **Exchanging Information**

_____ We will not ask our children to carry messages between us.

_____ We will share information about the children [choose all that apply]:

    _____ at least every _____ [specify interval of time].

    _____ with each exchange of our children.

    _____ the day or evening before an exchange.

    _____ as needed.

_____ We each will assume the responsibility to establish contact with the appropriate sources of information regarding

our children's [choose all that apply]:

    _____ health care

    _____ school

    _____ sports

    _____ other: _____ [specify]

_____ We will communicate with each other [choose all that apply]:

    _____ in person

    _____ by telephone

    _____ by letter

    _____ by e-mail

    _____ other: _____ [specify]

_____ We further agree that [specify]:

_____

_____

#_____ **Where Our Children Will Live**

_____ Our children shall live primarily with _____ [parent] and live with

_____ [other parent] as follows [specify; include days and times of exchanges]:

_____

_____

_____

_____ Our children shall split their time between us fairly evenly. They will alternate between our homes as follows

[specify; include days and times of exchanges]:

_____

_____

_____

_____ Our children's schedule for each month will be as follows [specify; include days and times of exchanges]:

Week 1: _____

Week 2: _____

Week 3: _____

Week 4: _____

Week 5: _____

_____ Our children will not live with either of us, but with _____ [other adult].

We will spend time with our children as follows [specify; include days and times of exchanges]:

_____

_____

_____

_____ Our children will reside at _____ school

and spend time with each of us as follows [specify; include days and times of exchanges]:

_____

_____

_____

_____ Our children will remain in one home. We will take turns living there as follows [specify; include days and times of each parent's arrival and departure]:

_____

_____

_____

_____ We further agree that [specify]:

_____

_____

_____

#_____ **Domestic Violence, Child Abuse and Child Neglect**

_____ If events such as _____ [specify] occur, _____ [parent] may seek a restraining order from the court which will [specify]:

_____

_____

_____

_____ Anyone providing care for our children other than a parent will be told about any existing restraining orders.

_____ [parent] will seek counseling from _____

_____ [provider] regarding _____

_____ [specify]; also [choose all that apply]:

_____ Parent and provider will be permitted to determine when the need for counseling has concluded.

_____ At the conclusion of parent's counseling, provider will send a letter to _____ _____ [other parent] indicating that counseling has concluded to the parent and provider's satisfaction.

_____ We will offer counseling and emotional support to our children as indicated in issue # _____ [Psychiatric and Other Mental Health Care].

_____ If our children are exposed to a violent or otherwise dangerous situation, the parent in whose care they are will remove them from the situation and, if necessary, find another adult to provide care for them.

_____ Our children may call _____ [adult's name] if they fear for their safety while in _____ 's [parent] care. This adult will care for the children until he/she receives different instructions from the other parent.

_____ We will seek an independent evaluation regarding _____

_____ [specify] for help in how we might best address this situation.

_____ The time the children are with _____ [parent] will be supervised by

_____ [other adult] to insure the children's safety and well-being. The supervised visits will continue until [choose all that apply]:

_____ Our children feel ready to spend time alone with _____ .

_____ A counselor indicates that the supervision is unnecessary.

_____ Other: _____ [specify]

_____ From _____ until _____ ,

_____ [parent] will not spend time with our children.

_____ During that time, _____ [parent] will maintain contact with our children via [choose all that apply]:

_____ phone

_____ letter

_____ e-mail

_____ other: _____ [specify]

_____ We further agree that [specify]:

_____

_____

_____

#_____ **Alcohol or Drug Abuse**

_____ _____ [parent] will attend a 12-step or similar program.

_____ _____ [parent] will seek counseling from _____

_____ [provider] to deal with the substance abuse; also [choose all that apply]:

_____ Parent and provider will be permitted to determine when the need for counseling has concluded.

_____ At the conclusion of parent's counseling, provider will send a letter to _____

[other parent] indicating that counseling has concluded to the parent and provider's satisfaction.

_____ _____ [parent] will modify his/her behavior around

our children so that he/she is "sober" as follows [choose all that apply]:

_____ Will not operate a motor vehicle within _____ hours of consuming drugs or alcohol.

_____ Will not consume drugs or alcohol for at least _____ hours before visits with the children.

_____ Will submit to a drug and alcohol screening test performed by _____

_____ [name of organization].

_____ The time the children are with _____ [parent] will be supervised

by _____ [other adult] to insure

the children's safety and well-being. The supervised visits will continue until [choose all that apply]:

_____ Our children feel ready to spend time alone with _____

_____ A counselor indicates that the supervision is unnecessary.

_____ Other: _____ [specify]

_____ _____ [parent] will prevent others

from consuming drugs or alcohol while our children are in [his/her] care.

_____ During that time, _____ [parent]

will maintain contact with our children via [choose all that apply]:

_____ phone

_____ letter

_____ e-mail

_____ other: _____ [specify]

_____ We further agree that [specify]:

_____

_____

_____

#_____ **Maintaining Contact When the Children Are With the Other Parent**

_____ Our children and _____ [parent] will make an

effort to talk at least every _____ [specify frequency] as follows:

_____ _____ [parent or children] will initiate each call.

_____ calls will be made between _____ and _____.

_____ If either _____ [parent] or children

will be unavailable at the usual time, the unavailable person will arrange a new time by:

_____ calling the other parent

_____ sending a note

_____ e-mail message

_____ other: _____ [specify]

_____ Our children and _____ [parent] will not call back and forth more than every

_____ [specify] unless something unusual happens or it is a special occasion.

_____ Our children will be given their own telephone line.

_____ _____ [parent] will be responsible to teach telephone rules.

_____ _____ [parent or children] will be responsible for telephone bills.

_____ _____ [parent] and the children can also communicate by:

_____ letter

_____ audio or video tapes

_____ e-mail or electronic conferencing

_____ other: _____ [specify]

_____ Visits with _____ [parent] will include

a mid-week dinner on _____ [day of week] as follows [specify time for exchange]:

_____

_____

_____

_____ We will arrange for our children to communicate with _____ [parent]

while our children are away on vacation.

_____ We further agree that [specify]:

_____

_____

_____

#_____ **Reinvolving a Previously Absent Parent**

_____ _____ [parent] has been absent

from our children's life for _____ [period of time], and now wishes to become

reinvolved. To make this transition easier for all of us, we agree as follows [choose all that apply]:

_____ We will both seek counseling.

_____ Our children will receive counseling.

_____ We will focus our attention and conversations on our children.

_____ We will build up the amount of time _____ [parent]

spends with our children as follows:

_____

_____

_____ _____ [parent] will retain the support systems and schedules

he/she established while _____ [parent] was absent, as follows:

_____

_____

_____ To make sure that _____'s [parent] re-entry into

our children's lives is for the long term, we will make necessary modifications to this agreement on or

before _____ [specify date].

_____ We further agree that [specify]:

_____

_____

_____

#_____ **Child Care**

_____ In securing child care, we will proceed as follows [choose all that apply]:

_____ Any child care provider will [choose all that apply]:

_____ be a licensed child care provider.

_____ be over the age of _____.

_____ be a relative or close friend.

_____ not care for more than _____ children at any time when our children are there.

_____ come into the home.

_____ other: _____ [specify]

_____ Each parent has the discretion to select the child care provider, but may not use [list names or traits unacceptable]:

_____

_____ Each parent will call the other first to care for the children in that parent's absence.

_____ We will try to share child care responsibilities with neighbors and friends.

_____ Our children can care for themselves, but _____ [other adult]

will check in with them.

_____ Our children can care for themselves as long as they follow these rules:

_____
_____
_____

_____ We further agree that [specify]:

_____
_____
_____

#_____ **Moving**

_____ We will resolve any issues concerning either parent's desire to move as follows [choose all that apply]:

_____ We will agree on a place to which both parents will move.
_____ _____ [parent] will move to _____ [specify].
_____ _____ [parent] will remain in the area.
_____ _____ [parent] will maintain two residences. One residence will be near the children and the other will be _____ [specify].

_____ We further agree that [specify]:

_____
_____
_____

#_____ **If Our Homes Are Far Apart**

_____ If there is a considerable distance between our homes, we agree as follows [choose all that apply]:

_____ The children will spend the school year with _____ [parent] and the summers with _____ [other parent].
_____ The children will live with _____ [parent] for _____ [specify grade or school level] and with _____ [other parent] for _____ [specify grade or school level].
_____ The children will reside at _____ [name of school] and will visit with each parent as follows [specify; be consistent with the options you chose under holidays and vacations]:

_____
_____
_____

_____ We further agree that [specify]:

_____
_____
_____

#_____ **Holidays**

_____ This agreement covers the following holidays:

_____ _____
_____ _____
_____ _____

_____ Holiday visits will begin at _____ [time] and will end at _____ [time].

_____ We will adopt an odd year/even year plan, as follows:
_____ In odd years, our children will be with _____ [parent] for these holidays:

_____ _____
_____ _____

and with _____ [parent] for these holidays:

_____ _____
_____ _____

In even years, the reverse will be true.

_____ The children will spend one-half of each holiday with each parent as follows:

_____   _____
_____   _____
_____   _____

_____ We will both celebrate the following holidays with our children:

_____   _____

Each parent will celebrate as follows:

_____
_____

_____ We will divide holiday vacation periods as follows:

_____
_____
_____

_____ Our children will always spend the following holidays with _____ [parent]:

_____   _____
_____   _____

and will always spend the following holidays with _____ [other parent]:

_____   _____
_____   _____

_____ We will plan for holidays as they come up. We will decide where the children will spend their holidays at least _____ [specify time, such as two weeks or one month] in advance.

_____ We further agree that [specify]:

_____
_____
_____

#_____ **Vacations**

_____ We will inform each other at least _____ [period of time] in advance of any planned vacation.

_____ We will provide each other with an itinerary of any trip, and contact information.

_____ Our children may accompany one of us on a vacation under the following conditions:

_____ Any time missed from a regularly scheduled visit with the other parent will be made up as follows:

_____
_____

_____ Travel will be restricted to:
_____ local area
_____ in state
_____ in the United States
_____ the following countries
_____ activities will be limited to _____.
_____ activities will not include _____.
_____ our children will not be away for longer than _____.

_____ We further agree that [specify]:

_____
_____

#_____ **Special Occasions and Family Events**

_____ Special occasions and family events are defined as follows:

_____
_____

_____ We will attend special occasions and family events together whenever possible.

_____ We will attend special occasions and family events as our children wish.

_____ We will attend special occasions and family events as we decide.

_____ _____ [parent] will attend the following special occasions and family events:

_____

_____

_____

_____ _____ [parent] will attend the following special occasions and family events:

_____

_____

_____

_____ We further agree that [specify]:

_____

_____

_____

_____

#_____ **Grandparents, Relatives and Important Friends**

_____ Our children will maintain their relationships with grandparents, other relatives and important friends as follows:

_____

_____

_____

#_____ **Transporting the Children**

_____ Transporting our children between our homes will be as follows [choose all that apply]:

    _____ We will meet for exchanges at _____ [specify time and location].

    _____ We will alternate transporting our children back and forth.

    _____ _____ [parent] will actually transport our children

    and _____ [other parent] will share in costs as follows:

_____

_____

    _____ _____ [parent] will travel to our children for visits.

    _____ _____ [parent] will bring our children for visits to the other parent.

    _____ Our children may travel on their own by train, bus or airplane when they reach age _____.

_____ We further agree that [specify]:

_____

_____

_____

#_____ **Improving Transition Times**

_____ We will make the transitions between our homes easier for our children by doing as follows [choose all that apply]:

    _____ Our children will start visits with _____ [parent]

    at _____ [specify time or event, such as after school or after work]. The visits will end at _____ [specify time or event].

    _____ When our children are changing homes, we will minimize the contact between us.

    _____ We will exchange information regarding our children the night before they change homes.

    _____ When our children are changing homes, the parent starting the visit will take time to give each child some undivided attention.

    _____ The parent starting a visit will let our children have some quiet time before any scheduled activities or trips.

    _____ _____ [parent] will try to establish and maintain a simple ritual to start and end his/her visits with our children.

    _____ We will try to be patient regarding any questions that the children wish to ask about the custody and visitation arrangements.

_____ We further agree that [specify]:

_____

_____

_____

#_____ Treating Each Child as an Individual

_____ Each of our children will sometimes need separate or special time with each of us. Therefore, we will set up short separate visits as follows [specify]:

_____

_____

_____

_____ Each of our children will sometimes need separate or special time with each of us. Therefore, we will set up separate time for each child while visiting together as follows [specify]:

_____

_____

_____

_____ Each of our children will sometimes need separate or special time with each of us. Therefore, we further agree that [specify]:

_____

_____

_____

#_____ When Parenting Styles and Values Are Very Different

_____ Although our parenting styles are very different, we agree to try the following strategies to minimize the effect of those differences on our children [choose all that apply]:

_____ We will focus our attention and conversations on our children, rather than on each other.

_____ We will encourage our children to explore the following aspects of each of our cultural heritages [specify]:

_____

_____

_____

_____ We respect the other's right to establish an independent life with our children, as long as it is not detrimental to our children.

_____ If our living arrangement exacerbates the problems our children experience because of our different styles and values, we will consider modifying that arrangement.

_____ We further agree that [specify]:

_____

_____

_____

_____ Consistency in Raising Children

_____ The standards for discipline in each of our homes will be as follows [choose all that apply]:

_____ We will abide by the same discipline standards.

_____ The following behavior rules will apply in both homes:

_____

_____

_____

_____ If either of us has a discipline issue with our children, that parent will explain the issue and response to the other so we can be consistent in our discipline.

_____ If our children complain about discipline in the other parent's home, we will encourage them to talk about it with the other parent.

_____ If we cannot agree on discipline standards that will apply in both homes, we will make an effort to understand and respect the other's right to establish behavior rules for our children.

_____ We further agree that [specify]:

_____
_____
_____

#_____ **Disparaging Remarks**

_____ We will refrain from making disparaging remarks about the other, his/her partner and his/her chosen life directly to our children or within our children's hearing.

_____ We further agree that [specify]:

_____
_____
_____

#_____ **Undermining the Parent/Child Relationship**

_____ We will encourage and support our children in maintaining a good relationship with the other. If either of us feels that the other is undermining our relationship with our children, we will proceed as follows [choose all that apply]:
_____ We will discuss the matter and try to reach an agreement.
_____ We will resolve the dispute through:
_____ counseling
_____ mediation
_____ arbitration
_____ other: _____ [specify]

_____ We further agree that [specify]:

_____
_____
_____

#_____ **Denying Access to the Children**

_____ If either of us is denied physical access to our children, contact with them or information about them, we will proceed as follows [choose all that apply]:
_____ We will discuss the matter and try to reach an agreement which will involve reinstating a visitation schedule.
_____ We will resolve the dispute through:
_____ counseling
_____ mediation
_____ arbitration
_____ other: _____ [specify]

_____ We further agree that [specify]:

_____
_____
_____

#_____ **When a Parent Needs to Develop Parenting Skills**

_____ _____ [parent] will work on improving his/her parenting skills as follows [choose all that apply]:
_____ Will attend parenting classes through _____.
_____ Will review written materials on parenting.
_____ Will attend counseling with _____ to deal with and resolve these issues.

_____ We further agree that [specify]:

_____
_____
_____

#_____ **When Nonrelatives Live in the Home**

_____ If either of us lives with nonrelatives, our children will have separate sleeping quarters from the adults.

_____ _____ [parent] will be responsible to make sure that no one in the house consumes nonprescription drugs, or becomes a danger to our children because of intoxication.

_____ _____ [parent] will be responsible to make sure the number of other visitors is kept reasonable.

_____ A nonrelative may not care for our children in the parent's absence.

_____ A nonrelative may not discipline our children in the parent's absence.

_____ We further agree that [specify]:

_____

_____

_____

#_____ **When Parents Have New Partners**

_____ We will resolve issues surrounding a parent's new partner as follows [choose all that apply]:

_____ Our children will always know that we are their parents, regardless of their attachment to a parent's new partner.

_____ Our children will refer to new partners as _____.

_____ The adults and the children will have separate sleeping quarters.

_____ Any new partner will participate in decisions regarding the children as follows [specify]:

_____

_____

_____ We further agree that [specify]:

_____

_____

_____

#_____ **Labeling the Custody Arrangement**

_____ The custody of our children will be as follows [choose one]: *(Note: Read Chapter 11 before completing this option. Your state may require you to differentiate between legal and physical custody.)*

_____ sole custody

_____ legal

_____ physical

_____ joint custody

_____ legal

_____ physical

_____ Joint custody to mean that we will make decisions and share time with our children as follows [specify]:

_____

_____

_____ split custody

_____ _____ [parent] will have custody of _____ [children's name(s)].

_____ _____ [other parent] will have custody of _____ [children's name(s)].

_____ _____ [other adult] will have custody of our children.

_____ We further agree that [specify]:

_____

_____

_____

#_____ **Making Changes**

_____ We will regularly review this agreement as follows: _____ [list dates or frequency, as appropriate].

_____ We will review this agreement when problems arise.

_____ Reviews will be:

_____ by telephone

_____ in person

_____ through:

_____ counseling

_____ mediation

_____ arbitration

_____ other: _____ [specify]

_____ Our children may participate in the discussions.

_____ Our children may participate in the decisions.

#_____ **Making Substantive Changes to This Agreement**

_____ If we negotiate a substantive modification of this agreement, _____ [parent] will prepare (or make sure that someone else prepares) a summary of the agreement so that we may obtain a court order incorporating our changes. Each parent will be responsible to review the agreement prior to its submission to the court, and to seek independent advice on the agreement to insure that it says what we intend it to say, accomplishes our objectives, and is within the general parameters of what a court is likely to approve.

_____ We further agree that [specify]:

_____

_____

_____

#_____ **Explaining the Agreement to Our Children**

_____ _____ [parent] will explain this agreement to our children. _____ [other parent] will be available to answer any questions the children might have.

_____ We further agree that [specify]:

_____

_____

_____

D. Responsibility to Prepare a Final Draft of this Agreement. _____ [parent] will prepare a final draft of this agreement. Both parents will be responsible to review the agreement for completeness and accuracy. By _____ [date], both parents will have made any necessary changes and _____ _____ [parent] will conform this agreement to the specifications of the _____ court for inclusion in an order of the court.

_____   _____
Signature   Date

_____   _____
Signature   Date

Index

CATALOG

...more from Nolo Press

	EDITION	PRICE	CODE

BUSINESS

	EDITION	PRICE	CODE
Business Plans to Game Plans	1st	$29.95	GAME
Getting Started as an Independent Paralegal—Audio	2nd	$44.95	GSIP
How to Finance a Growing Business	4th	$24.95	GROW
How to Form a CA Nonprofit Corp.—w/Corp. Records Binder & PC Disk	1st	$49.95	CNP
How to Form a Nonprofit Corp., Book w/Disk (PC)—National Edition	2nd	$39.95	NNP
How to Form Your Own Calif. Corp.—w/Corp. Records Binder & Disk—PC	1st	$39.95	CACI
How to Form Your Own California Corporation	8th	$29.95	CCOR
How to Form Your Own Florida Corporation, (Book w/Disk—PC)	3rd	$39.95	FLCO
How to Form Your Own New York Corporation, (Book w/Disk—PC)	3rd	$39.95	NYCO
How to Form Your Own Texas Corporation, (Book w/Disk—PC)	4th	$39.95	TCI
How to Start Your Own Business: Small Business Law—Audio	1st	$14.95	TBUS
How to Write a Business Plan	4th	$21.95	SBS
Make Up Your Mind: Entrepreneurs Talk About Decision Making	1st	$19.95	MIND
Managing Generation X: How to Bring Out the Best in Young Talent	1st	$19.95	MANX
Marketing Without Advertising	1st	$14.00	MWAD
Mastering Diversity	1st	$29.95	MAST
Small Business Legal Pro—Macintosh	2nd	$27.96	SBM2
Small Business Legal Pro—Windows	2nd	$27.96	SBWI2
Taking Care of Your Corporation, Vol. 1, (Book w/Disk—PC)	1st	$26.95	CORK
Taking Care of Your Corporation, Vol 2, (Book w/Disk—PC)	1st	$39.95	CORK2
Tax Savvy for Small Business	1st	$26.95	SAVVY
The California Nonprofit Corporation Handbook	7th	$29.95	NON
The California Professional Corporation Handbook	5th	$34.95	PROF
The Employer's Legal Handbook	1st	$29.95	EMPL
The Independent Paralegal's Handbook	3rd	$29.95	PARA
The Legal Guide for Starting & Running a Small Business	2nd	$24.95	RUNS
The Partnership Book: How to Write a Partnership Agreement	4th	$24.95	PART
Trademark: How to Name Your Business & Product	1st	$29.95	TRD

Book with disk

CALL 800-992-6656 OR USE THE ORDER FORM IN THE BACK OF THE BOOK

	EDITION	PRICE	CODE

CONSUMER

	EDITION	PRICE	CODE
Fed Up With the Legal System: What's Wrong & How to Fix It	2nd	$9.95	LEG
Glossary of Insurance Terms	5th	$14.95	GLINT
How to Win Your Personal Injury Claim	1st	$24.95	PICL
Nolo's Law Form Kit: Hiring Child Care & Household Help	1st	$14.95	KCHLD
Nolo's Pocket Guide to California Law	3rd	$10.95	CLAW
Nolo's Pocket Guide to California Law on Disk—Windows	3.0	$17.46	CLW3
Nolo's Pocket Guide to Consumer Rights (California Edition)	2nd	$12.95	CAG
Nolo's Pocket Guide to Consumer Rights (California Edition)	2nd	$12.95	CAG
The Over 50 Insurance Survival Guide	1st	$16.95	OVER50
What Do You Mean It's Not Covered?	1st	$19.95	COVER

ESTATE PLANNING & PROBATE

	EDITION	PRICE	CODE
5 Ways to Avoid Probate—Audio	1st	$14.95	TPRO
How to Probate an Estate (California Edition)	8th	$34.95	PAE
Make Your Own Living Trust	1st	$19.95	LITR
Nolo's Law Form Kit: Wills	1st	$14.95	KWL
Nolo's Simple Will Book	2nd	$17.95	SWIL
Plan Your Estate	3rd	$24.95	NEST
Write Your Will—Audio	1st	$14.95	TWYW

FAMILY MATTERS

	EDITION	PRICE	CODE
A Legal Guide for Lesbian and Gay Couples	8th	$24.95	LG
Child Custody: Building Agreements That Work	1st	$24.95	CUST
Divorce & Money: How to Make the Best Financial Decisions During Divorce	2nd	$21.95	DIMO
How to Adopt Your Stepchild in California	4th	$22.95	ADOP
How to Do Your Own Divorce in California	20th	$21.95	CDIV
How to Do Your Own Divorce in Texas	5th	$17.95	TDIV
How to Raise or Lower Child Support in California	3rd	$18.95	CHLD
Nolo's Pocket Guide to Family Law	3rd	$14.95	FLD
Practical Divorce Solutions	1st	$14.95	PDS
The Guardianship Book (California Edition)	2nd	$24.95	GB
The Living Together Kit	7th	$24.95	LTK

GOING TO COURT

	EDITION	PRICE	CODE
Collect Your Court Judgment (California Edition)	2nd	$19.95	JUDG
Everybody's Guide to Municipal Court (California Edition)	1st	$29.95	MUNI
Everybody's Guide to Small Claims Court (California Edition)	11th	$18.95	CSCC
Everybody's Guide to Small Claims Court (National Edition)	6th	$18.95	NSCC
Fight Your Ticket ... and Win! (California Edition)	6th	$19.95	FYT
How to Change Your Name (California Edition)	6th	$24.95	NAME

 Book with disk

CALL 800-992-6656 OR USE THE ORDER FORM IN THE BACK OF THE BOOK

	EDITION	PRICE	CODE
Represent Yourself in Court: How to Prepare & Try a Winning Case	1st	$29.95	RYC
The Criminal Records Book (California Edition)	4th	$21.95	CRIM
Winning in Small Claims Court—Audio	1st	$14.95	TWIN

HOMEOWNERS, LANDLORDS & TENANTS

	EDITION	PRICE	CODE
Dog Law	2nd	$12.95	DOG
For Sale by Owner (California Edition)	2nd	$24.95	FSBO
Homestead Your House (California Edition)	8th	$9.95	HOME
How to Buy a House in California	3rd	$24.95	BHCA
Neighbor Law: Fences, Trees, Boundaries & Noise	2nd	$16.95	NEI
Nolo's Law Form Kit: Leases & Rental Agreements (California Edition)	1st	$14.95	KLEAS
Safe Homes, Safe Neighborhoods: Stopping Crime Where You Live	1st	$14.95	SAFE
Tenants' Rights (California Edition)	12th	$18.95	CTEN
The Deeds Book (California Edition)	3rd	$16.95	DEED
The Landlord's Law Book, Vol. 1: Rights & Responsibilities (California Edition)	4th	$32.95	LBRT
The Landlord's Law Book, Vol. 2: Evictions (California Edition)	5th	$34.95	LBEV

HUMOR

	EDITION	PRICE	CODE
29 Reasons Not to Go to Law School	4th	$9.95	29R
Nolo's Favorite Lawyer Jokes On Disk—DOS	1.0	$9.95	JODI
Nolo's Favorite Lawyer Jokes On Disk—Macintosh	1.0	$9.95	JODM
Nolo's Favorite Lawyer Jokes On Disk—Windows	1st	$9.95	JODWI
Poetic Justice: The Funniest, Meanest Things Ever Said About Lawyers	1st	$9.95	PJ

IMMIGRATION

	EDITION	PRICE	CODE
Como Obtener La Tarjeta Verde: Maneras Legitimas de Permanecer en los EE.UU.	1st	$24.95	VERDE
How to Become a United States Citizen	5th	$14.95	CIT
How to Get a Green Card: Legal Ways to Stay in the U.S.A.	1st	$22.95	GRN
U.S. Immigration Made Easy	5th	$39.95	IMEZ

MONEY MATTERS

	EDITION	PRICE	CODE
Chapter 13 Bankruptcy: Repay Your Debts	1st	$29.95	CHI3
How to File for Bankruptcy	5th	$25.95	HFB
Money Troubles: Legal Strategies to Cope With Your Debts	3rd	$18.95	MT
Nolo's Law Form Kit: Buy & Sell Contracts	1st	$9.95	KCONT
Nolo's Law Form Kit: Loan Agreements	1st	$14.95	KLOAN
Nolo's Law Form Kit: Personal Bankruptcy	1st	$14.95	KBNK
Nolo's Law Form Kit: Power of Attorney	1st	$14.95	KPA
Nolo's Law Form Kit: Rebuild Your Credit	1st	$14.95	KCRD
Simple Contracts for Personal Use	2nd	$16.95	CONT
Smart Ways to Save Money During and After Divorce	1st	$14.95	SAVMO
Stand Up to the IRS	2nd	$21.95	SIRS

Book with disk

CALL 800-992-6656 OR USE THE ORDER FORM IN THE BACK OF THE BOOK

	EDITION	PRICE	CODE

PATENTS AND COPYRIGHTS

	EDITION	PRICE	CODE
Copyright Your Software	1st	$39.95	CYS
Patent It Yourself	4th	$39.95	PAT
 Software Development: A Legal Guide (Book with disk—PC)	1st	$44.95	SFT
The Copyright Handbook: How to Protect and Use Written Works	2nd	$24.95	COHA
The Inventor's Notebook	1st	$19.95	INOT

RESEARCH & REFERENCE

Law on the Net	1st	$39.95	LAWN
Legal Research: How to Find & Understand the Law	4th	$19.95	LRES
Legal Research Made Easy: A Roadmap through the Law Library Maze—Video	1st	$89.95	LRME

SENIORS

Beat the Nursing Home Trap: A Consumer's Guide	2nd	$18.95	ELD
Social Security, Medicare & Pensions: The Sourcebook for Older Americans	6th	$19.95	SOA
The Conservatorship Book (California Edition)	2nd	$29.95	CNSV

SOFTWARE

California Incorporator 1.0—DOS	1.0	$90.30	INCI
Living Trust Maker 2.0—Macintosh	2.0	$55.96	LTM2
Living Trust Maker 2.0—Windows	2.0	$55.96	LTWI2
Nolo's Partnership Maker 1.0—DOS	1.0	$90.96	PAGI1
Nolo's Personal RecordKeeper 3.0—Macintosh	3.0	$34.96	FRM3
Patent It Yourself 1.0—Windows	1.0	$160.96	PYW1
WillMaker 5.0—DOS	5.0	$48.96	WI5
WillMaker 5.0—Macintosh	5.0	$48.96	WM5
WillMaker 5.0—Windows	5.0	$48.96	WIW5

WORKPLACE

How to Handle Your Workers' Compensation Claim (California Edition)	1st	$29.95	WORK
Rightful Termination	1st	$29.95	RITE
Sexual Harassment on the Job	2nd	$18.95	HARS
Workers' Comp for Employers	2nd	$29.95	CNTRL
Your Rights in the Workplace	2nd	$15.95	YRW

ORDER FORM

Code	Quantity	Title	Unit price	Total

Subtotal	
California residents add Sales Tax	
Basic Shipping ($5 for 1 item; $6 for 2-3 items,	
add 50¢ for each additional item)	
UPS RUSH delivery $7–any size order*	
TOTAL	

Name _____

Address _____

_____

(UPS to street address, Priority Mail to P.O. boxes)   * Delivered in 3 business days from receipt of
order. S.F. Bay area use regular shipping.

FOR FASTER SERVICE, USE YOUR CREDIT CARD AND OUR TOLL-FREE NUMBERS

Order 24 hours a day	1-800-992-6656
Fax your order	1-800-645-0895
e-mail	NoloInfo@nolopress.com
General Information	1-510-549-1976
Customer Service	1-800-728-3555, Mon.-Sat. 9am-5pm, PST

METHOD OF PAYMENT

☐ Check enclosed

☐ VISA   ☐ MasterCard   ☐ Discover Card   ☐ American Express

Account # _____   Expiration Date _____

Authorizing Signature _____

Daytime Phone _____

Prices subject to change.   CUST 1.2

Visit our store
If you live in the Bay Area, be sure to visit the Nolo Press Bookstore on the
corner of 9th and Parker Streets in West Berkeley. You'll find our complete line
of books and software, all at a discount. We also have t-shirts, posters and a
selection of business and legal self-help books from other publishers.
Open every day.

NOLO PRESS 950 PARKER ST., BERKELEY, CA 94710

Take 2 minutes & Get a 2-year NOLO *News* subscription free!*

CALL
1-800-992-6656

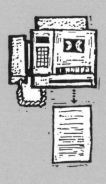

FAX
1-800-645-0895

E-MAIL
NOLOSUB@NOLOPRESS.com

OR MAIL US THIS POSTAGE-PAID REGISTRATION CARD

With our quarterly magazine, the **NOLO** *News*, you'll

- **Learn** about important legal changes that affect you
- **Find out first** about new Nolo products
- **Keep current** with practical articles on everyday law
- **Get answers** to your legal questions in *Ask Auntie Nolo's* advice column

- **Save money** with special Subscriber Only discounts
- **Tickle your funny bone** with our famous *Lawyer Joke* column.

It only takes 2 minutes to reserve your free 2-year subscription or to extend your **NOLO** *News* subscription.

REGISTRATION CARD

NAME _____ DATE _____

ADDRESS _____

_____ PHONE NUMBER _____

CITY _____ STATE _____ ZIP _____

WHERE DID YOU HEAR ABOUT THIS BOOK? _____

WHERE DID YOU PURCHASE THIS PRODUCT? _____

DID YOU CONSULT A LAWYER? (PLEASE CIRCLE ONE)   YES   NO   NOT APPLICABLE

DID YOU FIND THIS BOOK HELPFUL?   (VERY)   5   4   3   2   1   (NOT AT ALL)

SUGGESTIONS FOR IMPROVING THIS PRODUCT _____

_____

WAS IT EASY TO USE?   (VERY EASY)   5   4   3   2   1   (VERY DIFFICULT)

DO YOU OWN A COMPUTER? IF SO, WHICH FORMAT? (PLEASE CIRCLE ONE)   WINDOWS   DOS   MAC

We occasionally make our mailing list available to carefully selected companies whose products may be of interest to you. If you do not wish to receive mailings from these companies, please check this box ☐

CUST 1.2

"Nolo helps lay people perform legal tasks without the aid—or fees—of lawyers."

—USA TODAY

[Nolo books are ..."written in plain language, free of legal mumbo jumbo, and spiced with witty personal observations."

—ASSOCIATED PRESS

"...Nolo publications...guide people simply through the how, when, where and why of law."

—WASHINGTON POST

"Increasingly, people who are not lawyers are performing tasks usually regarded as legal work... And consumers, using books like Nolo's, do routine legal work themselves."

—NEW YORK TIMES

"...All of [Nolo's] books are easy-to-understand, are updated regularly, provide pull-out forms...and are often quite moving in their sense of compassion for the struggles of the lay reader."

—SAN FRANCISCO CHRONICLE